FIRE AND ICE

FIRE AND ICE

THE NAZIS' SCORCHED EARTH CAMPAIGN IN NORWAY

VINCENT HUNT

First published 2014

The History Press
The Mill, Brimscombe Port
Stroud, Gloucestershire, GL5 2QG
www.thehistorypress.co.uk

British Library Cataloguing in Publication Data.
A catalogue record for this book is available from the British Library.

ISBN 978 0 7509 5636 9

Typesetting and origination by The History Press
Printed in Great Britain

CONTENTS

LIST OF ILLUSTRATIONS

FRONT: Composite of Hammerfest in flames and German soldiers attacking through a burning Norwegian village during the 1940 invasion. Picture by Erich Borchert, provided by the German Federal Archive.

BACK: The church in Honningsvåg was the only building to survive the scorched-earth burning of Finnmark following the German retreat in October 1944. Picture used with permission of the Nordkappmuseet in Honningsvag.

ACKNOWLEDGEMENTS

The writing of this book has depended on much generosity and kindness from many people. Wideroe Airlines flew me across Finnmark and Troms to see for myself the locations of the incidents included here and to meet the people who talk about them so vividly. The hotel groups Rica and Radisson Blu helped too and Hilde Chapman at the Norwegian Embassy in London was a key figure in making this project a reality.

I am grateful to Mette and Øyvind Mikalsen for talking to me about the tragedy of Hopseidet. My special thanks go to Alf Helge Jensen of the *Finnmarken* newspaper for translating and Oddvar Jensen, owner of Mehamn's Arctic Hotel, for lending me his Mitsubishi Galant. Gunnar Jaklin was a treasure trove of stories and an encyclopedia of facts in Tromsø while artist Grethe Gunning told me tragic but wonderful stories in Djupvik and introduced me to Roald Berg, who gave me a carved wooden Sami drinking cup as a reminder of my trip. The evergreen Pål Fredriksen guided me around Nordreisa and climbed the Fals mountain to show me the Lyngen Line; Storfjord Mayor Sigmund Steinnes opened his secret files for me.

Film director Knut Erik Jensen was a mine of information in Honningsvåg, as was Rune Rautio in Kirkenes. Karin Johnsen made several important calls for me and told stories I could barely believe – then and now. Author Roger Albrigtsen of the FKLF cleared up many of my queries and offered advice on events in Porsangerfjord: Lieutenant Commander Wiggo Korsvik of the Norwegian Explosive Clearance Commando shared details of ammunition finds.

I am deeply indebted to Michael Stokke of the Narvik Peace Centre for his expertise on prisoners of war and his generosity and patience. I am extremely grateful to Torstein Johnsrud at Gamvik Museum, Yaroslav Bogomilov and Nina Planting Mølman at the Museum of Reconstruction in Hammerfest

(Gjenreisningsmuseet for Finnmark og Nord-Troms) and Camilla Carlsen, Bodil Knudsen Dago and Berit Nilsen at the Grenselandsmuseet in Kirkenes.

Thanks to historian Kristian Husvik Skancke for his time, knowledge and guidance, and to Professor Frederik Fagertun at Tromsø University who was kind enough to advise on aspects of the project.

Special mention must be made of Mrs Bjarnhild Tulloch, a survivor of the scorched-earth policy in Kirkenes and whose childhood memoir *Terror in the Arctic* – one of the few accounts of the time in English – was a significant research guide. For her kindness in recommending me to her friends Svea Andersen, Eva Larsen and Knut Tharaldsen, as well as Inga and Idar Russveld, I cannot thank her enough.

Curt Hanson, Head of the Elwyn B. Robinson Department of Special Collections at the University of North Dakota gave me permission to use the Nuremberg trial transcripts from his archive. Øyvind Waldeland kindly released pictures from the archive of Oslo's Defence Museum.

My friends Ian Muir, David Ford and Simon Price offered encouragement throughout, as did Shaun Barrington of The History Press. My thanks also go to Chris Shaw, who did the copyediting.

Finally, special thanks go to my wonderful wife Daiga Kamerade and my son Martins Vitolins. Their patience and humour helped keep me sane and sustained me in the many hours of research and writing required.

Vincent Hunt
Manchester, England

INTRODUCTION

This book is a collection of stories about the destruction and evacuation of northern Norway during the Nazi scorched-earth retreat of October 1944 to May 1945. Its focus is the counties of Finnmark and Troms lying to the far north of the Arctic Circle. Finnmark, west of the Tana River, was reduced to ashes in the retreat and emptied of civilians. The Nazi troops – Austrians, mostly – fell back to a fortified defensive line in the mountains near the Lyngen fjord where they planned a stand against an Allied invasion that never came.

This is a book of social memory: of towns bombed and burned flat with violent death and secret tragedies round every corner; of unspeakable cruelty, misery and brutality, with skinny malnourished children and hollow-eyed prisoners at every turn. The author crossed the region meeting ordinary Norwegians who describe extraordinary experiences or tell how their families and friends fared in a time of great disruption and dislocation. All these stories have been gathered by the author in English but they are Norwegian stories - of death, destruction and trauma in a beautiful land of rugged coastlines, jagged mountains and sub-zero temperatures.

Seventy years on, that land is still stained from its encounter with evil. There are Nazi bullets still in the ground and rusty barbed wire still around trees. Pensioners still have nightmares, and reinforced concrete gun bunkers are still standing, too well built to crumble. They seem as if they will never crumble but will always be there, gazing silently out to sea.

Even today, the war is never very far away in Finnmark. It's been bottled up in people's heads for seventy years and the fears have been passed down through two generations since. That third generation can walk into a forest today and still find traces of the war.

One elderly lady in the shattered, battered northern town of Kirkenes said to me: 'We used to say "Will we never be rid of this war?"'

The answer is no, not yet. The war is still here.

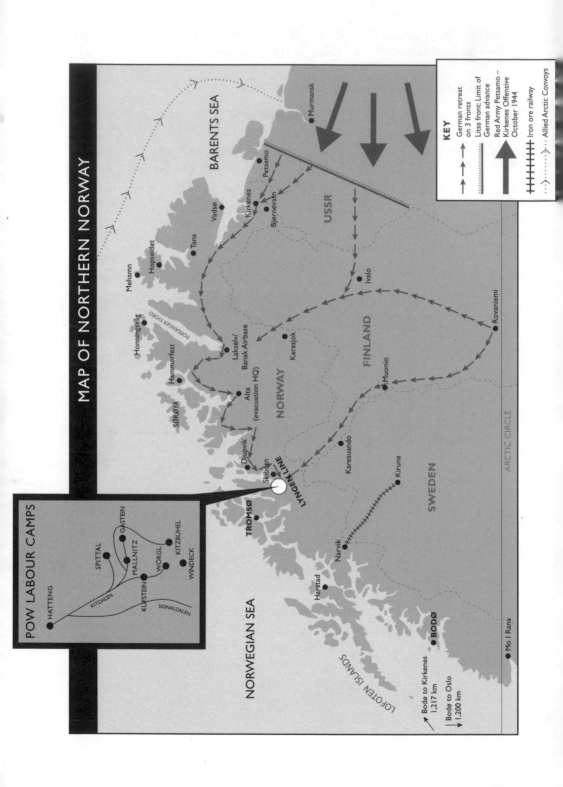

MAP OF NORTHERN NORWAY

POW LABOUR CAMPS

HATTENG
SPITTAL
GASTEIN
MALLNITZ
KITZBUHEL
WORGL
WINDECK
KUFSTEIN
KITDALEN
SIGNALDALEN

NORWEGIAN SEA

LOFOTEN ISLANDS

Mo I Rana
BODØ
Harstad
Narvik
TROMSØ
Skibotn
LYNGEN LINE
Djupvik
Alta (evacuation HQ)
SØRØYA
Hammerfest
Honningsvåg
FORSANGER FJORD
Mehamn
Hopseidet
Tana
Vadsø
Lakselv/ Banak Airbase
Karasjok
Bjørnevatn
Kirkenes
Petsamo
Murmansk

BARENTS SEA

NORWAY

FINLAND

Karesuando
Kiruna
Muonio
Ivalo
Rovaniemi

SWEDEN

USSR

ARCTIC CIRCLE

Bodø to Kirkenes 1,217 km
Bodø to Oslo 1,200 km

KEY

German retreat on 3 fronts

Litsa front: Limit of German advance

Red Army Petsamo – Kirkenes Offensive October 1944

Iron ore railway

Allied Arctic Convoys

1

'IT WAS ABSOLUTELY NORMAL GROWING UP PLAYING WITH AMMUNITION'

Two women and a man, all three of them elderly, are sitting on a red sofa opposite me in my hotel room in Kirkenes, Norway's most north-easterly town. We are 400km above the Arctic Circle at the final stop of Norway's famous Hurtigruten coastal steamers. The border with what was the Soviet Union is 7km east on the other side of the Pasvik river at a controlled crossing called Storskog.

The man, Knut Tharaldsen, worked for many years at the crossing as a border policeman. He grew up on a farm nearby close to a fjord called Jarfjord. As Red Army soldiers pushed the Germans out of the Soviet Union and back into Norway in October 1944, triggering the scorched-earth retreat, his farm was in the centre of the battlefield. Knut, then aged 8, looked on from a forest as the battle raged. As he is about to tell me, he saw things that no child should see.

One of the ladies, Eva Larsen, grew up in a place about 10km from here called Bjørnevatn, the site of an enormous iron ore mine. During the war 3,000 people from Kirkenes sheltered in the mine to escape the incessant bombing of the town and the fighting that liberated them. When Red Army soldiers reached the mine they were greeted with jubilation.

The third member of the group, Svea Andersen, grew up less than 1km from this hotel, down by the harbour. The Germans built a causeway across to an island in the fjord called Prestøia, which they turned into a military stronghold bristling with guns called 'Festung Kirkenes' (Fortress Kirkenes). Svea's was the last house before the checkpoint leading to the causeway. It's still there.

My three guests are about to tell me my first scorched-earth stories. I have a microphone and a tape recorder ready. They are the friends of a lady called Bjarnhild Tulloch, who grew up here and wrote about her wartime experiences in English. Her book – *Terror in the Arctic* – is one of the few accounts of the war in Kirkenes. Thanks to her generosity in putting me in touch with Svea, Knut and Eva, I have the chance to hear stories about a war I am not familiar with and which will touch me deeply.

Norway will never seem the same again. It is more than a land of picturesque fjords, tourists on Midnight Sun cruises and cheerful cyclists waving from the pages of holiday brochures. There are dark, disturbing chapters buried under the surface. I am at the start of a journey through a landscape of sadness, cruelty and bitterness.

Following the Nazi invasion and occupation of Norway in 1940, Kirkenes became increasingly important to Hitler's long-term aims. As the military build-up began in preparation for Operation Barbarossa, the strike against the Soviet Union set for the following June, Kirkenes became a vital strategic town. Tens of thousands of troops, mostly specialist Austrian mountain soldiers, or *Gebirgsjäger*, who were trained for the extreme conditions, were sent to Kirkenes for the northern punch through the Arctic against Murmansk and Leningrad.

Kirkenes was the ideal place: it was an ice-free port very close to the Soviet border with a direct road to Murmansk. German ships and commandeered Norwegian boats brought in tanks, lorries, fuel, weapons, building materials, food and liquor. Warehouses, stores and repair shops were built in the gaps between civilian homes and enough ammunition was brought into Kirkenes to support 100,000 men taking part in the offensive for a year. Soon the town was filled with vehicles, guns, barracks and stables and tens of thousands of men, horses and mules.

The German general in command of the strike was General Eduard Dietl. He had led German troops to victory in an intense two-month battle for Narvik twelve months previously against a combined force of Norwegian, French, British and Polish troops in difficult conditions in the mountains around Narvik, narrowly avoiding defeat when Norway suddenly capitulated in June 1940. On 22 June 1941 Dietl moved his Alpine troops across the Norwegian border to take control of Petsamo, home to a mine producing nickel, a vital component in the manufacture of armour plating. Supported by their Finnish allies, the German operation clicked into a second phase, Operation Platinum Fox, with the aim of pushing on and taking Murmansk. But before long, Dietl's men met fierce resistance.[1] The Russians landed reinforcements east of Petsamo, well before Murmansk, which slowed and then stopped the German advance across the tundra before the advance units could cross the Litsa river.[2]

Try as he might throughout July, August and September, Dietl could not get across the Litsa, despite repeated and often costly attacks. Soviet reinforcements were poured into the area to protect Murmansk and by late September, with supplies into Kirkenes now threatened by Russian submarines, Hitler was resigned to suspending the offensive for the winter. The Germans called off the attack in September and dug in, having already lost around 10,000 men. They had advanced just 25kms into Soviet territory.[3]

The lines were drawn for an Arctic war of attrition supplied from Kirkenes that would last for the next three years and claim tens of thousands of lives, not just through combat but also through exposure, frostbite and blizzards. The Litsa Front remained stable until 1944, but the entire situation in the Arctic north changed when the Soviets broke the year-long siege of Leningrad early that year. In the face of powerful Red Army offensives throughout the spring and summer of 1944, the Finns were pushed back from almost all of the territorial gains they had made since 1941 and suffered upwards of 60,000 casualties – military and physical losses that meant Soviet victory was inevitable. Finland's survival as an independent nation began to hang in the balance and they discreetly opened peace talks with the Soviets.[4]

To be ready for the increasingly likely event of a Finnish surrender, which would leave them exposed and vulnerable throughout the region, German commanders drew up contingency plans – Operations Birke and Nordlicht ('Birch' and 'Northern Lights') – to pull their 230,000 men and a mountain of supplies and weapons back to new defensive lines in the mountains surrounding the Lyngenfjord near Tromsø. Here they would regroup to stop any further Soviet advance or Allied invasion.

In late August the Soviets offered Finland a conditional peace deal. The war would end, but the Finns had to pay huge reparations, cede territory and get the Germans out within a fortnight, or turn their guns on their former friends. The Finns accepted the peace deal on 2 September and broke off relations with Germany. The armistice was signed on 19 September.[5]

General Dietl had died in a plane crash in June 1944 in the Austrian Alps on his way back from a meeting with Hitler to discuss tactics. His replacement was Generaloberst Lothar Rendulic, another Austrian and a veteran of the partisan war in Yugoslavia. As he took command the Soviets were building up their forces for the onslaught of the October 1944 Petsamo–Kirkenes offensive, which would turn the tide of the war on the Northern Front in the Arctic and trigger the German destruction of Finnmark in a scorched-earth retreat back to the Lyngen Line. This is where my scorched-earth stories begin.

Seated in the centre of the hotel room sofa, Eva Larsen, a former teacher in Kirkenes, speaks very good English. She has agreed to tell not only her story but also to translate Knut's for me. 'For many years people didn't want to speak about what they saw in the war. It was not for discussion,' she says. 'Knut's parents after the war didn't want to speak about what they saw. In October 1944 Knut was 8, so he had lots of memories – very clear and distinct.'

Knut nods. He understands English but doesn't speak it so well, so Eva translates:

We lived on a farm near Storskog, where you cross the border with Russia. The German general Dietl determined to stop the Russians at a defensive line near to my home. He went back to Germany and discussed with Hitler how to do it.

They built a series of short trenches in the hills from where the Germans could fire on the Soviets. We can see them today when we are picking blueberries.

Hitler told Dietl to get 5,000 soldiers to stop the Soviets but as it was the end of the war it was difficult to get that many. So he had to use youngsters, especially young boys from Austria, who were trained in mountain war.

The Germans had to retreat from the Litsa Front back to Norway on 17 October 1944. There was fierce fighting between the Russians and the Germans. On 22 October there was no more left of the German army. They were destroyed. There were German soldiers lying by the side of the road with their intestines outside their body, crying for their mothers. And later, Russians.

The fighting happened very close to my home. The Germans had taken over our house and one of their officers was wounded and died. It was winter – they couldn't bury him. So they threw him outside the house. He was lying there for a whole winter. If a German soldier was so badly wounded they couldn't save him, special German soldiers were commanded to kill their own. They would shoot him, put him out of his misery with a mercy shot.

It was not a big house, but thirty-eight people were living in it, on the floor and in every bedroom and in the hall and everything. There were two Germans living in the kitchen. When the house was modernised after the war you could still see the blood spots on the floorboards and in the kitchen from the wounded officers.

The fighting was coming from the air, from bombing, man-to-man fighting as the Russians attacked the Germans. The war was so close our house was used by both sides. At three o'clock in the morning the Germans left: by four thirty Soviet officers were in the kitchen.

There was fighting for many days. I saw it all. We were hiding in the forest in a shelter my father made, but we were close to the house. Fewer and fewer Germans were coming and more and more Russians. I saw a German soldier lying in the field next to the house shooting at the Russians but he had no helmet. He was hit many times and the front of his head was blown off. I was 10 metres away.

The Russians used to say: 'Bayonet the Germans in the back, above the belt, above his ammunition belt.' When they ran after the retreating Germans they would bayonet them in the back as the blade wouldn't stick. It was easier to kill them. The boys were lying by the side of the road, fatally injured, waiting to die, crying for their mothers.

Of course what you saw as a child affected people very badly: it made many children alcoholics after the war. It's a miracle I am not insane because of all I have seen as a young boy.

Svea and Eva were nodding solemnly and grimacing as Knut told his stories. Now they speak up. 'I think it was special that in Kirkenes we lived in a sort of friendship with the Germans,' says Eva. She goes on to say:

There were so many: seven Germans for every one of us. I remember a German soldier who drove a car and he stopped, opened the door and said: 'Come here.' My mother let me go and I got some sweets – 'bonbons' – from him. Maybe he had a little girl at home, just 3, like I was.

The Germans were clean and polite. They were very handsome men. We used to say: 'The Germans stole the girls' hearts, the Russians stole bicycles and watches.' My mother said: 'I'm so glad I was married because I am sure I could have fallen in love with one of those handsome Germans.'

At this point Svea leans forward:

There were two types of Germans: the green ones and the black ones. The green ones were OK but the black ones, with the death's head on their caps, they were no good.

Everything the Germans made they stamped with a German eagle and a swastika. They stamped the sacks of flour. One day a boat with flour and butter came to Kirkenes and was bombed. When the flour sacks floated up our people could grab them and make cakes and bread. When the sack was empty they made clothes out of them. I had a shirt made out of a flour sack, and when I took it off, it stood up on its own.

Kirkenes became vital to German military operations in the Arctic. It was a fortress town, a communications centre for the Litsa Front and the north of Norway and a base for air operations against both the Soviet ground forces and the Allied Arctic convoys supplying Stalin. It was a crucial link in the support and supply chain both into and out of the front line. Supplies and reinforcements went in and the dead and wounded came out, as well as troops being sent on leave or for redeployment. Soldiers wounded on the Litsa Front received initial medical care in Kirkenes and could then be shipped further south for longer-term rehabilitation.

The rapid and dramatic upgrading of the infrastructure of Kirkenes to handle this sudden influx of so many soldiers and so much cargo was carried out by Soviet prisoners captured in the fighting to the east. Kept in camps around the town, the prisoners were used for unloading the constant stream of ships bringing fresh war supplies, as well as on construction and roadbuilding projects overseen by the Nazi construction company Organisation Todt.

The docks became so busy the Germans even built their own railway to transport all the supplies around Kirkenes. Some 800 skilled civilian workers were brought in to build an air base at Hoybuktmoen, 12km from the town, which is the airport to this day. Soviet prisoners built a causeway to the island of Prestøia, which was turned into a military headquarters defended by batteries of anti-aircraft guns with a seaplane base alongside. Around the docks banks of anti-aircraft guns could throw up a fearsome field of fire, supported by artillery both along the coast and sited on the larger islands in the fjords surrounding Kirkenes to the east and west. The sea lanes were mined and U-boats and Luftwaffe bombers searched for targets in the Allied convoys heading for Murmansk and Archalengsk.

Because of the strategic significance of Kirkenes the civilian population found itself on the front line, gradually being bombed into oblivion. Only Malta was bombed more often in the war.

The German defences in Kirkenes were pulverised from the air by Soviet Ilyushin IL-2 Sturmoviks, ground-attack planes fitted with bombs and rockets with a rear gunner to watch their back as they delivered their deadly payload. The Sturmoviks bombed the docks regularly and also attacked German supply convoys in the Barents Sea. They earned the nickname 'The Black Death' from the anti-aircraft crews they terrorised and killed.

After one particularly intense attack in July 1944 had reduced much of the town to rubble, many civilians had had enough and left their homes for the safety of the tunnels at the iron ore mine at Bjørnevatn.

Civilian casualties in Kirkenes from the air attacks were mercifully low, especially as the German soldiers had built barracks and warehouses in the gaps between homes. Seven civilians died, among them Eva's grandfather-in-law. 'My father-in-law's father went out on the steps during an air raid,' she says. 'He heard planes and wanted to have a look and see where they were heading and he never came in again. One of the bombs fell nearby and the shrapnel killed him.'

I mention the prison camps the Germans set up in Kirkenes for the Soviet prisoners they brought back from the Litsa Front to use as slave labour, building roads, bunkers and bases. I ask if my guests have any memories of them.

'Near to my house was a camp with Russian soldiers who were prisoners,' says Knut. 'When the German guards saw that a prisoner couldn't work any more they pressed a bayonet into the back of their neck and pushed it up into their brain then twisted it. I saw that.'

Everybody in the room grimaces. Knut looks at me, pausing for Eva to translate. 'They didn't use a bullet. They just used a bayonet. Because they couldn't work any more.'

There is a silence, broken by Eva:

My mother told me that in the winter when it was very cold she saw a Russian prisoner working outside. She gave him a pair of mittens and he thanked her. But then instead of wearing the gloves, he put them in his pocket. Maybe he used them to get some food.

She sighs, and continues, 'There is a saying: "If you could gather the tears of all the Russian mothers, it would make a river bigger than the Volga".'

When the peace deal between the Finns and the Soviet Union was signed in September 1944, one condition was that the Finns had to get the Germans off their land within a fortnight. The Finns initially allowed the Germans to move men and supplies by trains and blow bridges and roads as they left, but Stalin tired of the delays and ordered them to use military force. When the Finns surprised the Germans with a landing at Tornio which threatened their withdrawal lines back into Norway the former allies fought bitterly, leaving hundreds of casualties.[6]

In a glimpse of what lay ahead for Norway, the last SS troops set fire to public buildings as they pulled out of the Finnish capital Rovaniemi in mid October 1944, but the fire spread to wooden private homes, and flames surrounded an ammunition train full of dynamite standing at the station. The force of the explosion wiped out much of the town. By the time the Finns reoccupied Rovaniemi, there was little left standing – perhaps 10 per cent of the town. This pattern was repeated throughout the Finnish settlements along the German retreat. Nearly a third of all the buildings in Lapland were destroyed by German forces withdrawing.[7]

A week before the burning of Rovaniemi, the Soviets launched the Petsamo–Kirkenes offensive in the northern Arctic, a joint land, air and sea operation setting 97,000 Russians against 56,000 Germans holding positions west of Murmansk. Despite advancing through boggy tundra strewn with boulders, and with hills offering defensive firing points over the single-track road through the battlefield, the Red Army quickly pushed the Germans back to the final river crossing before Kirkenes.

The German commander, Rendulic, had orders to hold on as long as he could so as many supplies as possible could be shipped out of Kirkenes. As the Germans fell back they sowed mines and set up rearguard positions to slow the Soviet advance, but by 23 October 1944 the Red Army was massing for the final push across the Pasvik river at Elvenes and on into Kirkenes.[8]

The next day fighting had reached the iron-ore mine at Bjørnevatn, only 10km south of Kirkenes. Streams of German columns were leaving town heading west. There were large explosions and fires as stockpiles of supplies and strategically useful buildings were destroyed. By 3 a.m. on 25 October, Soviet troops were fighting in the southern outskirts of Kirkenes. By 9 a.m. they were joined by tanks and artillery moving in from the south. The German rearguard fought pitched battles through the morning with three separate Soviet forces, but by midday the last organised resistance had been overcome. The following day Høybuktmoen airfield was taken and Highway 50 – the only road out – was cut. Any Germans left were forced to flee north to the fjord and escape in boats.

After defeating a German rearguard at Neiden, west of Kirkenes, Soviet commander General Meretskov decided that, with such rugged country and the polar winter on its way and with short days and sub-zero temperatures, the pursuit of the Germans should be called off. The Red Army moved up to the Tana River on 13 November and halted. Kirkenes was free.[9]

The conversation in my hotel room moves on to the liberation of Kirkenes by the Russians and conditions in the mine at Bjørnevatn.

'We lived in the tunnel at Bjørnevatn with 3,000 other people,' says Eva:

I lived there with my mother and father and aunts and uncles and grandparents. Ten babies were born in that time – one of them was my brother. One day I couldn't find my mother and I shouted: 'Mamma, where are you?' and my aunt said, 'Eva, you have a little brother now.' We went to a little cottage in the mine and we visited my mother. I can remember this little boy lying beside her wearing a yellow jacket. My aunt had made cocoa for my mother because it was very healthy, and I drank almost all of it. We didn't have sweet things then. I still remember this wonderful warm, sweet cocoa, and my aunt said: 'You mustn't drink all of that because it's for your mother – she's just had a baby.' All ten of those children are living today.

When the Soviet army came there was a celebration outside the tunnel. There was a Norwegian flag outside the opening and there was music and singing – 'yes, we love our country' – but I saw something very strange. I saw that people were embracing the soldiers and shouting 'Oh, I'm so glad!' Well, I thought that was strange, because I couldn't tell the difference between the Russian soldiers and the Germans. I had been taught to be angry with the soldiers and now everyone was kissing them!

Everyone laughs. It's clear the wartime memories are bitter-sweet.

Svea is next to tell a story. On the night of the liberation, her family were also hiding in a tunnel, but at Hesseng, nearer town than Bjørnevatn.

'My father made beds for us to lie in,' Svea says:

… and I had a little brother who was born in July 1944, so he was just a baby. That night we went to bed with Germans standing guard outside, particularly one man I remember who was working at a field kitchen. We didn't sleep very much because of all the noise but then we heard music and singing, and we could see Russians coming down from the ridge – 100, 200! The German with the kitchen had gone, and so had all the rest.

This was 25 October – liberation! By the time the Russians got to Bjørnevatn there weren't many Germans left. They were all on their way west, to Tana.

Hitler's order to burn Finnmark was issued only after the Germans left Kirkenes, but there was little left of the town by then anyway. The retreating Germans burned and blew up everything they could – storehouses, roads, administration buildings – and turned their coastal guns on the Soviets before the crews scrambled to escape in boats. Kirkenes was a wasteland, a town in ruins, with a handful of buildings remaining amid the rubble. Charred timbers and factory chimneys poked out of the ruins like bony fingers.

'Not many people from this eastern part of Finnmark were evacuated because the Germans were in too much of a hurry to get out themselves, so we were allowed to stay,' says Eva.

Svea nods in agreement. 'There were twenty houses left after the war in Kirkenes, and they were built for two families to share,' she says:

> We lived in one of the houses that were left and there were forty of us in there, all sleeping on the floor. When you got up in the morning you had to climb over all the other people. But if someone arrived in Kirkenes from the sea, we'd say, 'Stay with us. Lie down.' That was in 1945 but after that the town was built back up again.

Eva nods and leans forward. 'After the war, in 1944 and '45 there were problems,' she says:

> A few Norwegian soldiers came from Murmansk after we were freed, they were from Scotland, and they expected to be welcomed like heroes. But we were free, and they were not heroes at all. They were angry and irritated. They felt we had been too friendly with the Germans, but we had been living with them for four years. The Norwegian authorities put on a performance of Norwegian fiddle players, Norwegian costumes, just typical Norwegian things, and that was because they wanted to make sure we didn't forget we were Norwegians because we had been too friendly with the Germans – a rehabilitation. That was a number one policy in Norway.
>
> Many Norwegian girls had German lovers and they had children: Norwegian-German babies. In Oslo they say our sexual morality was very low because so many children were born at that time. History is written in Oslo, and Oslo is too far away; 2,500km is a long way.
>
> When Kirkenes was freed, they raised a flag in Moscow. The rest of Norway knows little about this. The Russians liberated Kirkenes. When the rest of Norway celebrated Freedom Day on 7 May 1945 we had been free for half a year; they don't know that. This 7 May doesn't mean so much to us – the important day for us is 25 October – that's Liberation Day. When the war ended and we saw the pictures of the king coming back, all the flags out in Oslo and everyone cheering and celebrating we said, 'Oh, this is in Norway – it's in our country?'

She pauses and tilts her head, almost wondering why this should be. Then she adds, 'Because it seemed so far away.'

We talk next about the dangers of life in a post-war town recently abandoned hurriedly by one of the best-equipped armies of recent times, which had stock-piled vast quantities of live ammunition in several camps.

Svea's next story is a tragic illustration of a situation that was commonplace:

After the war there were many very dangerous things left lying around which children played with. There were many young boys without fingers and just one foot.

I had two friends, a boy and a girl. We used to play with the shells they fired from those big guns. Once we had bashed the warhead off there was powder inside; some that was yellow in a flat tube and some that was brown. We mixed it together and tied it up in paper with a rubber band, then set fire to it and ran off into the sea before it blew up. It was very, very dangerous.

One day I had to go to Bjørnevatn 12km away to buy milk and that took all day because I had to stand in line, then I came back on the iron ore train and went back to my Mamma. Mamma said: 'Oh Svea it was very good that you had to buy milk today because your two friends are dead.'

I went to say goodbye to them. They were laid out in a shed and they looked like they were asleep. But under the sheet covering their head and shoulders there was nothing left. After that day I never played with the shells again.

Eventually our conversation comes to a close. We have been talking for hours. I see my guests out and take a stroll around the town to get some fresh air and soak up some of the history around me. I walk across the central square and past the white parish church (*kirke* in Norwegian) that gave the town its name. It's not the original one – that was destroyed in the war – but this new church was built on the same site.

The old harbour is to the left of an ugly modern hotel where tourists stir café lattes while gazing out across the fjord. Moored at the old piers are several battered fishing trawlers – one Russian, one Norwegian. Further along the harbour road and around a slight bend, I reach the dock where cargo ships are loaded with processed iron ore from the processing factory which dominates the hills I am now facing.

The Hurtigruten coastal steamer came in earlier this morning, just before my guests arrived, for its four-hour turnround at the end of its journey up the Norwegian coast. In a couple of hours it will head south again on its neverending shuttle. I've been most of the way along the coast on the boat but I've never made it to Kirkenes – until now.

The town is still bustling with temporary activity from the boat's arrival. Tourists can jump into minibuses for expeditions catching king crabs or canoeing down the Pasvik river separating Norway from Russia. Some wander the streets, peering into souvenir shops selling tacky gifts of trolls or sitting on a bench in the small central square smoking or eating sandwiches. The shopping streets have few attractions to hold anyone long: it's like a British market town on half-day closing in the 1970s. There are a couple of restaurants and cafes, a bookshop, a library and one or two tourist-standard hotels. A kebab van opens up hopefully each day in one corner of the square. The drivers at the town's only taxi firm have developed patience. Business in the Joker supermarket picks up briefly. There isn't that much to do in Kirkenes, to be honest, but it's a long four hours if you don't do something.

Some tourists find their way to Andersgrotta, an underground bomb shelter a few minutes walk from the town centre. Here you can get a brief glimpse into what happened to Kirkenes during the war. The shelter is open for an hour-long visit three times a day, twice in the morning and once in the afternoon, locked behind a thick steel door facing onto a street lined with yellow and grey wooden houses built in typical Norwegian panelled style, somewhere between sombre and cheerful.

A flight of concrete steps leads down to a gritstone path along corridors hewn from the rock, which open out eventually into an enormous cave. In the war around 800 people from the town sought shelter here. A platform of wooden benches fills the cavernous space, which at 4°C is noticeably chilly and 8m of rock separate the cave from the street above. A white screen fills one wall of the cave, which shows a 9-minute film telling of the German occupation between 1940 and 1944, the 328 bombing raids on the town and the liberation by the Red Army six months before the end of the war in the rest of Europe. Still photographs show German soldiers in the town with their weapons of war, the docks in flames and civilians fleeing air raids. The later sequences show flames licking at the wooden houses, locals embracing Russian soldiers liberating the town's population at the iron ore mine at Bjørnevatn and then scenes of the devastation inflicted upon Kirkenes. Vast swathes of the town are smoking ruins, punctuated by the brick chimneys rising from the charred timbers. In one picture only the stone steps of the bakery remain. Nine minutes is not long enough to digest what really happened here. And, sadly, some tourists simply don't believe it. During my time in Kirkenes I hear of American tourists apparently unable to accept that the Red Army liberated this part of Western Europe, and prepared to argue vehemently and unpleasantly until they were red in the face.

When the Hurtigruten steamer's enormous horn bellows out the ship's intention to leave, the tourists head back to the new quayside over towards Prestøia. On the way to the boat their minibuses pass more reminders of the war: along the quayside road there are still several ugly concrete bunkers that were once gun batteries and anti-aircraft positions. A wooden house clings to the top of one bunker, known to locals as the former offices of a post-war seaplane company. On the other side of the road is Svea's old house, rebuilt on the stone cellar blocks she sheltered in with twenty strangers, and now clearly home to a new generation.

I walk to the old piers to watch the final act of the Hurtigruten steamer's departure preparations. The adventure trips leave from here, just a short distance from the modern hotel. The deep-blue water of the fjord laps against the quayside, gentle waves breaking over jagged concrete blocks broken open to reveal steel wire reinforcements. Rusting in the water are the remains of a narrow-gauge railway goods wagon. Surely this cannot be a bogie from the wartime dock railway?

I am sure that, faced with the obliteration of everything they had worked for, some towns would have built a new Manhattan from their own ashes. The people of Kirkenes cleared up the mess, paved over the war, put up concrete prefabs in the 1950s and became an iron ore boomtown in the 1960s. But when iron ore slumped, so did Kirkenes – and you can almost feel that air of resignation as you walk its unremarkable streets.

The gigantic Hurtigruten steamer bellows for the last time, folds its cargo doors back inside its cavernous hold, slips its ropes and glides without fuss into the waters of the Boksfjord. By the time the waves the boat has made lap and slap against the quayside from where I am watching, it is heading for the Barents Sea and the journey south, and the people of the town are left alone with their thoughts. And what thoughts they are.

There were human settlements in Kirkenes well before the twentieth century but on a very small scale. It was a fishing village with a distinctive white church on its tip that gave the town its name: 'Kirke-nes' means 'church on the headland'.

It was the discovery of iron ore in 1866 10km inland at Bjørnevatn that caused something akin to a gold rush. Thousands of men and their families poured in to work at the mine and seek their fortune once engineers had developed magnetic separation techniques to make mining the ore commercially viable. A railway was built to transport the ore to a plant in the town where it could be separated and then transported to international markets by sea. Port, railway, mine and town all flourished. Swedes, Finns, Russians and Norwegians made their way to Kirkenes to create a community bound by iron ore, enjoying the benefits of prosperity. They built houses for the families and restaurants to cater for the population and numbers swelled, reaching 9,000 by the 1930s. Despite a slump in the 1920s, the mine exported 900,000 tonnes of iron ore in 1938. When the war came, it took them all by surprise.[10]

There were economic as well as military reasons driving Hitler's invasion and occupation of Norway in 1940. Exports of Swedish iron ore reached Germany through the port of Narvik halfway up Norway's Atlantic coast. Seizing Narvik protected this supply, crucial to weapons production – the iron ore at Kirkenes was a bonus. Secondly, the occupation of Norway would deny the opportunity for the Allies to launch a second front against Germany through Scandinavia, something Hitler was so preoccupied with he sent 350,000 men to Norway to prevent it.

The German invasion forced King Haakon to flee to London, along with his government, which operated in exile from there for the rest of the war. Norway capitulated and Hitler appointed loyal Nazi Josef Terboven as Reichskommissar. After several attempts to force the parliament to depose the king, Terboven declared he had forfeited his right to return and dissolved the democratic parties. Norway was now under the direct rule of the Nazis, controlled by Terboven, with a puppet regime in place headed by the leader of the fascist Nasjonal Samling party (NS), Vidkun Quisling.[11]

The Quisling NS party was roundly rejected by the Norwegian popula-tion and never registered any popular support – Terboven had barely disguised contempt for Quisling. In one famous incident in 1942 the country's teachers rejected en masse attempts to set up a new fascist-led teachers' union to help Nazify the school curriculum. As a punishment, 500 teachers were sent to work on hard labour programmes building roads in Kirkenes, held in camps alongside Soviet prisoners of war and treated in much the same way. But mass resistance to Quisling's plan and popular support for the teachers forced him to back-track, and by the end of the year he abandoned the idea and freed the teachers.[12] As a gesture of thanks the teachers paid for a new library to be built in post-war Kirkenes. The building still stands in Kirkenes but it has now been replaced by a new library. The old library is now used as a rest home.

The Nazi takeover and the Quisling regime of collaborators prompted a wide-spread and defiant resistance, directed from London, organising acts of resistance, sabotage and intelligence-gathering for the Allies. The Norwegian fascists coop-erated with and assisted the darkest deeds of the Nazis: rounding up Jews to be sent to concentration camps; setting up its own justice system and force of para-military thugs – Hird – based on Hitler's SA and its own political and secret police; betraying and executing Resistance fighters; and providing guards for the prisoner camps, who shocked even the Nazis with their brutality.[13]

Allied attacks on shipping off the coast of Norway following the German occupation led to the sinking of several of the Hurtigruten steamers carrying pas-sengers, mail and supplies from the south, and in 1941 the service was suspended, running only as far north as Tromsø.[14]

The combination of German levies on food and a reliance on imports meant the war had a drastic effect on supplies of staple goods for ordinary Norwegians. Shortages were common and worsened the further north one travelled.

By June 1943 conditions in Kirkenes were deteriorating. Essential food was in short supply and outbreaks of diphtheria, typhoid, dysentery and scurvy were common. Epidemics broke out despite mass innoculations. The basic diet was low in nutrition and calories, consisting of whatever could be found. Meals revolved around herring or turnips: herring soup, turnips with salt fish, turnips with her-ring – perhaps boiled turnips or turnips fried in cod liver oil. 'Coffee' was made from roasted grains or dried peas. Cigarettes were made from discarded stumps found on the streets, rerolled in plain brown paper. People made their own soap from caustic soda and fat. Potato starch was used in cooking and also as a talcum powder. And that was in the good times. The unpredictability of deliveries affected all aspects of life: foodstuffs, medicines, building materials, mail, clothing and even shoes.[15]

In the following passage, a nurse describes conditions in Porsangerfjord in 1943:

> Børselv [a village on the shores of the fjord] ran out of flour a couple of weeks ago, but on the west-side of the fjord it is much worse, as they have been out of flour much longer. Around Christmas there was a ship with potatoes. The westside and Børselv got potatoes but when the ship reached Hamnbukt, frost destroyed the whole load, and so Lakselv, Karasjok, Kjæs and Brenna didn't get any potatoes.[16]
>
> There was … a shortage of vitamins. Potatoes were an important source of vitamin C and had for the most part to be imported from other parts of the country. Potatoes transported to the county by boat could be drenched with salty seawater or even frozen on deck before they reached their destination.[17]

Pregnant women especially had a lower intake of calcium, iron and vitamin C. Medical reports note that 'one child, one tooth' was a common saying in Finnmark well into the 1970s.

Though once a plentiful part of the diet for local people, fishing became risky when the waters were mined. Freshwater fish were available with 'the right connections'. Daily butter rations for the staff at hospitals were the size of a thumbnail and flour was often of poor quality and difficult to make proper bread with. In rural areas, the water came from wells and sometimes small rivers and fjords, but there were health risks here too:

> Our teeth went bad. It was the water. We took water from the little lake in the marsh. So did the German soldiers who lived in the cottage in the neighbourhood. They also got bad teeth. Then their officer took water samples from the lake and there was a lot of iron in it, and they stopped using it. They got their water from a brook. We were a big family, and it was too far to bring the amount of water we needed from there, so we still took our water from the lake. And all the children got bad teeth.[18]

By 1944 the situation had become altogether more serious. The Kirkenes firefighters – volunteers to a man – were expected by their German masters to turn out during air raids and tackle fires, but were not now allowed to take cover. If they did they might be accused of being saboteurs, facing the possibility of imprisonment and even execution. Instead they dug trenches near the fire station so they could find at least some shelter from the bombs, now falling with increasing regularity.[19]

With the constant daylight of summer 1944, Russian bombers carried out round-the-clock attacks on the German defences dotting the coast around Kirkenes and at Vardø, Vadsø and Berlevåg. There were regular strikes against the big guns of Kiberg, a town across the Varangerfjord from Kirkenes armed with fearsome coastal guns facing onto the Barents Sea, from where they could shell the Allied Arctic convoys.

Much of the population of Kirkenes was living in the Andersgrotta caves more or less full-time by 4 July 1944, when the town suffered a devastating attack from the air. Bjarnhild Tulloch lived in the district of Haugen, a short run away from Andersgrotta. In her childhood memoir *Terror in the Arctic* she describes how she emerged from the shelter to find her life altered forever:

> stumbling from the darkness of the tunnel into bright sunlight was a blinding albeit sobering experience. A strong smell of smoke filled the air. Slowly picking our way through the rubble up to Haugen we looked around in disbelief. The Haugen we knew and loved was almost unrecognisable. It was a beautiful summer day but wherever we turned there were ruined houses and smouldering fires ... The destruction seemed to be widespread with smoke curling and rising from ruins where houses had been.
>
> Our house was still standing, but only just. The house diagonally across us from the square was gone, blown off its foundations. The house across from our kitchen had burned down. The steps and landing [of our house] had disappeared and the outside door was missing ... Where there had been windows, there were now only gaping holes. The walls were peppered with shrapnel and there were signs of fires having been put out. The floor was covered by a thick layer of pulverised material, which had been all our dishes and food, and probably the window as well. The kitchen table and chairs, along with the rest, had been turned into rubble. One cupboard door, left on the wall and peppered with holes, was swinging slowly from one hinge. We were now destitute. All we had was the clothes we were wearing.[20]

In the library across the square from my hotel I'm looking through a book of pictures from the wartime occupation, which deals in some detail with the fighting on the Litsa Front. The book is called *Kirkenes–Litsa* by Kalle Wara. The scale of the German presence is enormous. In one picture a ship at the docks has unloaded twenty-four artillery field guns which have been lined up side by side on the quayside I walked along earlier this afternoon. There are barrels of fuel and oil and sacks of food as high as the soldiers beside them. Perhaps Svea's shirt was made from a sack like this. In the background I spot the old school house that was taken over by the Nazis and destroyed by Russian bombing. Other pictures show thousands of soldiers on parade, tanks driving away from the docks and 300 horses in makeshift stables being fed before being moved to the Litsa Front. The Germans would find the tanks of little use. Facing enemy artillery on a single road surrounded by swampy marshland and rocky tundra, lack of manoeuvrability under fire would become a key issue. They were soon withdrawn from a combat role.

I turn another page. Here there are Stuka dive bombers on their way to attack Murmansk, horses and reindeers pulling supplies in snowstorms and a column of trucks loaded with soldiers driving along a waterlogged, muddy road led by a motor-cycle sidecar outrider. The next picture shows a U-boat slipping into Kirkenes from a patrol hunting Allied supply ships heading for Murmansk – the photo alongside shows black smoke belching from one ship hit by Luftwaffe bombers.

Another page shows the aftermath of a Soviet air raid. A bomb has torn the entire end from a wooden house. Wallpaper peels from an upstairs bedroom wall and there's a pile of timber and unidentifiable belongings in a sad pile outside. Another house has had its back broken by a bomb blast. The front has collapsed while the back has reared up on its foundations like a sinking ship.

Another photograph shows the aftermath of a direct hit by an incendiary bomb on a timber store at the docks. Thick black smoke and flames rise high into the sky. Hundreds of people look on from a safe distance, but the smoke is so dense and the picture taken from so far away I cannot distinguish with certainty whether they are Germans, prisoners or civilians, but, judging by the ship stand-ing off the quay, that looks like where I stood an hour or so ago watching the Hurtigruten steamer leave.

At the back of the book I find a series of maps showing the German defences around the town. Kirkenes certainly lives up to its billing as a fortress. There are searchlights and air defence guns all along the coast, dotted around the fjords and inlets. There are three airfields: Høybuktmoen in Kirkenes, Bardufoss near Tromsø and, in between, Banak near Lakselv on the Porsangerfjord. There are marine bases and barracks for 10,000 to 15,000 men for the coastal defences and the 45,000 men going to and from the Litsa Front. Ships or aircraft approaching Kirkenes would have to run the gauntlet of a network of coastal artillery guns that packed a deadly punch. Across the fjord at Kiberg there were three 28cm cannons. An island in the centre of the fjord facing Kirkenes had four guns which could point either out to sea or at the town.

The town itself was guarded by a coastal battery of three 15cm guns. There were air defence batteries of four 88mm guns in three separate places round the town and coastal air defence guns on the beach, with vast storehouses and ammunition dumps in several places round the town. Up near the three lakes heading out of town towards Murmansk, marked with barbed wire, was one of the biggest pris-oner of war camps in the area, a 'fangeleir'. There were minefields, bomb stores, ammunition dumps, barracks, workshops, coastal bunkers and seaplane harbours ,including the one alongside the fortress island of Prestøia.[21]

Great thought and vast amounts of effort had clearly gone into the defence of Kirkenes, and it's not difficult to see why. The town was the centre of the German command structure along the coast of Finnmark and to the Litsa Front in the east, linking to the front-line troops both in Finland and the areas of the Soviet Union under German control. A network of telephone cables laid across land and undersea connected Kirkenes with coastal batteries at Vardø, Kiberg, Vadsø, Bugøynes and along the coast to east and west. Knocking out the communications centre in Kirkenes would have dealt a severe blow to the effectiveness of the German army along this whole front.[22]

From the library in the town centre I walked up a steep hill to the Borderlands Museum (the Grenselandmuseet) which overlooks the town. Here I would get an insight into the war through the eyes of the Soviet pilots sent to attack Kirkenes and who had to fly through fearsome defensive fire to deliver their bombs.

The museum is an amazing place, being built around one of the few remaining Sturmovik ground attack planes. It was ditched in a fjord during the war and remained there for forty-five years before being rediscovered. When it was salvaged the Russians took it back across the border, restored it free of charge and then presented it to the people of Kirkenes. The two-seater plane, painted blue on the underside and camouflaged a mottled green above, with a red propeller spinner and a reindeer with antlers painted just below the cockpit, fills the main hall. The pilot for its final flight was Alexander Chechulin, commander of a squadron of Sturmoviks from the 214th Airborne Assault Regiment in 1944.

'I remember Kirkenes very well,' he said in an interview after the war. 'Every time we flew over Kirkenes there was so much shooting I had to close my eyes. When you are the first to attack you close your eyes, then you open them and let the bombs fall. We would fly over again to take pictures before returning home.'

The Germans hated Sturmovik attacks, hence the nickname 'The Black Death'. One captured NCO told Russian interrogators, 'The Sturmoviks were what the soldiers dreaded the most. When they appeared both soldiers and officers spread out seeking shelter wherever possible. Almost everyone is convinced the Russian planes are better and that the Russian pilots are more skilful and braver than the Germans.'

Another NCO prisoner said, 'The aircraft's effect on morale was enormous. Anti-aircraft defences covered the battery for fear of attracting the attention of the planes. In fact it took hours to calm down the aircraft defence squad after such an attack.' And yet another soldier said, 'Everyone hides behind rocks in fear, waiting for the planes to pass over. After the attack they thank God they are alive. One does not wish either friends or enemies the terror of such moments.'[23]

The following morning a tall man wearing a black and white check shirt takes his place on the sofa in my hotel room. Rune Rautio is a Second World War military historian specialising in the Arctic Front war. One of my new Norwegian friends put his number into my hands and suggested I call him. From his very first words I can see that his expert knowledge will answer some of the questions gathering in my mind.

'The scorched-earth order to destroy everything was first given by Hitler on 16 October, a week after the start of the Petsamo–Kirkenes offensive,' he says:

That was an order that the German troops should withdraw after destroying their own buildings and fortifications, but it didn't specify destroying the civilian houses. Then Hitler changed his mind and ordered the destruction of all civilian property. That was issued on 28 October but because of communication difficulties the troops didn't receive the order until the following day, and by that time the Germans were long gone from Kirkenes.

There wasn't very much to burn in Kirkenes by then anyway, especially after the Soviet bombing of 4 July. The Russians dropped cluster bombs, incendiaries and 1,000kg bombs which ruptured the water pipes so once the fires took hold of the wooden houses they couldn't be put out.

The order on the 28th was too late for Kirkenes to be classified as a 'scorched earth' destruction – it arrived after the liberation by the Russians. By then the Germans had left for the west, and it was only after the Battle of Neiden several kilometres outside Kirkenes that the Germans began what you would describe as a scorched-earth retreat; that is, burning everything in their path. They started burning on the 28th, so the first place that was burned according to the instructions was Bugøyfjord, a small village between here and Varangerbotn.

Many people round here will tell you that the relations with Germans were good and even very good, as you had reservists manning the coastal fortifications in small places. They were older, family men with a wife and children at home, mature, and they came into close contact with the civilians. Many of them established relations that would last the rest of their lives.

A lot of those Germans came back frequently to Norway to visit friends from this area, even shortly after the war. Some units receiving the order [to destroy everything] did not pay attention to it as they were in a hurry to save their own skins and escape from the Russians, while other units simply ignored it and left, like in Bugøynes.

There was no road then to the fishing village of Bugøynes 95km west of Kirkenes – the only way in and out was by sea. The village survived intact because the commander of the German garrison made a deal with the locals that if they let him use their fishing boats to get his men out, he wouldn't burn the town. They did, and he and his men left peacefully. The commander was received like a hero when he returned to visit after the war.[24] Rune continues:

People say the only time they were really afraid of the Germans was when those battle-shaken maniacs without nerves came from the front during the withdrawal in October 1944. Then you had all those youngsters that had been going through all those terrible traumas withdrawing from here to the Lyngen Line. A lot of those people were unstable and extremely dangerous and there were a number of incidents. They were trigger-happy, extremely nervous and violent. You had to be extremely careful. There were cases when the 6th Mountain Division withdrew this way and they started to burn buildings according to the order from Hitler, and in some cases they also murdered people. Some people who didn't get out of the house quickly enough were burned inside it and sometimes the owner of the house would argue and they'd shoot him and throw him in the fire. We had incidents like that.

Rune looks out of the window at the town:

And it's not true that Kirkenes was the second most bombed place in Europe after Malta. It's a good story but it's not true, because that claim is based on inaccurate logging of plane movements over the town. A plane may have flown over the town to attack shipping in the fjord but that's been logged as an alarm. The town of Kirkenes was actually bombed very little. Most of the bombing attacks were directed against ships either in the harbour or in the fjord.

There was the bombing of 4 July 1944 when much of the town was in flames and there was another attack in August, but Kirkenes itself wasn't attacked more than three or four times in the war.

I can see that Rune is a stickler for detail and not afraid to go against the grain. That comparison with Malta is everywhere in the town, but I take his point. He continues:

Once the German attack on Murmansk was stopped at the Litsa river there were 100,000 troops here who needed food, supplies, fuel and shelter. The Arctic Front became a war on the supply chain. Between 1941 and 7 October 1944 the Russians were trying to rupture the Tromsø to Kirkenes supply line in the same way as the Germans were trying to stop the Arctic convoys bringing supplies into Murmansk.

Rune has spent many years working on Finnmark's war years and his detailed knowledge adds interesting dimensions to the family stories I've heard so far. He has plenty to say about why the Russians didn't remain in Kirkenes and also the post-liberation situation in the town:

The Russians stayed for a year and went back in September 1945. As soon as the Petsamo–Kirkenes operation was over [in November 1944], all the ground forces, aircrews, special forces units and commandos were sent to the Berlin offensive and also to the fighting with Japan. They only left what was strictly necessary and gave a lot of tasks to the increasing number of Norwegian troops coming from Scotland via Murmansk to this area from November onwards. Most of this province was formally under Soviet command but with Norwegians taking care of the daily duties. You mostly found the Soviet units between the border at Kirkenes and Neiden, 2,000 to 3,000 soldiers, something like that.

A lot of women in Kirkenes had had German boyfriends so the Norwegian troops who were coming in started cutting their hair off. That was not an uncommon situation in Europe because it had happened all over but it was definitely not popular here so they got a very clear message, even from the priest, to stay away. Ironic songs were even written about their behaviour: 'They came from Scotland, had never been in a war, their bellies were full, good life. And then they came here to people that had been under occupation for four or five years. They had no idea about how life had been and then they started to teach them.'

That was totally unacceptable. This municipality had about 10,000 people living here during the war. That means on a permanent basis there was one German soldier for every person. Then with all the movement of troops to the front and for rest here, in reality it was two to three soldiers for each person here. In situations like that you can't avoid getting close to people. Since they were not isolated in camps but mixed in between the civilians in barracks all over the town – side by side – to talk about making a civilian 'cold front' in a situation like this is bordering on stupidity.

There was one story in my home town Vardø. There was an educated woman – a piano teacher – who didn't like the Germans at all, and she was forced to have a German officer living in one of the rooms in her house, which was quite common. She treated him like he didn't exist and one day she came home and heard some beautiful piano playing coming from her house. Of course it was him playing. They began talking and he was a music lecturer from Vienna. It's impossible to have an enemy in a situation like that when you have a common interest.

Without prompting, Rune moves from subject to subject, so I don't interrupt him. He's clearly a man who has a great deal of knowledge on this subject and I'm thankful to have had an hour of his time:

Many people have asked why the Russians withdrew. They'd taken this area, they could have kept it, and of course the Norwegian government-in-exile were extremely nervous about it. We even know from recent historical research that the Russian general staff tried to convince Stalin not to withdraw but to go into a long-term lease of ports in the north – Kirkenes was ice-free, Tromsø was a superb port – so they wanted to have a kind of arrangement where they could stay after the war, but Stalin was very clear that they would withdraw. And this is in my mind because of the 'Percentages' deal with Churchill. Churchill and Stalin reached an agreement [in Moscow in October 1944] about how to separate Europe after the war, what should be the British sphere of interest, the Russian sphere of interest and what could be a mix. They had an agreement and Stalin kept to that.[25]

With that, Rune looks at his watch and says he has to go – he has an article to write. I go down in the lift with him and say goodbye on the street. It's a beautiful morning, warm and sunny with a clear blue sky. It feels odd to be talking about terrible events from seventy years ago on such a lovely day but they feel strangely close at hand.

I need only look around the town to see the aftermath of the war. Reconstructed around a central square, the town's buildings are mostly basic, flat-fronted 1950s blocks of drab brown or grey. There's nothing historic in Kirkenes. It could be East Germany in the bad old days.

In the centre of the square is a rather beautiful statue of a woman carrying a baby in swaddling clothes with a boy sitting by her side. The woman is proud and defiant, despite being barefoot and clad in a simple dress and shawl. The monument is dedicated to the mothers of Kirkenes for their efforts during the war.

An elderly VW Golf pulls up alongside the hotel. It's Svea Andersen again, keeping her promise to take me for a drive to show me some of the areas we have been talking about. We begin by skirting the shopping area, noting the 1950 prefabs that got the town back on its feet. She turns right, down a road of large but basic wooden houses, all painted different colours.

'Before and after the war Kirkenes was an iron ore town,' she says:

My father was a fisherman who came from Nordkapp with his brother to work at the mine. There were lots of communists at the mine. This area was known as 'Little Moscow' because of all the communists who lived here. The boss of the Bjørnevatn mine lived around the corner on a road lined with trees, in a big wooden house with a large garden.

She turns left and we pull up outside a picturesque wooden house set in spacious, carefully tended gardens, with antique street lamps lining the drive up to the front door.

'There,' she says. 'That was the boss's house.' We laugh: the distance between the communists and the boss is literally 100m. 'It was in everyone's interests for the mine to be successful,' she says, pulling away from the kerb again:

In the 1960s Kirkenes was a boom town again due to the iron ore and the
Sydvaranger factory. The processing building survived the war. Lots of the town was
rebuilt in the 1950s and 1960s. The church was rebuilt in 1959 and the area around it
dates from that. The school was bombed because the Germans made it into a headquarters. In reality, only the stone buildings survived. There are one or two wooden
buildings left – here, this is one.

She pulls up again. We get out of the car. A wooden-panelled, wooden-roofed
two-storey house stands in front of us. There are windows to the side on the
ground floor but not above, only in the gable end. A single chimney sits in the
middle of the roof ridge. The eaves curve downwards slightly as they reach
the edge of the house to allow snow to slide off. Around the side is a wooden
verandah and a small garden with a tree growing in it. The house is painted an
unremarkable brick red. There are no signs or plaques identifying this as one
of the few pre-war buildings in Kirkenes and, as such, having some historical
rarity value. I guess the whole town looked like this before its date with destiny.
The old red house sits in an estate of more modern prefabricated wooden buildings, mostly grey. This area is called Haganes, and leads up a hill to a victory statue
of a Soviet soldier carrying a submachine gun. Engraved into the stone base are
the words: 'To commemorate the brave Soviet soldiers who liberated Kirkenes in
1944.' Around the base is a large floral bouquet. It's fresh. Clearly people here have
long memories.

From the statue, Svea drives me out of town past the three lakes, heading for
Jarfjord to see where the final stages of the Petsamo–Kirkenes offensive were
played out. It's an area of small lakes and marshy swamps punctuated by streams
and occasionally rivers, close to Knut Tharaldsen's farm at Storskog on the
Russian border. This was the battlefield.

The marshland is dotted with steep, rocky outcrops several hundred metres
high in some places. The lower slopes are covered by dense woods of pine trees.
Higher up, where the rocks are sheer, vegetation is sparse and cover is limited.
A single road, now named the E6, runs through the marshland. It's the same road
used by both armies in their clashes of October 1944.

The role of Red Army engineers in keeping the road operational throughout
the twenty-four-day offensive was crucial. Three times the usual number of engineers supported the attack, working directly behind the front-line troops to clear
mines and repair and improve the road as soon as the Germans had been pushed
back. Combat units not engaged in fighting were assigned to help.[26]

Their achievements were considerable: in Arctic tundra, with little cover
and often under fire, Soviet engineers built 15km of road for wheeled vehicles,
210km of tracks and paths, 33 temporary bridges (up to 16 tons), 20 bridges (up
to 60 tons), 2 pontoon bridges and 3 assault bridges. They organised 4 assault

crossings, built 30 fords for armoured vehicles and cleared and restored 500km of road, removing nearly 16,000 explosive devices totalling more than 50 tons of explosives.[27]

The commander of the engineers on the Karelian Front, Lieutenant General Khrenov, said, 'Absolutely untrafficable terrain does not exist. The degree of trafficability depends on the quality of engineer support.'[28]

We pass Knut's farm on our left. I think of the German and Austrian boys dying by the roadside with their guts spilled, waiting to die, calling for their mothers. At reunion dinners many decades later, Red Army veterans with their tongues loosened would tell how they shed tears when they turned the dead German soldiers over to find they were just teenagers.

After a short drive further east we reach the shores of Jarfjord, a stretch of water that's been a summer fishing retreat for generations of Norwegians, including Svea and her family, with small woods of young silver birch trees growing alongside the road. We stop briefly, imagining the scenes of war that must have shattered this peaceful region. Then we head back past occasional barns and fishing cabins, past typical two-storey Norwegian wooden houses, painted red or white or brown, until we reach the bridge across the Pasvik river at Elvenes.

This is the last natural obstacle before Kirkenes. The bridge that once stood here was blown up by German soldiers hoping to slow their foes down and buy time to save their lives. But under cover of darkness Red Army pioneers paddled across the river below to silence German machine guns dug into the rocks opposite. The chasm was quickly breached by Soviet engineers using pontoon bridges.

Following intense exchanges of fire the Germans were driven back. The Petsamo–Kirkenes offensive was in its last stages, having cost the lives of an estimated 15,700 Soviets and 9,000 Germans.[29] But the road to Kirkenes lay open.

There were some things that Rune had said to me earlier that morning that I'd found scarcely believable, so when I got back to the hotel I listened to my tape of the interview again to check I'd heard him correctly. I had.

Rune grew up in Vardø, an island town 50km from Kirkenes by road, at the extreme north-east of Norway. Lying off the tip of the Varanger Peninsula across the fjord from Kirkenes, Vardø was just north of the fearsome coastal batteries at Kiberg. Boats leaving Kirkenes would go straight past there to get to the open sea.

'My entire childhood was spent fascinated by all the remains of the war physically around us,' Rune said:

> The Germans had an airstrip on the mainland and three coastal batteries on the island plus a lot of other fortifications. There were remains everywhere, some destroyed during the retreat, some complete. Since we were curious kids running around playing in the caves and the bunkers we found a lot of ammunition. Shells, grenades – thousands of them.

We had a game where we'd make a fire on the beach and put a shell on it. This was totally normal. So now when we read that in Oslo someone has found a 75mm shell in the garden and the police have evacuated everyone in the area, we don't understand that.

On a mental level we grew up hearing all those stories from our fathers and mothers about the war. In 1959 the war hadn't been over very long. We heard dramatic stories about the bombing of the town by the Soviets, the retreat, the scorched-earth burning. They didn't burn Vardø but they burned nearly everything else. Those stories triggered our fantasy and that's when I became interested in history. There was nothing in writing in those days about the war in this area: plenty about what happened in the south. We feel closer across the borders in the north than we do with the south.

There were a number of incidents directly after the war, in 1945 to '47, of kids playing with mines or accidentally stepping on mines and getting killed but in my generation there were surprisingly few. I was seriously injured myself when one of the shells we put on the fire didn't detonate. Finally after a long time I went to the fire and the shell exploded right in front of me when I was a metre away. That cost me four months in hospital. I remember it like yesterday. I took the blast right in the chest and a lot of shrapnel hit me in the arms and stomach and went quite deep.

He shows me white scars along his wrist and arm:

One piece missed the main artery in my arm by a centimetre. We found two boxes of 37mm anti-aircraft shells at the German airfield near Vardø and took them over to the island. We'd worked through both boxes and had great fun for two days. The one that fooled me was the last one, I think.

He laughs at the memory:

We were quite professional and didn't take too many chances. The first thing you did was kick off the casing and use the gunpowder inside for other purposes. We only put one shell on the fire at a time because, if you put more on, one would explode before the other and you wouldn't have any control over the other one. Sometimes the shell wouldn't explode properly because they were damaged by time – rotten, we used to say. So there wouldn't be a detonation, just a 'pffffff'. I went to the fire to look at this one and it exploded.

I was extremely lucky, as well as not being lucky. I was severely injured in the stomach, but if I had been a second closer I'd have been killed instantly. A second later I'd have taken the blast across more of my body and my neck and head and I would have been fatally injured. A few centimetres to the right or left and I would have been killed. I was also very lucky that the senior doctor at Kirkenes where I was flown was a professor with surgical experience of dealing with war wounds. I think he saved me. My parents were extremely shocked.

I'm not surprised. But Rune's brush with death is one of a number of similar incidents in the area from that time involving dumped German ammunition:

I remember another case, of a boy who found a shell at the seaside with some friends, quite a big calibre. They took it to his bedroom at home to examine but then it was dinnertime so the friends had to go home. They agreed to come back after dinner but this boy couldn't wait. He started to examine it and the shell blew up. That was a nasty story.

All around Kirkenes, all over Finnmark, there were people damaged by the war – one eye, reduced hearing, lacking one or two fingers – because of similar accidents. The Germans dumped truckloads of ammunition in the river of a Sami town in the central part of Finnmark called Karasjok. Even today the military is collecting hundreds and even thousands of pieces of live ammunition there. Here in Kirkenes, near to the second lake as you go out of town, the Germans had a big ammunition store. Even today the mine command of the army are doing clean-up work and each summer they find 1,000 to 2,000 pieces of ammunition – different calibres, even mines. That's seventy years later. When we were kids we'd walk in lakes with a clay bed and we'd find shells in there that weren't rusty at all. They looked like they'd been dumped there yesterday.

I switch off the tape, still a little stunned by Rune's matter-of-fact accounts of young children carrying around shells with incredible destructive power, some-times with tragic consequences. The more time I spend in Kirkenes the more incredible the stories seem to become, but then, of course, if you mix curious children and live ammunition then perhaps it's not so surprising. What I am find-ing a little odd is that there is no central museum dedicated to a proper display of what happened here – a record of this remarkable human experience.

Apart from a tacky souvenir shop in the square, the only museum, the Borderlands museum, is at the top of a hill outside the town. It's a reasonable distance away from the centre, badly signposted and a stiff walk up a steep hill: no silver-haired Americans are going to climb that. Only the Andersgrotta cave seems to have any kind of historical story-telling for the tourists who take the trouble to get off the boat.

I come across an account by the first Allied officer into liberated Kirkenes, an American, Colonel Paul Boyd. He flew by Catalina flying boat from Shetland into Murmansk in early December 1944 and from there made contact with the Norwegian military mission under Colonel Arne Dahl, which moved into liberated Kirkenes soon after the Russians.

His report reads:

> Along the road were evidences of war. Farmhouses and small towns were totally destroyed. From the standpoint of civil affairs the situation is bad. About half of the population remain in Kirkenes, and they are sleeping at least ten people to the room. There is a diphtheria epidemic, scabies is prevalent, and a lot of dysentery. The food situation is bad, and there are no potatoes or fish available. Some flour has been supplied by the Russians, but they have been given to understand that that cannot be continued. Fortunately the Germans left good stockpiles of coal, and they succeeded in destroying only a small amount. A truck was secured to return to Petsamo with us and pick up the medical supplies (1,000 lbs brought from Shetland).[30]

It's becoming clear to me that the children of Finnmark have had a different upbringing than most. What I'm about to hear shocks me even more, because it seems the impact of the war wasn't restricted to the immediate generation that lived through it, or their children, but has been transmitted down to a generation that wasn't even born: the children of the war children.

Just before five o'clock that evening I call in at a new travel agency office that's operating at the front of my hotel. It's called Destination Kirkenes and is run by Karin Johnsen, a relative of one of the families Bjarnhild Tulloch suggested I talk to. I simply popped in to say hello and tell her what I was doing, but, after a brief chat about why she started her business, I realise that our conversation has turned to the subject of the war. I ask her if she'll talk more after she closes for the day and she agrees, readily.

Taking her place on the red sofa in my room an hour later, Karin begins an account of a little girl's childhood that is just extraordinary. Her first words take my breath away. 'It was absolutely normal growing up playing with ammunition,' she says:

> We all collected ammunition. My brother and the other kids used to find ammunition belts and start a fire in a barrel. He'd put the ammunition belt in it and then crawl away, otherwise they would have been shot. The bullets would heat up and go off and there would be bullets flying everywhere. This was in the 1960s.
>
> I think most people here collected ammunition: old people, young people. Like – 'I have a secret.' The secret was the ammunition. I always wanted to go

to school so I started wearing a backpack when I was 4 years old, so everything went in my backpack. I trusted my brother – if he said 'carry this' I would do it. But I knew I had to because they would search him. My mother used to search my brother, but I used to carry the explosives. My brother said I looked so innocent. Everybody did it. Kids would say: 'We've got something.'

The thought of a 4-year-old girl carrying live and unstable ammunition in her backpack fills me with horror. Karin continues:

Everybody collected ammunition. Up that road there [she points from the window] some kids found some shells from an anti-aircraft gun so they blew them up, and everyone around lost their hearing. Not one of those kids was older than 15. We still laugh about it now.

She laughs; a hard, scornful laugh that I will hear many times before her story is told.

My mother had three white scars on her back and arm, like stripes. It happened in a bombing – she was hit by bomb fragments, I think. But she said: 'Don't ask.' So we never talked about it. We had a teacher with no hands. He lost them in some kind of ammunition accident, but he had the nicest writing in school. He'd put the chalk between his stumps and write on the board.

This was all directly related to the war. I shouldn't say our parents didn't care but they had enough problems in their head. I grew up with everybody arguing about what happened during the war or what happened afterwards and always screaming and shouting at each other. We were so used to it. I thought they were all raving mad, all of them. It was like growing up in a mental hospital. We grew up with people talking about the war, so we made our own war. We would beat the other kids up, or if we were bored we'd go round town looking for kids from Bjørnevatn, beat them up and send them home. They were not allowed to come into the centre – it was our town. Children from other places in town were terrified to come into town. Before my time our kids had a prisoner camp down by the quayside.

We were from Haganes, we were supposed to be the really evil place. If we went to town the police stopped us and they'd say: 'Where are you from?' And if we said 'Haganes' they'd say 'Go home.' We were tough kids. Most of us had parents and grandparents who were messed up after the war, and they had enough to do taking care of themselves. So we started these gangs. It reminded me of *Lord of the Flies*, with the children in charge. When I first read that book, I thought it was about us: the children were in charge. The war was normal for us, so I can easily identify with children who've grown up after a war.

I am not a psychologist but it seems the war has scarred the people of Kirkenes quite deeply and profoundly. There seems to be some truth in what Karin says about the experiences of survivors not really having been acknowledged. The scorched-earth stories of their parents seem to have driven a younger generation to act out the anger and the fear in the very air in ways that seemed unthinkable. This was a town at war with itself, young against old, children from one area against others, doing what you did in a war.

'You would get a crisis psychiatrist or medical help if you went through that kind of traumatic experience nowadays,' Karin says:

> You'd be in therapy for years. But there was nothing. That's why the kids took over, and we were ruling the town. Because we knew the grown-ups had their problems with screaming and shouting and drinking and everybody was more or less nuts, so that's what happens.
>
> When it was a clear sky in the winter, my grandmother would say, 'Look out, it's bomb weather.' And when there was a thunderstorm she'd say, 'Put your boots on and go to the basement because now we are going to die.' She'd have these flashbacks and if there was a big explosion or planes passing low over town, she'd be hysterical. I'm still scared of thunderstorms. My grandfather was crazy too. He taught me how to use a Luger. He said I had to bend my arm or the recoil from it would break my arm. He had a bayonet that he'd stolen from the Germans during the war. He sent me home once with it to scare my grand-mother after getting me drunk.

Karin has called a few of her friends from the same gang to come and add their stories to hers while I am in town. When she spoke to one man, now approach-ing 60, he said: 'Now people will believe me.' The chaos and craziness of post-war Kirkenes seems to be on another level entirely, but I am beginning to sympathise with the frustrations of war survivors and their descendants who took such a beating and yet can find no validation or evidence of it in the history books.

'I think lots of people were very bitter because their history was never men-tioned,' Karin says:

> Nobody talked about it. I thought my grandmother was raving mad because she was talking about the war and there was nothing in the history books. In 1949 when Norway joined NATO it wasn't politically correct to write that the Soviet Union had saved this place, so they wrote nothing, and that's a big injustice to the old people. They were living in their own world, so we lived in our own world too. The parents and grandparents didn't have a clue what was going on.

Then they tell me that Norwegians came here [in November 1944] and started to punish people for being friendly with the Germans. No wonder people are messed up. All the medals handed out were in the south, and there wasn't a war there – it was an occupation. The war was here. They talk about giving medals to the Alta Battalion (who fought against the Germans in Narvik and nearly defeated them) but it's too late. And it's a shame. I wonder when Norway will write the history books correctly?[31]

As I will discover, the hostility in Finnmark towards the official history written by 'Oslo' also covers Resistance fighters. In the north they were called 'partisans' and were mostly communists, trained in Moscow and sent back to Norway in small groups. The distinction between 'Resistance' and 'partisan' opens up an entirely different chapter of bitterness in Norway's wartime history. This place really is two countries.

Being so close to the USSR, with strong fishing links and a history of communist organisation already, Finnmark almost naturally looked to Moscow during the war. Some men sailed east to train as partisans rather than live under the Nazi yoke; others stayed and helped support communist partisans, who returned after training in Moscow to operate in three-man cells to carry out surveillance of the German convoys or report on troop movements, hiding in caves and radioing regular reports.

Little or no official recognition was given to their part in the war, when up to 100 people from Finnmark went east to become agents for the Soviet Union, many leaving from the fishing village of Kiberg. Before long the Germans realised the arrival of the Soviet planes and submarines attacking their convoys was no coincidence. They launched a concerted counter-intelligence operation involving 1,000 troops sweeping the Finnmark coast in the summer of 1943, which effectively smashed the partisan network.

In the crackdown eighteen agents were killed – some fighting to the death in caves when they were discovered, sometimes being killed by flamethrowers. Another twenty-three people who had helped with information and food for the agents were executed and a further thirty were sent to German concentration camps.[32] In one notorious episode, eleven partisans were beaten to death near Kirkenes by German guards after having been forced to dig their own graves by the side of the road.

After the war the surviving partisans returned home but honoured an agreement they signed in the Soviet Union not to talk about their operations. When relations deteriorated because of the Cold War these communists became the subject of suspicions and surveillance. In 1992, the Norwegian King Harald V visited Finnmark and unveiled a monument in their honour. He offered an apology on behalf of the Norwegian authorities saying, 'I am afraid that we may have unjustly inflicted great personal strains on some people in the shadow of the Cold War.'[33]

In 2006 a forgotten partisan hideout was discovered at a remote headland over-looking the mouth of the Varangerfjord, through which every boat heading for Kirkenes had to pass. The three partisans who had operated from there – Gunnar Halvari, Andrei Kasereff and Modolf Hansen – were set ashore in 1944 with enough food and equipment for three months. They lined the cave with reindeer skin, peat and a parachute and set up a radio transmitter reporting observations every day to Murmansk. After two months they got word the area was freed, so they came out, linked up with Russian forces and were sent to Murmansk for debriefing. They returned to Norway at Christmas 1944 but kept silent about their activities, which remained unknown until their cave was discovered sixty years later complete with oars, batteries, boots, cooking materials and skis, untouched since the day they left it.[34]

Kåre Tanvik shot to fame in Norway in 1968 at the age of 15 when he starred in a film called *Scorched Earth* about wartime events in the north. He later had a successful career as a documentary film producer and now runs the tourist Snow Hotel in Kirkenes, as well as the Andersgrotta shelter in the centre of the town. He's a very busy man because he's moving the Snow Hotel to a new location and has a team of workmen doing the rebuild, so it takes a few days before our paths cross. We arrange a meeting shortly after breakfast at the Borderlands Museum and over coffee he tells his story, which seems, like every story in Kirkenes, an extremely personal and painful one. '1944 is Year Zero here,' he says:

> Everything was burned. I don't have anything of my grandparents. No memories, nothing. Everything was destroyed. I was born in 1953; my whole childhood was spent hating Germans. I couldn't learn German in school. My father said, 'It's a war language – we don't like it.' He was a postmaster. The official language of the postal service is French – so I learned French.
>
> I was born in a barracks sent from Canada. That's all we had to live in after the war. We had a big quilted jacket in my childhood – my mother called it 'the Englishman'. It was aid from the war. It was 1cm thick with a big stick-up collar, a military light green. When it was cold in the cabin in the evening and we were sitting by the fire my mother used to put 'the Englishman' around her.
>
> My father and mother had a handicraft shop, a souvenir shop. She imported wool and knitting needles so people could make sweaters in 1946. When we started the shop the first cruise ships came with Germans. They came to see what they had messed up. When I say Germans that's not quite correct because 80 per cent were Austrians – *Gebirgsjäger* – specialists from the Alps, because of the cold and the snow. But we called them 'Germans'.
>
> When I was about 13 or 14 my mother took the fur of the reindeers to the jetty and I made a small shop there to sell the skins to the Germans. One man asked me:

'Are they polar bear skins?' They were quite white so I said, 'Yes, and for you my friend, very cheap.' And he bought them. My mother was very happy and everyone was laughing that I could fool them. And, really, that's how I felt inside me. War is war but we can't understand why they had to burn everything down.

I work with Germans a lot now, a younger generation who had grandfathers and fathers here, and they have never heard about the buildings being burned down here. But they sit in the Andersgrotta crying, for what they have done, for the evil of the war.

When the *Scorched Earth* film was made in 1968 it was the first time people in the south had heard about what happened in the north. I was famous and I decided to go into movies – not acting, but making them. In the 1990s I asked the council if I could have Andersgrotta and they said yes, so I made a film about the war and opened it up to the public.

The post-war realignment of Europe into the North Atlantic Treaty Organisation (NATO) versus the Soviet-dominated Warsaw Pact drew political and military lines that would last for the next half century. Norway was one of the founder members of NATO in April 1949. When West Germany was admitted in 1955, Soviet leaders immediately created the Warsaw Pact of communist states. At a stroke communists in Norway were viewed with suspicion.

I sense an underlying anger in Kåre's comments. 'Yes I'm angry,' he says:

I'm angry about the burning and also that the Norwegian government went to bed so early with Germany in NATO. And I'm angry that the structure of this area was changed after the war. Lots of people moved out and went to the south. We lost our identities in Finnmark. A person is the result of what is around him. House, chairs, history, everything. And, when everything is burned down and you rebuild it, you try and rebuild it either the same or maybe brand new. And then you think maybe something is missing or it doesn't fit right. Maybe it's not as good as before?

Kåre pauses. 'Maybe mentally something happened here,' he says. 'Everything was destroyed: the houses, the boats. We don't have any history.'

Kåre looks at his watch. We have talked for a while and the builders are due to arrive. He needs to go but there are things he wants to get off his chest first:

Politically it's like this: the guys in the Resistance are always heroes, but not here, because most of them here were communists. The guys in Oslo had no impact on the war but here they did because they were partisans. My wife's father was helping the partisans and his brother took the partisans in his boat to Russia. He was tortured and shot at Christmas 1941 – the first victim of the Nazis in this area.

My wife's family were all communists and her father was without a job for six years in the 1960s. The Social Democrats – the Arbeiderpartiet [elected to power after the war and dominating government for three decades afterwards] – were the worst for hunting down communists – for thirty years.

When they declassified the records we found my father-in-law's file. His phone was tapped, he was followed when he was cycling, he couldn't work for many years. For seventeen years he ferried passengers by boat from a seaplane that landed on the harbour. When the airport reopened in 1962 the guys in Oslo said, 'You can work with us up there.' But the police blocked him from the job. They said he would report military movements at the airport to Russia. So he didn't get the job. We found the letter from the police in his file.

All the Resistance guys in the south got the best jobs in Norway but for thirty years my father-in-law was harassed because he was a communist and his brother was executed for fighting so we could be free here.

I'm beginning to realise that coupled with anger is a sense of deep injustice that sits deep in his heart and close to everything he holds dear. What happened in Finnmark changed the course of Kåre's family, his life and the life of his loved ones. It wasn't just a wooden house that was burned down. The foundations of his being were destroyed.

'When I opened Andersgrotta in 1992 King Harald came to the opening,' he says:

I asked him to sign a stone by the entrance and when he did I said, 'Now you have also signed that you shall not forget the partisans because they have never had dinner in your castle. They have been harassed by the police. We have the third biggest police station in Norway here – seventy police in Kirkenes because of the communists.'

It's not so much bitterness as righteous indignation. 'But now we have the oil, huh?' he says. 'Now we have a value because of the oil.'[35]

On my final evening in Kirkenes I met Karin Johnsen outside the hotel. She was smoking a cigarette and chatting to a very tall man who turned out to be a journalist at the local paper, the *Sor Varanger Avis*, which has an office across the street. This journalist introduced himself as Yngve Gronvik, and, when I told him I was gathering stories about the war, he promptly offered a story that once again made me wonder if the war actually ever did end here. He emailed it through to me later that night.

'Ever since I got my first Airfix kit as a kid I have loved the airplanes of World War Two,' Yngve wrote:

The beauty of them, the power. Number one was the Spitfire, and number two the Mustang.

My grandfather was engaged in the battles north of Narvik [with the Alta Battalion], where they were the first in the war to stop the German army and actually beat them. It was just a matter of days before the Germans would have to surrender when Norway capitulated. He told me a few stories, showed me his guns and so on, but I was just a kid.

As a teenager I moved with my parents to Kirkenes, and after a few years I learned a lot that we didn't learn at school, like the first occupied country to raise the free flag in Europe was Norway, and that happened in Bjørnevatn, in the mines in October 1944, and the Soviet army was the liberator.

Later I learned that the airport was originally built by the Nazis by Luftwaffe engineers and slave workers and that from there and nearby airfields they led the bombing of Murmansk, the Litsa Front and the Allied convoys. I heard about the bombing of Kirkenes with more than 1,000 air raid alarms during these three to four years and the dog fights. I never knew all this happened in Norway. An old man once described watching German and Soviet airplanes fighting in the skies above Kirkenes. 'They looked like a swarm of flies,' he said.

When I was older my grandfather told me about how they at first hesitated to fire at 'real people' in the fighting, and about the nightmares that followed him all his life. His buddy was hit in the back by a grenade and his body exploded into pieces. 'I wake up every night covered in his bloody guts,' he told me. I was starting to learn about another side of the war.

I was told there were lots of crash sites of wartime planes in Sør-Varanger [the municipality surrounding Kirkenes on all sides, an area of 3,700km² of mostly fjords, forests and barren land]. The first one I visited was a Russian Ilyushin IL2 Sturmovik. It had metal wings with the red star still on them. It was smashed to pieces. I started thinking about the two people that had been inside. Later I learned the two crew survived an emergency landing and hid in the forest for several days before they were united with the advancing Red Army.

I started collecting maps and stories and visiting all the planes I could find: American, British, Russian and German. There are many of them still out there.

One day a friend of mine told me about a crashed plane on top of a remote mountain where there might be human remains. We had to take a boat there and climb for several hours. It was hunting terrain and, though a few people knew about the plane, it wasn't common knowledge. We found the plane and there were bones. They had been hidden under small rocks but someone had put the rocks to one side — as though to look at the bones — and then not covered them again.

I thought about my grandfather. If something like this had happened to him, I would want someone to collect his bones and give him a proper burial. And I would have liked to know about it. I felt ashamed they were there, almost on display. So I decided there and then that he should be buried in Russia, and I had to find his identity and his family. This was in 2000 and the borders and archives were opened. 'It shouldn't be too difficult,' I thought.

It was an American plane, a Bell P-39 fighter, that the Russians got thousands of through the Lend-Lease deal. The Americans didn't like it, neither did the RAF, but the Russians loved it. It was modern and fast and had a huge gun that blew right through German armour.

I asked local historians and the Russian consul general in Kirkenes for help and sent lots of letters but nobody could answer my questions, and, to be honest, I didn't really know much about the plane in the first place. Then about a year later a local hunter came with some photos taken in the early 1980s. One was of the tail of the plane and it still had the numbers on. The whole tail had been missing when I was there. He also told me he was the one who made the 'grave'. I sent the number to everybody I had been in contact with.

The consul general told me they had found records of the plane in the archives in Moscow and a report that said when it went missing, but had no details about the pilot. I asked my friend Rune Rautio for help. He looked the date up in the Northern Fleet operational diary and there it was! We found that in November 1943 two P-39s went missing that day and when they wrote the report they had mixed up the names. With the help of two Russian historians we worked out which pilot flew each plane. Every pilot had a number – a code for each assignment – and that was the last two digits in the plane's number. So, finally, after four years, we had it. The bones in the cardboard box were of Junior Lieutenant Dimitry Petrovich Pisjauk.

But how was I to get him buried in Russia? And what about his family? Did they even know? Nobody had seen the plane shot down, so he was reported missing in action. Now I had a copy of his personal records with a photo. I asked the Russian authorities in Kirkenes to help, but nothing.

Then, a breakthrough. A young Russian woman who had married a man from Kirkenes had done lots of work finding the Russian fathers of wartime children in the area. The Russians had stayed until September 1945 and the result was a number of children being born in 1945–46. She met the same wall of silence until she wrote directly to President Putin.

A month later I received instructions from the consul general to meet an official on the other side of the border on a certain date. I would be taken to the Litsa Valley cemetery for the burial of Junior Lieutenant Pisjauk with full military honours. This was on Putin's personal orders.

I packed the bones as respectfully I could, had the box sealed and stamped by the consulate and went to the border. I don't speak Russian and watched nervously as border guards ran the box three times through the X-ray.

Finally I was led to a big black Russian car. In it was a small man in a black coat who spoke a little German and a little English. He was an ex-general leading the work of finding and burying soldiers that were still unaccounted for from the battles in Litsa between 1941 and 1944. He spent all his free time looking for lost soldiers in the area. Later I learned that he was much loved and respected because of this.

We had to stop twice on the way to meet different people in different uniforms. I was presented and we drank vodka. It was dark when we got to his quarters and met his men. They turned out to be veterans of the wars in Afghanistan and Chechnya.

We had a hell of a party that night and everybody wanted to talk to me. I became everybody's brother. They could not understand why a Norwegian – from a NATO country – had shown such interest in one single Russian soldier. For them, that was totally crazy.

The burial was the next day, and in addition to my pilot they were burying more than 100 soldiers killed in 1941 found during the past year. Only 8 or 9 had been identified. It was a big day. There were 1,000 spectators, speeches by generals and veterans, big crowds of children and youth organisations watching. The Northern Fleet played Chopin's funeral march and military salutes were fired. I gave interviews to several TV networks and was seen as the hero of the day. And I had a terrible hangover ...

Later there were more speeches, much toasting of each other, the drinking of copious amounts of vodka and another big party. It was quite overwhelming really, and when I got home I had lots of pictures and a great story for my newspaper.

But I was still searching for the pilot's family, and I had discovered in Russia they have a website similar to Facebook called vkontakte.ru (or just vk.com). I made a profile and put on a search for the name Pisjauk. From 30 million users I got one hit, a young girl!

The name caused me problems, as it sounded like a dirty joke nickname in Russia. Nobody believed it was his real name, but it turned out he was from the south, from the Black Sea region, close to Ukraine. The girl was the granddaughter of one of Pisjauk's brothers, and she told me his younger sister was still alive, the last person in his family, living in Ukraine. I wrote a long letter, telling everything I knew: his mission that day, how he had been shot down, reported missing, the burial, everything. I had it translated into Russian and sent it.

The answer I received was heartbreaking. She had been just a little girl the last time she saw him, and the family didn't get any news of him until 1947, and that news was 'probably killed'. That made his mother so ill she almost died of sorrow. His sister told me he had dreamed of being a pilot, but his parents thought it was too dangerous. But then came the war and that changed everything. He was only 21 years old when he was killed.

This was mission accomplished – almost. I wanted her to come and see his grave and even got her an invitation, all expenses paid by the Russians, but she said she was too old and too weak to travel. So that was that.

It took me seven years from collecting the bones to the burial in Russia. A couple of years later I got a medal from the Russian Minister of Defence 'given to individuals who have made a special effort to honour the memory of dead soldiers'.

I was proud, but I feel I share it with so many who helped me. And it's tricky too, given my political views on states like Russia and their relations to neighbour countries. But there is also another side. Norway is the only neighbour of Russia that they have never been to war with. The relationship has always been good, even in the Cold War. And they pulled out in 1945. As Stalin said: 'We have an agreement about the border, signed in 1826, and we intend to keep that agreement.'

I know that there are still more soldiers and pilots out there waiting to be found, but I don't know if their stories will be known or get the same ending as this one. We'll see. Right now there is another plane I am looking for.[36]

Having liberated the town on 25 October 1944, the Red Army remained in Kirkenes to help the local population prepare for the coming winter. Colonel Arne Dahl's Norwegian military mission arrived from Murmansk on 10 November and began to enlist the help of any available men. Detachments of Norwegian soldiers from Sweden were airlifted in and the exiled Norwegian government was allowed to send naval vessels into Kirkenes harbour from early December. By January 1945 there were 1,350 Norwegian troops in Kirkenes, rising to 2,735 by May. Soviet forces withdrew from Norwegian territory in September 1945. The Red Army had lost 16,000 soldiers clearing the Nazis from the Arctic North; the Germans lost 9,000 trying to stop them. The largest military offensive on Arctic terrain in history was over.[37]

But the German rearguard action before Kirkenes fell had saved the lives of tens of thousands of troops now falling back through Finnmark to the new defensive fortifications being built at the Lyngen Line.

As the Germans retreated, the operation began to evacuate the 60,000 people who lived in Finnmark before the petrol squads moved in to systematically burn every building to the ground. Hitler's order for 'scorched earth' was about to become reality.

2

'PITY FOR THE CIVILIAN POPULATION IS OUT OF PLACE'

In two months German army fire patrols destroyed 11,000 houses, 6,000 farms, 4,700 barns, 27 churches, 140 buildings owned by religious organisations, 53 hotels and inns, 21 hospitals and smaller medical institutions, 420 shops, 306 fish factories, 106 schools, 60 local authority administrative buildings, 230 buildings for craft and industry, 108 lighthouses, 350 bridges, 350 boats with motors, thousands of rowing boats and countless numbers of telephone poles.

Norge I krig: Frigjoring (Norway at War: Liberation)[1]

On 28 October 1944 the chief of operations of the German High Command, General Alfred Jodl, issued the following order to the commander of the 20th Mountain Army, General Lothar Rendulic:

Because of the unwillingness of the north Norwegian population to voluntarily evacuate, the Führer has agreed to the proposals of the commissioner for the occupied Norwegian territories and has ordered that the entire Norwegian population east of the fjord of Lyngen be evacuated by force in the interest of their own security and that all homes are to be burned down or destroyed.

The supreme commander, Northern Finland, is responsible for the Führer's order to be carried out without consideration. Only by this method can the Russians with strong forces, and aided by these homes and the people familiar with the terrain, be prevented from following our withdrawal operations during this winter and shortly appear in front of our position in Lyngen. This is not the place for sympathy for the civilian population.

It must be made clear to the troops engaged in this action that the Norwegians will be thankful in a few months that they were saved from Bolshevism, and that the barbarian methods of the air war against our German country and her cultural shrines have brought a thousand times more misery to our people if compared with the humane evacuation and destruction of homes in northern Norway, which is necessary for our war effort, and which, if it is not done, must be paid with the blood of German soldiers.

The population, whose livelihood is fishing, in northern Norway, furthermore has enough shipping space at its disposal to be able to get out of the way en masse across the water. A large part of the small Norwegian ships which are kept hidden at present can be used for this, and can later also be used for our own transportation needs.

The danger of the formation of guerrilla bands on the part of the Norwegians appears to be negligible since they will no longer be able to use the houses during the winter.[2]

The next day, 29 October, Rendulic issued his own orders to his commanders outlining the instructions of the High Command, including the following paragraphs:

It is the responsibility of the Commander-in-Chief of Northern Finland that this order be carried out ruthlessly so that the Soviets supported by dwelling places and a population which knows the country will be prevented from following our withdrawal with strong forces. Pity for the civilian population is out of place.

Execution of the Evacuation: (to be complete by 15.11.44)
a) The entire evacuation area is to be emptied of people.
b) Evacuated settlements are to be destroyed unless they are to be used by troops marching through (that is, at the latest by the rear guards).
c) The operation must be a sudden one and the officers of the Reichskommissar of Norway must participate and Norwegian authorities must be harnessed for it: the latter, however, only from the beginning of the operation.
d) The seized population is to be led to the nearest ports under military guard (also small ports with docks suitable for cutters).
e) Local and district commanders are to erect reception camps in or near these ports.
f) Men capable of working and marching and in the western districts women capable of marching also, are to be coupled to the marching units furthest in front and to be taken along.

g) In as far as the population still has small ships available they are to be used for the deportation of the evacuees. Military cover!

h) All ships used by the Wehrmacht (freighters and army transports) are to be loaded additionally with as many evacuees as possible.

i) Columns on Reichsstrasse 50 to be formed only to an unavoidable degree; invalids, women and children to be assisted by loading them on trucks. Only men really capable of marching to join the march columns!

It is requested that the Reichskommissar Norway will make available as much shipping space as possible as otherwise numerous casualties among the Norwegians will be unavoidable during the evacuation.

I request all officers concerned carry out this evacuation with the sense of it being a relief action for the Norwegian population. Though there will be necessities here and there to be severe all of us must attempt to save the Norwegians from Bolshevism and to keep them alive.[3]

The later consideration of these orders by Rendulic – who'd served in the vicious Balkan campaign before taking up his command in Norway – is revealing. After the war he was tried at the Nuremberg war-crimes trials of the Nazi leaders in 1947. The scorched-earth devastation in Finnmark and the forced evacuation of the population of 75,000 were dealt with in a series of hearings called the 'hostage' case, which also included events in the Balkans, Yugoslavia and elsewhere where the civilian population were involved in a military action.

In his evidence at his trial, he said:

There is one sentence which I would like to draw to your attention. It is the last sentence in the second paragraph, and it reads: 'Compassion for the civilian population is uncalled for.' [Transcript translation of 'Pity ... out of place'.]

This sentence should not be regarded as an invitation to take harsh measures. It is to be understood in connection with the next sentence, which is the first sentence of the next passage, where it says, 'The troops carrying out this order must be made to understand that within a few months the Norwegians will be thankful for having been saved from Bolshevism, etc., and that the whole operation is in the interest of the Norwegians.

It had to be expected that the people would be kind and would comply with the requests of individual Norwegians to exempt them from evacuation, and that these men would not know that thus they would face a deathly danger. There was an oral explanation of this order to the effect that Hitler attached particular importance to the measures ordered for Finnmark because he counted on the Exiled Government's landing and settling in Finnmark if this area was left completely intact.[4]

Rendulic added: 'A person who orders something like this cannot desire cruelty and ruthlessness, but I am not in a position to put a general next to every lance corporal to make sure that the orders are carried out in a proper way.'[5]

The stage was now set for the forced evacuation of all civilians from the north of Norway and their relocation south – or at least, out of Finnmark. From 29 October 1944, the scorched-earth policy was active and the compulsory clearing of human settlement from Finnmark was under way.

On 1 November, the Germans issued proclamations informing the Norwegian population of what they were required to do. They were signed by Rendulic and countersigned by the feared and fanatical Reichskommissar of Norway, Josef Terboven, who had gained a reputation for loyalty and ruthlessness for ordering the execution of thirty-four Norwegian civilians in a crackdown designed to restore law and order in Trondheim in October 1942. The proclamation warned of dire consequences for anyone who disobeyed:

TO THE POPULATION:
The evacuation of a part of northern Norway has been rendered a military necessity as a result of the treachery of a Finnish Government clique.

The evacuation necessitates the removal of the civilian population, as the enemy has proved that, in those territories occupied by him, he ruthlessly and brutally forces the civilian population to give him active assistance in achieving his aims.

This means that no shelter or means of existence of any kind can be left to the Bolshevik enemy in the fighting zone. All such installations as housing accommodation, transport facilities and food stocks must be destroyed or removed.

The population in these districts will therefore be deprived of the basis for their existence, so that, in order to be able to survive, they must evacuate to those Norwegian territories which are still protected by the German Wehrmacht.

He who does not comply with these unequivocal instructions exposes himself and his family to possible death in the arctic winter without house or food.

(signed) by TERBOVEN,
Reichskommissar for the Generaloberst, Occupied Norwegian Territories.

(signed) by RENDULIC,
Commander-in-Chief 20th Army.[6]

Among the accounts of the scorched-earth policy given to the Nuremberg war-crimes tribunal was that of Trygve Schance, who had been a police director in Polmak, a settlement on the banks of the Tana River in Finnmark close to the Finnish border and on the only road west out of Kirkenes.

Schance had been a police sergeant major in Vardø (a treeless island in the far east of Finnmark) since 1935 when he was 28. He had spent the war in Vardø but was moved to a new post as police director in Polmak on 1 February 1945. In Vardø he had been responsible for keeping petty crime – thefts and minor violations of the law – under control. He estimated that between 80 and 85 per cent of the town was destroyed when the Nazis pulled out in early November 1944, though he had been living in a small village further west at that time. He had learned of the German pull-out from Finnmark in a telephone conversation with his mother-in-law, who lived in the tiny settlement of Finnkonckeila. Finnkonckeila was a tiny fishing village squeezed into the mouth of an impossibly narrow gorge between two mountains, accessible only by boat. It was home to several hundred people with its own fishing fleet and fish processing industry. The Norwegian government refused to allow it to be rebuilt after the war because of the fear of landslides, and it is now an eerie ghost town.

In his evidence to presiding judge Justice Edward F. Carter, Schance described how his experience unfolded on 30 October 1944:

> She told me that a German detachment had been in the town of Finnkonckeila. These Germans told the population that the town was to be burned and the population evacuated in boats. The population had decided not to go away. They did not want to evacuate the town, and began at once to leave for the mountains.

> The childrens' home had been transferred to Finnkonckeila from Vardø at some previous date. There were twenty-three children from the ages of 1 to 15 years, and we had four women looking after these children. My mother-in-law wanted to know whether I could possibly help to take these children from Finnkonckeila to a safer place, and I answered that I would. Eleven young men accompanied me across the mountains. At six o'clock in the morning of 31 October, we began our trip and arrived in Finnkonckeila at about two or three o'clock in the afternoon. The population had already gone into the mountains overlooking the village. A German detachment had arrived in a motorboat and stayed near the village. I saw that boxes of dynamite were taken from the boats to shore and also cans of gasoline.

> I went down into the little town with one of my comrades. It was my intention to obtain clothing which I had previously sent to my mother-in-law, and it happened that I struck up a conversation with the leader of this German

detachment, a lieutenant. I asked him whether it was true that this town was to be burned. He answered, 'Yes, this place is to be blown up. This is not only to happen here, but in the whole of Finnmark.' He added that the population was to be sent to the south in small boats. I asked him what would happen if the population should decide to go to the mountains. He answered that afterwards a detachment would arrive which had the task of fetching the population.

He said those who should refuse to come along would be arrested and taken into German captivity, and risked being shot. We were told to leave the place at once because the blowing up and burning down was to begin at once. We went back to the camp which the people had in the mountains. The other ten who had been with me had begun to make preparations in order to take the children away with them over the rocks.

At about half-past three in the afternoon, they began blowing up and burning down the houses. There were three fish processing factories, producing all kinds of fish products. These were blown up with dynamite. The Germans went from house to house with their cans of gasoline, smashed the windows with the butts of their rifles, and a moment or two later the houses began to go up in flames. The procedure was quite systematic.

I sat up above the village and watched what was going on until about five o'clock in the afternoon. By then the whole place was a sea of flames. At that time we began our retreat [south through the mountains] to Skjanes with the children. We had a very strenuous trip. The children were badly equipped for such a trip, with only thin shoes, and the smallest had to be carried on our backs. The way back took us 18 hours.

Schance told the Nuremberg court that the Norwegians lodged the children at the school and about 11 p.m. that night more German soldiers and marines arrived in landing boats and set fire to the warehouse in the town:

Soldiers were posted around the village, and others went and told the population that they would have to be on the landing craft within, at the latest, one hour. The leader of this detachment was a German lieutenant. This officer went to the school building where the children were, and he ordered that all of them should be brought to the boat instantly. The superintendent of the children's home came running to my house which is situated about three or four hundred yards from the school, and they asked me to try to intervene.

I talked to the lieutenant. He said his order was to collect these people and my objections and pleas were of no interest to him. He said exactly the same as the lieutenant in Finnkonckeila, that those who remained behind would either be made prisoners of war or possibly shot on the spot. This conversation took place on the stairs outside the school building.

It was night and the children were in their beds, and the officer ordered his soldiers to start taking the children to the ship. I saw them taken out of their beds without any opportunity to put on clothes, and they were taken to the ship as they were. I saw that I could do nothing. I went back to my house, where my wife, mother and children were.

I was stopped by the German lieutenant, and he told me to go to the boat. I pointed out that I was in my pyjamas and only had an overcoat apart from that, and slippers. I told him he should give me an opportunity to prepare myself better for such a trip, and that I had a family to look after. He ordered a soldier to take me to the boat at once. I said there would not be any harm if I could go back to the house and prepare myself and my family for the trip, whereupon he gave me permission to do that. The soldier said in an hour at the latest we should be on the boat.

In that time we succeeded in leaving our house and getting into the mountains. Later it appeared that the rest of the population had done the same. The country around Skjanes is very rough. It is very easy to get away and hide. The ship left after an hour with the children and the people [who had been looking after them].

The next day – 2 November – an armed fishing boat came to Skjanes, a kind of auxiliary war ship. Germans landed from the ship and started to burn down houses and the village. By then the civilian population was in the mountains in the neighbouring district. We tried to get as close to the village as possible to see what was going on.

The same thing happened as in Finnkonckeila. Explosive stuff such as gasoline was taken into the houses. The windows were broken and soon after this the houses burst into flames. Those domestic animals the population were not able to bring to safety were taken by the Germans. Some were slaughtered on the spot; others were taken onto the ship.

Altogether there were 130 [people gathered in the mountains]. The eldest was 86 years old, the youngest was a girl 4 days old. We had taken this little girl and her mother on a stretcher into the mountains shortly before the burning started. None of us had anything except our clothes and what we could carry.

For three days we stayed out in the open. In the meantime we tried to build houses out of turf which we call '*gamme*'. After three days we had enough houses but very little to eat and few clothes.

We ate cattle which we slaughtered, cattle saved from the Germans. We were in the mountains for seventeen days. In the first days we saw German ships coming continuously to and from the fjord, and German aircraft flew over our heads. We had no communications with other villages by telephones or road.

We knew Finnkonckeila had been burned to the ground. We had seen the sea of flames in Berlevåg. We sent small patrols of two or three men to Gamvik and

Mehamn to see what was happening there and we discovered there that these villages were completely destroyed. They had been blown up and burned down and the population compulsorily evacuated to the south.

On 17 November, a [Norwegian] motor boat came from Batsfjord and we discovered how conditions further east in Finnmark were. I went with the motorboat when it went back east, as far as Vardø, where I worked. After all, I had a job.

I got there on 19 November. My job was to collect information about the population which had remained behind, so that we could help them. It turned out that we had a few Norwegian motorboats left, boats which we had succeeded in saving. So far as it was possible, we used these motorboats to transport people who were still in the open, but it must be remembered that the German controls had to be avoided. In addition my job was to interrogate people who came from West Finnmark. It turned out that a few motor boats there had also been saved.

As soon as it became a little quieter there – as soon as there weren't so many German ships there – these boats started out to eastern Finnmark. There were also boats coming from Lofoten. They made a large bend in the north and then they landed in eastern Finnmark.

After we had listened to the people who arrived in this way, we learned much more about what had happened in the various villages. Slowly but surely, we discovered the whereabouts of people, and where help was most needed. The Norwegian soldiers had arrived at this time in Finnmark, and Lt Colonel [Gunnar] Johnson was appointed leader of the expedition to help the civilian population.

We listened to what these people who came from the other parts of Finnmark had to say, and discovered how the Germans had acted in the various districts. Slowly but surely we succeeded in bringing the people who had been living under the most difficult conditions to Eastern Finnmark. In the meantime we received news that the Germans had also been carrying out destructions in Western Finnmark.

In his evidence, Schance told of a conversation he'd had with a German soldier at his mother-in-law's house in Finnkonckeila, as the population was being rounded up and herded onto the landing craft:

I met a German soldier who was forcing some drawers, etc. I do not know what he was looking for. He saw that I took various pieces of clothing and tried to put them into my rucksack, and he said to me, 'Leave it, you don't need anything.' He said, 'If you should succeed in getting away into the mountains, you are going to be shot anyway, and if the Russians come, then you will be used for forced labour in Siberia, and you don't need any of these things there.

Schance explained that he'd travelled through much of the east and west of Finnmark in the immediate post-scorched-earth period assisting refugees, visiting Skjanes, Vardø, Berlevåg and Polmak regularly. The Russians didn't come, he said, and the Norwegian population regarded the destruction which had taken place – and the evacuation – as 'pure vandalism'.[7]

Initially there were no German plans to fortify northern Norway but once Hitler's plans to strike the Soviet Union through Finnmark became known, orders were given to begin strengthening defences and preparing the region as an assembly area.

The road and railway network in Norway was not extensive, especially in the north, so from 1941 the port of Honningsvåg became an important staging point in the supply route north by sea. Materials, fuel and supplies were unloaded there from large boats and transferred to smaller vessels for the journey east to Kirkenes and on to the Litsa Front. German High Command decided batteries should be built along the coast and on outlying islands, in particular, offering a field of fire across the entrance to the large Porsanger fjord. To protect against a landing from the sea, mines were laid, defensive positions built and beach defences improved at Mageroya. Alongside the 2,500 inhabitants of Honningsvåg, 500 to 700 soldiers were billeted; 200 men were stationed at the battery at Porsangerfjord alone. [8]

Hitler's belief that there would be an Allied invasion in the north tied up large quantities of men to man these batteries, materials to build these vast defences and significant strategic weapons, such as the battleships *Scharnhorst* and *Tirpitz* that lurked in the fjords. Once the defences were built, the morale of the soldiers manning the garrisons was not good, as Norwegian historian Einar Richter Hansen noted:

> Many suffered from the so-called Arctic melancholy (the Germans called it being mountain sick: *bergkrank*) and the number of suicides increased from 1943. This was mostly due to the long distance away from home and the problem of getting leave. The dark long polar nights were also hard to bear. The Germans were quick to react to the most trivial of things and there was often wild shooting.[9]

Around the Nordkapp, all activity was connected to the sea: the catching, freezing or transport of fish or activities related to fishing or boats. But the war, especially since the invasion of the Soviet Union, made fishing a much more dangerous activity due to bombing, submarines and minefields. In 1942 fishermen negotiated extra rations of flour, coffee, syrup, meat and canned fish if they fished in the area of the Lofoten Islands, a more exposed offshore location. The following year, for every 1,000kg of fresh fish delivered to the German fish freezing company in

Hammerfest, crews received 100g of coffee and 100g of tobacco. It was also possible to work as a fisherman and be employed at the same time in the German construction industry improving the roads or new coastal defences, or to get work at the docks in Porsanger or the harbour at Billefjord. The Germans paid well and the work went on all year round. There was no unemployment because the Germans didn't allow it: they conscripted all those without jobs.

By night German patrols rigidly enforced the blackout and by day identification cards were compulsory and subject to spot checks. Mail was searched and it was forbidden to give the Russian prisoners food. 'Un-German activities' could result in imprisonment in a German concentration camp. Newspapers were censored but still produced, though full of German propaganda, and radios had to be handed in. Rumours began to replace facts, in the absence of reliable information. Shortages became more commonplace after the sinking of two Hurtigruten coastal steamers in 1941, the *Richard With* and the *Vesterålen*. Following these sinkings a replacement service (known as 'Aerstninga' or 'substitute') took over the northern stretches from Tromsø to Kirkenes to keep mail, passengers and supplies moving. [10]

When Soviet forces took Kirkenes and moved swiftly west to Neiden, Reichskommissar Terboven suggested that Hitler order the immediate scorched-earth clearance of Finnmark by issuing a 'führerbefehl' or 'Hitler command' that had to be obeyed. This done, Terboven and Rendulic jointly ordered the compulsory evacuation of the civilian populations in Finnmark and Nord Troms. Copies of this announcement were printed on pink paper and posted on noticeboards and on the walls of houses.

The plans to evacuate the civilian population were drawn up by Terboven's deputy Obersturmbannführer Hans-Hendrik Neumann, with the Norwegian Nazi puppet leader Vidkun Quisling appointing ministers Jonas Lie and Johan Lippestad to oversee it. A former adjutant of Reinhardt Heydrich and a long-time Nazi, Neumann had been in charge of training and indoctrination for the Nasjonal Samling party and its SA equivalent, Hird, before becoming Terboven's deputy. [11]

Lie drafted the Norwegian government's call on 17 October for the population of Finnmark to embark on a voluntary evacuation, but this was widely ignored, except by members of the Norwegian Nazi party. The first boat left Kirkenes on 22 October with twenty-two people on board – most were National Socialists and sympathisers. [12]

Lippestad sent a telegram to all police chiefs in the west of Finnmark:

> You are herewith ordered to compulsorily evacuate the population within your district. Publicise this by posters and via all telephone stations and contact the German authorities for immediate initiation of the compulsory evacuation which has been ordered by the German authorities. Inform us immediately by wire, particularly whether additional transport is required. [13]

Lie set up headquarters for the evacuation in the town of Alta, where the Tirpitz had been anchored until the month before. Repeatedly attacked and damaged by British midget submarines and torpedo-carrying bombers, the pride of the German fleet had been towed to nearby Tromsø for repairs. The other feared battleship in northern waters, the *Scharnhost*, had been sunk by the British in the Battle of the North Cape in December the previous year with the loss of nearly 2,000 lives.

Organising a team to take care of reception areas, billets and provisions Lie set a deadline of 10 November 1944 for the evacuation of Finnmark. Early in the evacuation he proved himself ruthless in the pursuit of this goal. He gave short shrift to the chief steward of one Norwegian boat, who suggested raising a white flag and surrendering if Russian ships intercepted them on the way from Vardø to Hammerfest, a dangerous journey through mine-infested waters with the ever-present threat of Russian submarines, Allied bombers and warships.

The steward – Ragnvald Waernes – was arrested, brought before a special tribunal and shot on the orders of Lie. His grave had been dug before the hearing convened: he was executed as soon as the sentence was passed.[14]

The German scorched-earth strategy involved preventing any Allied force that might land in Finnmark, Soviet or otherwise, using harbours, roads or bases that would help them launch an offensive against the retreating 20th Mountain Army. 'Denial of advantage' extended to food supplies and to animals for haulage, so on Saturday 28 October and Monday 30 October the Germans ordered the local population to hand over all cows and horses. Lief Lukassen of Tverrelvdalen near Alta recalls:

> On Monday the madness began: first all horses in the district were to be handed over. Several hundred horses were driven down to the monsters. Next came the compulsory handing over of cows. All those who had cows were ordered to appear at Ovre Alta slaughterhouse at 10am. Those who did not appear would be severely punished and the cows would be taken in any case. Many people had more than 20km to walk and on bare ice practically all the way.[15]

People were only allowed to take with them the property they could carry and everything else was to be burned, so they began to hide valuables and equipment. Simon Simonsen, a farmer on the far side of the bay from Alta, remembers their attempts to stash valuables:

> The farm was a so-called combination farm with both agriculture and fishing. Consequently we had tools for both industries. We loaded nearly all the fishing tackle in boats and stored it in a cave approximately 2km away. You could only get there by boat. We were not allowed to stash away property and things.

Everything was to be burnt, nothing was to remain. We therefore had to do this by night and luckily the weather was fine during this period, with temperatures a little below zero but no snow.[16]

Silverware, jewellery and photo albums were buried. So were sewing machines, fishing tackle, guitars, armchairs and even, as one display cabinet at the Hammerfest Museum of Reconstruction proudly shows, a barber's chair imported from Chicago.

Rowing boats were filled with stones and sunk in deeper water to be recovered later. Salted and dried meat and flour were stored in barrels in accessible places. Sometimes these hiding places were plundered and the contents stolen. Church valuables were packed up and sent south into storage.

Idar Russveldt and his family fled Kirkenes for the safety of Tana during the bombing. From there he watched the German retreat:

> The people in Tana all went to the mountains when we heard the Russians were coming. We hid in the valley, 40 or 50 of us living in a *gamme*, a hut with a turf roof. There were so many of us you couldn't lie down to sleep. We had to sleep sitting down.
>
> One night someone suggested we go up the mountain to look over the Tana River. From there we saw the German retreat. We saw one house burning, then the next, then after an hour the next house burning and so on. I can remember being on the top of that hill seeing them moving along the road burning all the houses, just like it was yesterday.

Idar's wife Inga had also fled Kirkenes with her family. She spent the later stages of the war in Nesseby, a small village on the other side of the fjord from Kirkenes, again offering safety away from the bombing:

> We lived in a cowshed with a turf roof. The Germans burned everything and they tried to burn that too but the roof was new and wet. We ran away but found the bridge across the river had been bombed. I remember following a tall man through the river. He said, 'Only tread where I put my feet, because it's mined.'
>
> I wasn't scared. It was exciting – I was only 8. We had fish more or less every day and we gathered berries from the woods. Lots of people had dried salted meat with cloudberries [a sharp tangy red berry found in Norway]. But I don't know how the grown-ups could live with so little food, in the autumn.[17]

The evacuation organisers requisitioned 250 fishing boats for the movement of people south from Finnmark and Nord Troms. Among these were German transport ships, Norwegian cargo boats and the tourist ship *Stella Polaris*. One of the places people were ordered to head for to catch the boats was the slate quay at Bukta in Alta. Lief Lukkassen recalls:

> Monday 4 November was probably the saddest day in the history of Alta. Along the road in [my village] Tverrelvdalen there were large groups of people. Tiny infants lay in baskets, old men and women between 80 and 90 years of age sat on the roadside. They were all waiting for transportation to be taken away from their homes – into the unknown among strangers. German vehicles came, one after the other, and picked up people and drove them to Bukta, the place of embarkation. They had to stay there until Tuesday morning, as the boat which was to take them did not sail until then.[18]

The burning began on 6 November in the villages of Skarsvåg, Karmoyvaer, Tufjord and Gjesvær, followed by Nordvågen on 11 November and Honninsgvåg two days later. Almost everything was destroyed. On Thursday 7 November the German ship *Dichtmark* left Bukta fully loaded with 700 to 800 evacuees, 1,000 German soldiers and ammunition. In case of mines, the troops were put at the back of the boat, the evacuees at the front. The weather was good and the ship arrived without incident in Tromsø in less than twenty-four hours. There the evacuees were disembarked, registered, fed and housed before moving either further south or to stay with relatives in the area. Many travelled on the coastal steamer *Dronningen* to Mosjøen; others took smaller boats to their families on surrounding islands.

Fishing boats were packed full of people, setting sail on a two-day journey to Tromsø. Some evacuees ended up on the German freighters *Carl Arp* and *Adolf Binder*, which were overloaded, lacked proper hygiene and became insanitary. Dysentery broke out; lice spread like wildfire. The Germans filled barges with meat from slaughtered animals and abandoned cooking utensils and sent them south.[19] Some civilians rode bicycles south along Main Road 50; others packed into the few remaining civilian cars that hadn't been requisitioned by the Germans.

Along with the 200,000 soldiers, 60,000 horses, mules, trucks, motorcycles, guns and military equipment, the Germans also brought Russian POWs. On some days these undernourished men had to walk 30km, tottering and staggering along in wooden shoes, with rags or paper bags for socks. One Russian prisoner wrote of the experience:

> Most of the time I could not feel my own feet. It was like wearing pieces of wood and they were blue. Where did we sleep? Outside! When evening came we looked for a hollow near the road, a gravel pit was fine. We sat as close to each other as possible and we gathered sticks and twigs and lit small fires.

We walked for the whole of November. I think we arrived in Alta at the end of November. Or was it early December?[20]

Some POWs tried to escape. One eye witness recalls:

The prisoners came late in the evening and were not given anything to eat. Nine or ten of them then tried to escape. They suddenly ran towards the forest which wasn't far away. The guards immediately shot at them and several fell down. Those who were not hit ran towards the forest except two men who came back. At a distance of 10–12 paces the guards waved at them not to come any closer and shot them down.[21]

In the three weeks of 1 to 21 November an estimated 35,000 evacuees passed through Tromsø, which was the main evacuation centre for those being moved south. Between 10,000 and 11,000 evacuees were staying in the town at any one time. With 10,000 German soldiers also stationed there and a resident population of 10,000, the number of people in Tromsø trebled. German officers and soldiers had requisitioned all the available rooms in private houses, so the evacuees were put up in churches and village halls. The provision of meals developed into a system: all the large soup pots in town were gathered to feed the evacuees and hospital kitchens fed 1,000 people a day. Even the cheese moulds in the town's dairy were pressed into service, as they could hold 2,000 litres of soup. Somehow 10,000 people were fed every day.[22]

From Tromsø evacuees moved further south, to reception centres at Narvik, Mosjøen and Harstad. If elderly people died, they were left behind. Relatives were not allowed to stop. The stream of refugees continued from Mosjøen to the Lofoten Islands and along the coast south of Tromsø. The original plan had been to relocate the majority of evacuees south of Mosjøen, but most had to move on via Trondheim to southern Norway, arriving in Oslo by train. One evacuee recalled:

When the train stopped at Ostbanen [Oslo's main station] we were received by the police in Nasjonal Samling [Quisling's Norwegian Nazi party] uniforms. We were going to a restaurant in Karl Johans gate [one of Oslo's main streets nearby]. We were a sad procession. At the front walked two NS policemen followed by a group of exhausted people with their meagre belongings. There were children and old people from nursing homes who had to be led by the hand and people from the inner regions of Finnmark in their worn sweaters.[23]

Evacuees sent south were sometimes met with accusations of cowardice or of being Nazis, as the newspapers were full of propaganda about the population fleeing the Bolsheviks in the north. There was no mention of the forced evacuation programme.

Special commando groups carried out the scorched-earth destruction. Bridges, harbours, roads, military installations and power stations were blown up, along with power lines and thousands of telegraph poles. Wells were destroyed or poisoned with animal carcasses and minefields were sown alongside existing ones. An entire forest was cut down and the timber transported south to prevent invading soldiers using it.

As civilians were cleared from villages and the retreating German forces passed through, the burning squads moved in. Sometimes civilians such as Agnes Hansen of Storekorsnes saw their own homes being destroyed:

On Saturday 11 November the Germans began burning property on Korsnes. Our summer cowhouse was the first one they set fire to. Erik and Karl Vensel had taken our stove outside to hide it. Then other Germans arrived and smashed it. After this the house was burnt down.[24]

A secret German report of 25 November 1944, signed by Colonel Herrmann, leader of the evacuation staff, assessed the success of the evacuation. It gives a detailed breakdown of where the population was moved to: 29,000 people to the south, 3,500 to the Lofoften Islands, 10,000 people left behind in eastern Finnmark, 8,500 Sami who were not evacuated and 200 people who evaded capture. The report details how tens of thousands of people were 'forwarded' by the Hurtigruten ships and notes with pride how 'voices in the Swedish press' had praised the operation. Humanitarian aspects of the compulsory evacuation are addressed in section five of the report, with emphasis placed on rations being offered from field kitchens, care and assistance offered to pregnant mothers, children provided with milk and transport laid on for the sick, injured and elderly. Help evacuating the latter category is considered especially important so as to deny the enemy material for propaganda purposes:

Army Headquarters, 25 Nov. 44
War Diary High Command 20 (Mountain Army O.Qu.
/Evacuation Staff
No. 31/44 Secret: The Evacuation of Northern Norway

Mission
The intention to induce the population of Finland and Ostrom to evacuate these territories voluntarily failed because of the limited willingness to support this demand. Accordingly, the Führer ordered the forced evacuation of the territory east of the Lyngenfjord in order to protect the population from

Bolshevism. The Führer-order to the Wehrmacht commander, in Chief of North Finland contains the following demands:

> The territory is to be emptied of human beings so that the enemy cannot rely on the working potential and local knowledge of the population. All quarters, traffic and economic installations are to be destroyed so ruthlessly that the enemy is deprived of every possibility of living in this area. Whatever can be evacuated in important goods is to be salvaged.

> The initial time period set for evacuation, Porsanger territory by 9 November, Alta/Hammerfest territory by 12 November, and East Troms by 15 November 44 could be prolonged until 20 November 44 as a result of a change in the situation.

> Accordingly a salvaging of economic goods in excess of the first planned amounts was possible. The territory to be evacuated corresponds to 1.5 times the size of Denmark. The distances on the single National Highway, the National Highway 50 amount to 1,000 kilometers from Kirkenes to Narvik and from Hammerfest to Tromsø, 500 kilometers. Furthermore this highway was occupied by the marching movement of the army, so that first of all the sea lane came into the question with regard to deportation.

> For the purposes of the execution an evacuation staff was formed with the High Command of the 20th (Mountain) Army, to which a representative of the Reich Commissioner for the occupied Norwegian territories was added.

Means

The possibility was merely offered as far as the sea lane was concerned to utilise the unused transport space on ships of the Reich Commissioner for Naval Transport (German Commercial Flag) and on Ships of the Navy (Reich Service Flags and Reich War Flags). Beyond that, Norwegian local ships and numerous cutters were utilized.

On land, the population wandered off individually with their own trucks (trucks, omnibuses, and horse drawn vehicles). The young folk also made use of bicycles frequently for the march to Narvik.

Execution

The inadequate records of the Norwegian resident register were the basis for the seizure of the population. According to them, the territory to be evacuated, including the nomadic Lapps has before the war a population of about 62,000. The (apparently very restricted) number of those persons who fled the evacuation can accordingly only be estimated. On account of lack of time the order to the population for evacuation could only take place in the form of an appell decreed jointly by the Commander & Chief of the 20 (Mountain) Army and by the Reich Commissioner for the occupied Norwegian territories.

Assembly points for the deportation by sea were erected in Billefjord and Honningsvåg for the area Porsanger and East Finland, in Hammerfest for the Island territories, and in Alta–Sopnes–Burfjord for the territory Alta with Kautokeino. The felder traffic took place with trucks and omnibusses, from the sea with cutters, or from the Islands and the coastal localities in North Varanger by units of the Navy.

Deportation from the Porsanger area took place in the main through two mass transports with 1,700 and 1,060 persons on the steamers *Karl Arp* and *Adolf Binder* from Billefjord. In Alta, through a mass transport of 750 persons on the supply ship *Dithmarschen*. Deportation for the rest, with Norwegian local ships and cutters.

Rounding up organisations were set up through civilian offices for quarters and further transport of the deported population in Tromsø, Narvik and Harstad. Forwarding to Mosjøen and Trondheim took place with ships of the Norwegian Hurtigrute.

Besides them, the following ships were utilized. the steamers *Brabant*, *Dronning*, *Sigurd Jarl*, *Stella Polaris* as well as the hospital transport ships *Lofotes*, *North Star*, and *Polar Ice*. This forwarding was finished by 25 November 1944, in the main.

Supplies, including quarters and medical help could not be guaranteed by the civilian sector in this wide area to a full extent. The Wehrmacht helped accordingly on a generous scale:

through the provision of rations where supplies could not be managed in such bulk by the civilian sector. In the reception stations on land as well as on board the German ships warm rations were given out from field kitchens.

through the provision of barrack camps as quarters at the assembly points, Billefjord and Sopnes.

through the help of the unit during transport to the coast, as well as during embarkation, especially by assisting families with children.

through large-scale care of sick, injured, pregnant women, and mothers with small children by doctors and medical installations. Admission of women for confinement into hospitals, further transport on hospital ships, provision of small children with milk, etc.

The transport of sick and injured from outlying homes for the aged and homes for tubercular cases whose evacuation was necessary, in order not to afford the enemy propaganda material, required an especial regulation. The deportation from Karasjok, Boerselv, Kautokeino, and Talvik and/or Korsfjord took place under the responsible leadership of Oberarzt Dr.Gaebler with medical trucks of the Wehrmacht and our own boats used for this.

The population could only take what baggage they could carry, on account of the restrictions of the transport space. The cattle had therefore to be taken over by the Wehrmacht against memoranda receipt, as far as it could not, in individual cases, be taken along. After extension of the evacuation time an extensive salvaging of important economic goods was also ordered for the civilian sector. Here the execution was the responsibility of the Wehrmacht. Furthermore, a final search was carried out by the Norwegian police detachments on the islands and outlying localities. Destruction will accordingly only be ordered by the subordinate sector commanders and/or rear guard officers in agreement with the evacuation commissioners when the salvaging of valuable economic goods (especially fishery equipment) is finished, or impossible.

Salvaging of the reindeer herds took place by an order to the Lapps to drive their herds to the west over Kautokeino–Helligskogen into a reception territory in Tromsfylke. A retreat to the south was prevented by a blockade on the Swedish border, a lock at Helligskogen made possible the driving through of the reindeer herds by the march movements of the unit on to the highway Finland–Skibotn. This action cannot be finished yet, since on account of the slight snowfall, the expedition of the Lapps could not be put into operation yet to full extent. Where a herd could not be transmitted farther, part of the animals were taken over against memoranda receipts by the Wehrmacht; the Lapps were nevertheless left the minimum necessary for existence.

Results (see Table of Evacuation)
In the reception organisation, including the fisherman already settled on the Lofotens 36,914 persons were taken all together. About 5,000 persons migrated before the start of the evacuation up till October from East Finland. About 1,100 persons have migrated by means of self-aid without passing through the reception organisation. A smaller residue of workers of the Wehrmacht is to be moved off later with the unit.

About 10,000 persons have remained in the area of Kirkenes, as a result of the war events. In West Finland and East Tromsø only about 8,500 persons, in the main Lapps, are left behind, whose deportation was only of interest in connection with the finding back of reindeer herds.

The evacuation in the territory between Lyngenfjord and Porsangerfjord could therefore be carried through almost completely. Even voices of the Swedish press had to admit the success of the action and speak of an almost 100% evacuation of the population.

The success of the action was made possible through the excellent co-operation of all participating offices of the Wehrmacht, the Reich Commissioner and the Norwegian administration.

Experiences

Orderly evacuation under the conditions imposed is only possible if an orderly method of seizure is present in the hands of an administrative medium. Both were not at hand. The Norwegian Lensmaenne (civilian police) were partly the first to leave their realm of their own accord. The administration in Hammerfest and in Talvik worked well.

Even in short periods for evacuation, a frictionless development is possible, if a calendar is also at hand in civilian offices for the evacuation of important goods. Idleness and avoidable losses of important goods result from improvising.

It contributes in any case to the quieting of the population if every family can have at their disposal a memorandum with the individual orders for carrying out the evacuation. Such a memorandum was to be issued by Minister Lie according to the suggestion of the Army HQ but came too late to have any great effect on the population.

Some untoward events, such as the execution of the 'Law concerning hand and span services' with the separation of the men from their families to be deported and with guarding like prisoners, burning down of houses in the presence of the inhabitants even where an immediate destruction was not necessary and shelling of the locality Kjollefjord by units of the navy hinder the readiness of the population to follow the officially proscribed way.

(sgd.) Herrmann, Colonel
Leader of the Evacuation Staff [25]

Enclosure to High Command of the 20th (Mountain) Army
Table of Evacuation As per: 25.11.44

No. of residents to be evacuated on 9.4.1940:

East Finmark	circa 25,000
West Finmark	circa 27,000
Troms, eastwards Lyngenfjord	circa 10,000
Total	62,000

Carrying out of the evacuation: People evacuated

Via Tromsø to South	29,014
Via Narvik	circa 3,400
Via Harstad	circa 1,000
On the Lofoten Islands	circa 3,500
Total	36,914

Moved to the South without registering	1,101
Moved from East Finmark up to October	circa 5,000
Workers employed by the Werhmacht, etc,	285
transported with the troops	
Total	43,300

People not evacuated: No longer able to leave East

Finnmark	circa 10,000
Laplanders remaining in West Finnmark (mainly Nomads)	8,500
Fugitives who have avoided evacuation	circa 200
Total	18,700
Total population	62,000[26]

Only a scattering of buildings escaped the destruction in the two counties of Finnmark and Nord Troms. In Honningsvåg only the church and burial chapel remained, while one house each was spared in Skarsvåg and Gjesvær. The military batteries in the area were blown later, on 12 and 13 December.

Some houses were used as billets for German guards who patrolled the area right up to the liberation. Others were left standing as a lure to people who had fled the initial evacuation. Often churches were spared, sometimes they were not.

Some Norwegians living in areas to be evacuated decided to take their chances by hiding out in caves, mountain crevices and under upturned boats covered with turf instead. They heard broadcasts by the Norwegian government-in-exile urging them to take to the mountains, as liberation by Allied forces would happen 'shortly'.[27]

German patrols which were left behind after the initial withdrawal used dogs to search for cave dwellers throughout the winter and up to the capitulation in May 1945. They used speedboats and sometimes Norwegian fishing boats in the searches. Sometimes the people they found faced an uncertain fate. Some were sent south, others were shot.

The Nuremberg trial transcripts contain a short but painful chapter telling of the death of a farmer's wife at the hands of a German landing party at Veidnes, a settlement in one of the fjords at the very tip of the north of Norway:

Report to: Police Chief Vadsøe submitted by Police Officer L. Naess. Subject: Compulsory evacuation and arson in Veidnesklubben and the killing of Frau Wilhelmine Soerensen.

Interrogated on 2 July 1946 in Veidnesklubben: The witness: Wilhelmine Soerensen. He is familiar with the incident and understands his responsibility as a witness. He is ready to make a statement and declares:

On 16 December 1944 the witness was on the trip by motorboat to Ifjord. At that time most of the residences in Veidnes had been burned by the Germans, but the entire population had fled to the mountains and was living in adobe huts. No Germans were left in any camps in Laksefjord, which made the population feel secure from the Germans.

Arriving at Ifjord the witness and the other people in the motorboat suddenly became aware of a warship lying in the Trollbukt near the shore. Dawn had just broken and the moment the people in the motorboat saw the warship, automatic weapons from there shot in front and behind the motorboat so that there was no possibility for flight.

When the commander of the warship heard that the families of the people had remained in Veidnes, the destroyer went to Veidnes.

There the German lieutenant with 14 soldiers went ashore with a Norwegian (Martin Mikelsen) who had orders to show the way to the families.

The witness and the other people on the motorboat remained aboard and were locked into the boxes where the ropes are kept. There they remained locked up until 2100 hours when the Captain arrived and issued an order to some others to go ashore.

The witness and two other people remained aboard in the box where the ropes are kept all night. The next day at 12:00 the witness was permitted to come out of the box and to move around the deck freely.

About half an hour later the Norwegian Julius Mattisen came aboard. The witness inquired of him concerning the witness' wife and for the first time he heard that she had been shot to death by the Germans up in the mountains the afternoon or evening before. The witness then tried to talk to the Captain. However, the latter had gone ashore.

At 2:00 the same afternoon the commander came aboard and the witness could talk to him. The Captain related that the wife of the witness had been killed unintentionally. Civilians, some of them armed, had fled at the arrival of the Germans. The commandos had opened fire from the ship and thus the wife of the witness had been hit.

The Captain further related that the wife of the witness had been buried in a lake in the country. The witness then wanted to go in order to get the body. He was not permitted to do so and now the Captain said she had been buried in the ocean.

The name of the wife of the witness was Wilhelmine, nee Eriksen. Her body has not been found.

After the Germans had burned down all the remaining houses in Veidnes the destroyer left for Honningsvåg in the evening of 17 December.

Adult males above 50 years of age were sent as prisoners to the prison camp of Kroekeberg. Later they were interrogated by uniformed Germans. Having been detained from 11 to 12 days, all prisoners from Veidnes were released from the camp together with some other prisoners.

Read to and agreed to:
signed: Egil Soerensen.[28]

German patrols continued searching for civilians who had escaped the evacuation until the end of the war. This newspaper report details the fate of two men on the same day:

Anders Henriksen, [from] Lille Lerresfjord, who was out fishing with his son when they were discovered by a German patrol boat, suffered a sudden death. They managed to get ashore and were trying to escape uphill when Henriksen was shot. That was on 6 April this year. Martin Aslaksen, Gammlevaer, was shot on the same day by soldiers from the same patrol boat when he tried to escape after being discovered.[29]

Those who chose life in the caves faced a tough existence. They had to stay out of sight or risk discovery by German patrols and forage for food when they could. Stockpiles of salted meat and dried fish were packed into the caves. The men went fishing at night to avoid detection, gathering their nets from hiding places in the mountain and burying them again after they had caught enough fish to keep them going for a while. Some women gave birth in the caves. One group of a hundred people – families with children – sought refuge in a cave on the island of Sørøya that could only be reached at low tide. But one day a German patrol passed that way and spotted them and they were all forced to go to southern Norway.

The villagers living in caves knew where others were hiding and would often visit each other to keep spirits up and listen to the news from London on the radio. Children were only allowed out of the caves in poor visibility or when it was snowing. Laila Thorsen kept a diary of her childhood experiences during the burning of Finnmark:

> We are finally allowed out for a while but with strict orders to stay near the cave. We are so happy that we behave just like cows when they are let out in the spring. Shhhh, did you hear that?
>
> A rumbling sound is coming closer and closer. It becomes louder and louder and the mountain is shaking. German airplanes! Get down and lie still! While I'm shouting to the others I take Odd by the hand and we drop face down on the ground. We lie there and listen to the noise from the airplanes. They fly low over us. Dear God, don't let them see us.[30]

The 300-strong Norwegian military mission led by Colonel Arne Dahl, which had arrived in Kirkenes in November 1944, began operations to find and rescue cave dwellers along the coast. The search parties were led by another colonel, Gunnar Johnson, who had been head of the medical service with the Norwegian Ministry of Defence in London. Travelling in fishing boats, often in bad weather, in poor light because of the polar winter and without lighthouses or lights from the shore to steer by, Johnson's teams evacuated nearly 900 cave dwellers back to liberated East Finnmark by Christmas 1944. Throughout the winter, from his headquarters at Bjørnevatn near Kirkenes, Dahl and his fellow officers who were carrying out Operation Crofter began to recruit volunteers from Finnmark and Norwegian exiles who had been training in so-called 'police' units from Sweden to help with the relief work. By February 1945 the force had swelled to around 3,000 men, delivering supplies to people living in caves along the coast and inland. In January 1945 Johnson heard about the desperate plight of some 1,000 people who had sought refuge on an island off Hammerfest called Sørøya. He drew up plans for a daring evacuation by Royal Navy destroyers. On 15 February,

502 men, women and children were rescued by four British destroyers and taken first to Murmansk and then on in convoy to Scotland.

Around the same time, a German army counter-propaganda unit found plenty of reason to crow about the success of the evacuation. The following extracts are from a secret propaganda report sent to German Army Command HQ in Narvik on 4 January 1945:

Subject: Evacuation. Counter propaganda

Towards the end of October 1944 the Bolsheviks invaded Norwegian territory and occupied Kirkenes. The Norwegian population which by and large had shown itself loyal and, more than that, even helpful and obliging toward the Germans during the four years of occupation had to be preserved from the grasp of Bolshevism. The procedure of the Bolshevists in Rumania, Bulgaria, Poland, Finland, Estonia and Lettland shows what kind of fate the Bolsheviks had in store for the Norwegian population also. They would have employed the Norwegians ruthlessly and brutally for their own purposes. They would have killed all Germanophile Norwegians, raped the women and brought starvation to the country.

In order to safeguard the German march movements the Soviets had to be prevented in the course of their advance from finding billets and working forces available which might be employed in combat against the Germans. Cases of espionage participated in by individual Norwegians, who had remained in Finnmark, show that the Bolshevik would have found supporters also in the indigenous population. North Norway and north Finland were evacuated for this reason and all residences and installations were destroyed.

A large part of the sensible Norwegian population gladly and willingly followed the call of the German government in October 1944 to evacuate voluntarily. The English radio broadcast a proclamation to the Norwegian population in the Norwegian language not to follow the orders of the evacuation authorities but to move off into inaccessible side valleys. Unfortunately there were a number of Norwegians who fulfilled this demand with their women and children. As far as the German Command was concerned it could have left the Norwegians to their fate. No doubt they all would have perished in the mountains.

But in order to help these misled people and to preserve them from certain death the German Wehrmacht employed patrols to comb through fjalls [*sic*] and fjords to pick up Norwegians there who were full of gratitude to their last hour saviours. This for instance: 212 Norwegians were found during a search operation by a Mountain Jaeger regiment in the area west of the road Lakselv–

Kistrand on 5–7 December 1944 in the area north of Kistrand and Repparfjord. These rescue operations were carried on at a time when the Wehrmacht itself had to accomplish marches of an extraordinary extent. If at present some individual Norwegians still keep hidden in the caves they alone are responsible for their miseries.

The evacuation of the territory evacuated by the Wehrmacht and the complete destruction of all roads, billets, transportation and food stores prevents the Bolsheviks from a thrust into north Norway. That produces a great disappointment to the Soviets. Their planned continued march will have to be delayed for the time being. That is why they agitate against the evacuation of north Finnland and north Norway and why they are trying to incite the neutral countries on this issue. And for all that it was Stalin who during the withdrawal of the Russian troops in 1941 for the first time caused the Russian population to evacuate and all residences to be destroyed.

Because Germany is fighting this struggle for her existence she must reply to the Russian methods of warfare with the same means unless she wants to lose.

During the evacuation all Norwegians were treated decently. The German soldier has assisted all Norwegians requiring his help and thus he helped to mitigate to a great extent the emergency produced by the evacuation. In individual cases he has shared his rations with Norwegians and he helped … the women loading their baggage.

The population was evacuated by means of ships or motor trucks. All available shipping space was mobilised. In order to cite one example: two large transports with about 1500 Norwegians each left for Tromsø in the first half of November from Billefjord and Hambukt in the Porsangerfjord [the notorious ships *Carl Arp* and *Adolf Binder*, which have gone down in evacuation infamy]. The space put at the disposal of the Norwegians was intended for transportation of German Wehrmacht goods. All German motor vehicles as far as space permitted took along Norwegians. The young Norwegian capable of marching was permitted to go along on the ship or the motor vehicle only in order not to separate him from his family.

For this the German soldier managed long stretches on foot and had to spend the night outdoors.

If it did happen that in individual cases single family members were separated from their families, the Germans did everything in their power to reunite the family.

German Wehrmacht doctors cared for the civilian population while en route and in the interim billets. The troops themselves furnished sufficient rations and established the billets.

And all these measures were carried out at a time during which the Germans themselves carried out one of the most difficult march movements.

In as far as Norwegians had to leave their personal property behind, measures were taken to compensate them. As far as the transport situation permitted the rest of the entire Norwegian possessions, particularly household equipment, clothing, fishing equipment, stoves, lighting fixtures were salvaged and evacuated.[31]

3

'THE DESTRUCTION WAS AS COMPLETE AS IT COULD BE'

The Finnmark region is more than 48,000 square kilometres. That means it is larger than Switzerland or Denmark. In this area about 60,000 people were living, mostly rather poor people and most of them fisherman. The main part of the population was living along the coast. The climate at that time of year is very severe and the Polar Circle is very far south of this area.

The mean temperature in December is about 14 degrees Fahrenheit. In January it is about 11 to 12 degrees. In the inner part of the country it is far colder and the temperature may drop to 40 below, even more. The country is very high so that the northern winds coming right in from the Arctic Ocean have a tremendous bite.

There is not a very great amount of snow: I might say, generally speaking, about one metre. But because of the heavy storms, especially from the north, this snow is drifting up in large drifts and that again means that it is very difficult to keep the roads open. Not so much because of the amount of snow but because of the drifting snow and I would like to point out that even with the assistance of a great number of Russian prisoners of war, the Germans were not able to keep Main Road 50 open all the year around.

Major General Arne Dahl, liberator of Finnmark,
giving evidence to the Nuremberg war crimes
hearings on conditions in the north of
Norway at the end of the war.[1]

Allied support for the Norwegian government-in-exile in London and for the Resistance in Norway (known as Milorg) had been considerable from the fall of Narvik in 1940 onwards, even if there had been sharp differences over strategy, priorities and the inclusion of Norwegian views in the decision making. Airdrops were a vital part of the resistance and intelligence strategy pre-liberation, especially given the challenging geography and remoteness of some areas – which was also at times a distinct advantage to the Resistance.

Allied aircraft flew a total of 717 successful missions out of 1,241 into Norway, dropping 208 agents, nearly 1,000 containers and three times that number of parcel drops with arms, ammunition, explosives, radio equipment, medicines and uniforms.

The 'Shetland Bus' sea route was another supply lifeline. From 194 trips, 190 agents and 385 tons of arms and equipment were landed in Norway, with 345 agents brought back to England. Instructors and wireless operators were shipped in and out, with the frequency of the trips rising dramatically in the final year of the war, increasing Milorg's capacity to strike at the German infrastructure and undermine their effort.[2]

With regular supplies of weapons, instructors and agents, Norwegian troops in Scotland waiting for their opportunity to return, and an extensive intelligence network supported by the local population feeding information back to the UK, everything was in place for a strike against the German military machine when the time was right.

The scorched-earth withdrawal from Finnmark in autumn 1944 caused concern that this destruction might be repeated further south, so Milorg made detailed plans to stop Germans destroying communications, ports and industries. To help with operational planning London sent in more than 100 officers to link up with agents already in Norway and establish a network of bases of hand-picked men in forests and mountains. They were under the leadership of the SOE, acting on orders from London and ready to attack German units at a moment's notice. The strength of Milorg Resistance fighters in the spring of 1945 was estimated at 40,000 trained and well-disciplined, though lightly armed, young men.[3]

The Allied fear was that with hundreds of thousands of fresh, well-trained, battle-hardened and well-equipped soldiers dug into well-prepared defences in remote, difficult to reach parts of mountainous Norway, the more fanatical Nazi leaders might decide to go down fighting in a short-lived but murderous Fortress Norway ('*Festung Norwegen*') blaze of glory.

Another factor was uncertainty about how the Soviet Union would respond having pushed the Nazis out of Finland and back into Norway. Norway's government-in-exile was concerned that should it be less than proactive about the liberation of the north of their own country, the Red Army might sweep the Nazis back across Norwegian borders, follow the retreat, hammer home its advantage and then not withdraw.

So the Norwegian government sent to Finnmark Colonel Arne Dagfin Dahl, considered a hero for his efforts as a commander of the famous Alta Battalion in the unsuccessful defence of Narvik against the Germans in 1940. His job was to demonstrate to the Soviet leadership that, with the Petsamo–Kirkenes offensive having successfully broken the Nazi Arctic frontline, the Norwegians were capable of taking care of the liberation of their own country.[4]

Dahl would co-ordinate the transition back to Norwegian administration after nearly five years of control by the Nazi and Quisling regimes. He would oversee the return of Norwegian fighters from Scotland and also Norwegian nationals from Sweden, where up to 50,000 exiles had crossed the border to seek refuge. Up to 15,000 had joined so-called 'police' battalions set up in Sweden to train for action as peacekeepers and policemen for a transitional administration once the war ended its final stages. That time was now. But the scorched-earth policy meant Dahl had a bigger job on his hands than he had expected.

Arne Dahl had been Norway's military attaché to the UK and Belgium during the First World War and even saw action at the front line with British forces at the Somme in 1916.[5] In 1939 he took command of the Alta Battalion, which the following year, with the help of French, British and Polish forces, was on the verge of defeating General Dietl's *Gebirgsjäger* at Narvik when RAF and Royal Navy support was diverted to oppose the German invasion of France and the Low Countries. In virtual secrecy, the Allies evacuated 24,500 troops by sea in early June 1940. Suddenly abandoned, Norway capitulated.[6]

After disbanding the Alta Battalion and escaping from Narvik by boat Dahl took command of Norwegian troops evacuated to Scotland. Later, he was appointed head of a military mission to the US and Canada, where he attended the Command and General Staff College at Fort Leavenworth in Kansas. In 1944, then with the rank of colonel, he was made commander of the Norwegian military mission to Russia, which had the task of liaising with the Soviet forces which had liberated Kirkenes and parts of eastern Finnmark.

Though pushed back from the Litsa Front by the Soviet Petsamo–Kirkenes offensive of October 1944, the German rearguard action before Kirkenes had bought valuable time for the withdrawal west. The extraction of close on a quarter of a million men, 60,000 horses, tens of thousands of prisoners, trucks, field guns, ammunition and supplies had been a feat of phenomenal logistics and co-ordination. This vast army headed west through Finnmark in two groups: in the north marching along the only road, Main Road 50, or pulling back further south along the border with Finland, heading for the town of Skibotn. Both army groups were heading for the Lyngen Line, a narrow neck of land in the mountains and fjords of the Lyngen Alps. But having withdrawn such an enormous force to the Lyngen Line, Allied military strategists were not sure what the Germans would do next.

Norway had not been high on the list of Allied priorities. The Normandy landings of June 1944 had been the number one consideration and every effort had
been put into ensuring their success. Despite Churchill pushing the idea of a joint
operation with the Soviets – codenamed Operation Jupiter and involving landings
in northern Norway, possibly at Porsangerfjord – Allied planning remained focussed
on the Normandy beaches. The assumption was that the liberation of Norway
would happen after the D-Day landings and a push across Western Europe.[7]

On entering the war as an ally of the west in 1941, the Soviet Union had given
full recognition to the Norwegian government-in-exile and treated Norway as
an allied power under enemy occupation.[8] In May 1944 the Norwegians signed
an agreement with the approval of the Western Allies agreeing that Norway was
in principle a Soviet area of operations.[9] During the Petsamo–Kirkenes offensive the Red Army had waited for permission from Moscow before crossing the
border into Norway, and Soviet commanders welcomed Norwegian participa-
tion post-liberation. Churchill wrote to Stalin on 23 October 1944:

> At Moscow [the 'Percentages' meeting that month] you said you would let me
> know whether there was any way we could help you in northern Norway. I
> understand that a token force of 200 Norwegians will be sent. Please let me
> know whether you have any other requirements and I will immediately make
> enquiries whether and to what extent they can be met.[10]

Having led a 97,000 strong offensive against the Germans, the Soviet commander
Lieutenant General Shcherbakov was somewhat surprised and disappointed when
Colonel Dahl arrived with a small number of staff for his military mission and
the 230-strong 2.Bergkompani (Mountain Company) as part of Operation Crofter,
Norway's move to re-establish a Norwegian administration in the far north.[11]

Dahl returned to Norway in November 1944 in an Allied convoy to Murmansk.
This was a symbolic entry point: the retreating Germans had destroyed many of
the landing stations along the Finnmark coast. He went straight into talks on
6 November with Shcherbakov, who readily agreed to his requests for help with
transport and supplies so he could take over from the Red Army. Dahl re-entered
Norwegian territory on 10 November 1944 with a team of deputies from the
Norwegian government acting for the police, justice, social affairs, finance and
information departments.

What greeted him was the wholesale destruction of ports, the devastation of
towns, the deportation of all inhabitants, the shooting of livestock, the burning
and blowing up of every form of shelter from the elements in an Arctic winter
and possibly thousands of people sheltering in caves with little or no food.

Concerned that the German army might repeat this further south, on
15 November the Norwegian prime minister in London raised the idea with

British foreign secretary Anthony Eden of a joint British and American operation north of Mosjøen to cut off the German retreat. A landing at Bodø was one option considered. Eden's response was, the Norwegians 'ought to know there were no British soldiers available for such an expedition'.[12] There would be no Allied military intervention to stop the disaster unfolding in the Arctic.

The advance Soviet patrols had halted on the Tana River. By the time Dahl reached them on 10 November the last contact with the Germans had been four days previously. He quickly discovered the Red Army did not intend to pursue the Germans any further. The main Soviet force was transferred south for the assault on Berlin; only a token force would stay in Norway.

By the time Dahl's main force arrived on 27 November, the Germans had a three-week headstart. Pursuing them seemed pointless when there was important relief work to do to save the population from freezing or starving to death in the coming winter.

One unit of Norwegian troops was sent to follow the Germans along Main Road 50, the only road west. Dahl considered it a futile effort but went too.

He shared his thoughts at the Nuremberg trial, when he was a key witness for the prosecution case against Lothar Rendulic, commander of the German 20th Mountain Army, which carried out Hitler's order for the destruction of Finnmark. 'I saw the scorched-earth policy as I have never seen it before,' Dahl said:

> When we got to Kirkenes part of it was still burning. There were epidemic diseases spreading, some cases of typhus, but rather large epidemics of diarrhoea and dysentery. There were no doctors. As far as I know there was only one doctor left in the whole district who had made his escape. Now there were epidemic diseases, cold, hunger and so on and no doctors, no hospitals.
>
> The destruction was as complete as it could be. Practically all of the territory west of the Tana line was completely destroyed. There was nothing left. When we got to these places, they could not offer us any shelter. First of all they were burned, and secondly the concrete fundaments of the buildings were blown up by dynamite so that the building could not even be repaired.
>
> All the communications were destroyed. The roads were blown up and mined; the bridges, the quays, the telephone and telegraph centres; the telephone poles were either cut down or blown up, and in the craters along the few roads were a great number of both Teller mines and personnel mines.
>
> Also the housing was destroyed – not everything in the easternmost part of Eastern Finnmark because the Russian attack had prevented that destruction. Otherwise, speaking of the line west of the Tana River, everything was completely destroyed – housing, historical buildings and churches. Not all of them but more than half of the churches were destroyed. And this destruction took place – as far as I know – from October until rather late in the spring of 1945.

The destruction [didn't always] take place at one particular time. There were places which were raided two or three times.

I thought it was wanton, and I could not see that it was a necessity for the German forces to destroy the country so completely. I can understand that communications were destroyed but I cannot understand that ... housing, for instance, especially along the coast where there could not be any advantage, [was] so destroyed, and monuments, churches and hospitals.[13]

The scale of the humanitarian disaster unfolding in Arctic Norway even reached the pages of the Canadian forces newspaper *The Maple Leaf*, which carried this report in its edition of 20 November 1944:

Norwegians driven out into Arctic winter

London – According to Norwegian government circles in London, terrible scenes are being witnessed here in the far north amid the gloom of the Arctic light. Thousands of men women and children are being driven out of their homes and sent wandering over snowbound roads in a temperature of 20 degrees below freezing.

Germans are carrying out ruthless scorched-earth policy, not only to hamper the advancing Russians but also to put those Norwegians who seek to evade evacuation in a well-nigh impossible situation.

Invalids and young children are dying by the wayside and those who try to hide from so called 'voluntary' evacuation are hunted out and shot. Homes of people are being burned down and their stocks of food taken away in order to compel them to evacuate.

This chaotic and horrible turmoil has been created by the Germans very largely for propagandist and political reasons so that they may concoct a story of the 'panic flight from the Bolsheviks.'

Hammerfest, for example, the most northerly town in the world, is now a 'dead' town. Tromsø, receiving centre for evacuees arriving from the north and with a peacetime population of 10,000, is now fantastically overcrowded with both German troops and Norwegian evacuees.

A letter written by an inhabitant of Tromsø to a friend in Oslo reads: 'Another 30,000 are arriving and accommodation must be found for them.' What worries evacuees most, apparently, is the fear that the world may think they are fleeing from the Russians.

To quote again from a letter from Tromsø – 'Tell the world that it is not the Russians we are fleeing from but the Germans. They are destroying everything.'

The Germans will no doubt try to hold the Lyngen line covering Tromsø until as many as possible of their troops in Finland and northernmost Norway have been withdrawn. But withdrawing to the line running from the Lyngen Fjord to the Swedish frontier, the Germans would provide themselves with a short defence line which could not be taken in the rear – except by an allied landing on the west coast.[14]

On 5 December 1944, the Allied supreme command Supreme Headquarters Allied Expeditionary Force (SHAEF) ordered the Norwegian Resistance Milorg to launch its 30,000 fighters in large-scale attacks against the railways in Norway. The aim was to stop large numbers of German troops being sent from Norway to central Europe to join the fight against the Americans and British. Milorg obliged, but the withdrawal of German combat troops from Norway was still considerable, despite its attacks. German records show seven divisions were pulled out of Norway in the first four months of 1945.[15]

There was no longer any need for two armies in Norway and far more pressing need for troops to defend the German homeland. The army of Norway was dissolved and its non-Nazi commander Colonel General Nikolaus von Falkenhorst retired, to be replaced first by Rendulic and – when he was transferred by Hitler to the Courland Pocket in Latvia a month later – by General Franz Böhme, another Austrian. It would be Böhme who would sign the German surrender in Norway in May 1945.[16] Böhme had invaded Poland in 1939 and France in 1940 then ruled Serbia with unflinching cruelty, executing 100 Serbs for every German soldier killed and fifty for every German wounded.[17] Böhme would cheat justice while awaiting trial at Nuremberg in May 1947 on charges of massacring civilians by jumping from a fourth-floor prison balcony. His fall was broken by a catwalk two floors below – he died two hours later.[18]

One possibility that could not be discounted – and which appeared increasingly likely with the war seemingly lost in Europe – was that of a last stand by the Hitler regime and loyal diehard troops in a scenario termed 'Fortress Norway' (Festung Norway). The Reichskommissar of Norway, the ruthless Hitler loyalist Josef Terboven, was considered among those who favoured this option.

The viciousness of Terboven was well known. As mentioned earlier, during the imposition of martial law in Trondheim he had personally ordered the execution of thirty-four civilians. They had been executed in retaliation for the killing in April 1942 of two Gestapo officers in an operation to capture Resistance agents landed by the 'Shetland Bus' at the village of Telavåg. An elderly fisherman who had arranged the secret smuggling of agents and weapons from Scotland was taken to Gestapo HQ in Bergen to be tortured, and nineteen other men thought to be involved were taken to concentration camps. All the remaining men from Telavåg were sent to Sachenshausen concentration camp near Berlin: thirty-one of these died. The women and children were taken to a prison camp near Bergen. Terboven then ordered the total destruction of Telavåg and the removal of its name from all maps. Every house was blown up and burned, all animals were taken away and all boats were sunk. The destruction was so complete that not even the wells remained.[19]

Another shocking incident three months later illustrated what Terboven was capable of: the massacre of 288 Yugoslav political prisoners at Beisfjord. The camp was sealed off after an apparent outbreak of typhus among the 900 prisoners held at the camp, about 10km east of Narvik. Norwegian sources say the SS marched out prisoners considered healthy and the remainder were then ordered to dig graves and stand in front of them, so when they were shot by the guards they would drop into them. The prisoners were killed by the guards twenty at a time. Prisoners too weak to stand were left in the barracks, which were set on fire. Those who jumped out of the windows were mown down by a machine gun in the watchtower. Seventeen members of a paramilitary force of Norwegians loyal to Quisling, known as 'Hirden', took part in the killings. During a total of four months, 748 of the 900 prisoners died.[20]

In March 1945 Terboven summoned Böhme and Kriegsmarine Commander Otto Ciliax to ask if they could guarantee the loyalty of troops in Norway 'in the case of German collapse on the continent'. Details of the meeting were relayed back to London in April by the Norwegian intelligence agent 'Edel' (in real life Jens Christian Hauge, head of the Norwegian Resistance Milorg, later defence minister and one of the most powerful men in Norway). 'Terboven was then apparently playing with the idea that Hitler, Himmler, etc., should come to Norway,' he wrote. 'The two commanding chiefs could not guarantee the loyalty of their troops.'[21]

The war had entered its final stages and the liberation of all Norway was a matter of weeks away.

4

THE VILLAGERS THAT ESCAPED AND THE TOWN FULL OF NAZIS

A tall man with light brown hair and a beard opens the door of a museum in Gamvik, a small coastal village on the very far northern tip of Norway. It's a very beautiful and natural place to be – idyllic even. The museum is housed in a wooden former fish processing factory which stands on stilts, jutting out into a small inlet from the sea. On a slope down to the sea to the left of the entrance, fish-drying nets made from orange twine stretched across a wooden frame are a throwback to bygone, simpler times. A single road leads away from the museum, snaking left and right through a scattering of houses and eventually up into jagged ,brooding mountains in the distance.

Between 1942 and 1944 there was a garrison of 150 German and Austrian soldiers stationed here, manning a battery of coastal guns trained on the sea channels not far offshore. Gamvik has a tale of two wars, almost: two years of reasonable, peaceful co-existence with the garrison and then two months of terrifying raids from SS landing parties. These troops burned all the houses to the ground and tried to round everyone up and deport them.

I have borrowed an old Mitsubishi Galant from the owner of my hotel so I can drive through the mountains to Gamvik to meet the curator of the museum, Torstein Johnsrud. Torstein has arranged for me to meet relatives of six fishermen killed by the Germans in one of the darkest chapters of the scorched-earth episode, the killings at Hopseidet two days before the war ended.

First, I have come to see his museum, as Gamvik is also a significant place in the war. Despite three raids by the SS landing parties, almost every one of 300 villagers managed to escape the forced evacuations. Only 13 people were caught by the patrols: the rest hid in caves.

It's clear as we talk that the museum doubles almost as a community centre. People pop in to do some photocopying and to have a chat. There's little evidence of another place – like, for instance, a shop – that would perform the same function. As Torstein talks, Gamvik's wartime history unfolds:

The Germans built big cannons into the hill behind the village because they expected an invasion here. The guns were to protect the sea where the German ships passed for Kirkenes and also to support attacks on British convoys to Murmansk. But a shot was never fired in anger from here, only in training.

There were 150 soldiers stationed here in Gamvik. They were reservists – family guys from Germany and Austria. There are still elderly people here who remember these times and they say these guys were very nice: well disciplined and never any trouble. Probably it had a bit to do with the fact that if they did anything wrong the penalty was the Eastern Front where the possibility of getting home to Mum wasn't exactly the same as sitting here and behaving well.

So the local population had – well, I wouldn't say friendly relations, but they got on well enough in their daily lives from 1942 until 1944. Then came Hitler's order in late October that everything should be burned. The nice guys left and a week passed and nothing happened. People wondered: 'Is the war over? Are we free?' but then the SS guys came with their Schnellboots that could move in fast and do their job. They burned Finnkonckeila [a nearby village] on 5 November. People escaped here over the mountains and you could see the smoke from here – it was on the eastern side of the peninsula, about 20–30km away from here as the crow flies. It was a very narrow little valley crammed with buildings and drying racks for fish. It was like a little city. Amazingly intense.

When they burned Finnkonckeila everyone knew the Germans were coming here next, so when they arrived the day after everyone went up to the mountains. Both German and Allied forces wanted to tell the local population about what they should do, how they should behave. The Germans said: 'Come with us. We are going to evacuate you south away from the horrible communists who are going to kill and rape you.' And the Allied propaganda said: 'Hold on, we're coming to rescue you.' And that didn't happen either.

So on 6 November when the Germans came people ran into the hills and watched them destroying the village. They came down when the Germans left for Mehamn and that was burned the day after. Three weeks later the Germans came back and again the people ran away. That was in late November. The Germans destroyed what little the local people had managed to rebuild.

Some people from here had gone east because the eastern part of Finnmark was liberated before the Germans managed to destroy it, but others stayed. Of 300 people in Gamvik, 287 dodged the evacuation. They hid in tens and twenties and in single families all around the coast and in the hills. I've heard astonishing stories of people sitting on the beach in the winter night, completely quiet, trying to hear if any Germans are coming, or sitting under piers while the tide is rising, keeping a lookout.

In that time some soldiers [from Arne Dahl's military mission] had arrived here and when the Germans came back a third time on 13 December this time they were met with fire. It's said that a German soldier was killed but no Norwegians were killed. The Germans didn't catch anyone.

Torstein shows me some of the collection of photographs and maps in the museum's collection. There are hand-drawn maps, showing the caves and hideouts around Gamvik where families sought refuge away from the main village, as well as photographs of the conditions they survived in after the Germans destroyed everything. 'In Norwegian history it's unparalleled in recent times,' says Torstein:

There are stories of families trying to run away with children and the elderly. There's a cave here – you can see it on this map – that housed twenty to thirty people on the night after the first burning. This map shows the hideouts people went to after the burning. Some of them were very small, on the coast and in the hills. It was winter and so people stayed near the coast so they could get fish and perhaps in the hope that a boat would pick them up.

It's incredible what people were doing to get away, and amazing how they managed. There's an image here of a family that has built a roof over their heads with this half-boat – the Germans destroyed all the boats too. They've rescued what they can to shelter from the Arctic winter. The attack happened late in November and there's almost no light then. All the sheep and livestock were killed, so there was very little to eat. It's probably a desperate situation. Some boats were saved though, hidden from the Germans, so little by little people could do some fishing and keep themselves going.

Torstein points to another photograph which shows a family standing outside a shelter made from a driftwood frame lashed together and covered with cloth and rags, their only protection against snow, ice and wind:

This little hut here [Oswald Johansen's hut at Tverrikvannet, see illustrations] housed forty people the first night. It's 20m² and it's just made of timber, rags and turf. There's no forest here so all they had was driftwood and turf. They were the only building materials they had. Even the school was made of turf. It's a traditional technique connected with Sami culture so people knew how to do it.

And here are the records of the people who were captured by the Germans.. where and when. Some on 5 November and some on 13 December.

Only thirteen of a population of 300 were captured and after the Germans had
burned the place three times…

He tails off as the phone begins to ring. I look at the list of names of the captured
villagers in amazement: a father, grandfather, the neighbour, his wife and sons;
another man, his daughters. The astonishing thing is that, like this list and like in
these pictures, everyone has names. In this museum, this history is personal and
local. Every single person is named. The family probably still live here.

Torstein returns from his phone call. 'There was one building left standing,'
he continues:

> That was the chapel where they kept the dead bodies before burial. Everything
> else was made of wood, soaked with petrol and set alight. One or two build-
> ings were rebuilt like they were pre-war, while people remembered how they
> looked. But nothing is older than the war. Rumour has it that after the war the
> Social Democrats weren't too upset that Finnmark had been burned to the
> ground because it was considered a backward part of the country and old fash-
> ioned in its ways, difficult to industrialise and modernise. And now you could
> start from scratch. And for the planners in Oslo – well, of course it's sad but it's
> an opportunity.

'To modernise the society with living standards higher than before the war?' I ask.
Torstein nods:

> Of course the merchants, the guy who owned this factory for instance, would
> have had a nice house whereas the common people would have lived in
> houses made of turf, at least until the 1910s and 1920s. The idea after the war
> was that you are not going back to that, you are coming with us into the
> future. And it's not going to be a communist paradise – it's going to be a social
> democrat paradise.

'Did people resent that lack of freedom to choose?' I wonder. 'It also seems that
people weren't too unhappy about that,' Torstein replies:

> They got help from the authorities to get better houses than before the war,
> and they weren't used to that either. Funnily enough it was another war that
> did for Gamvik. The fish factory had to close in 1969 because of the war
> in Biafra. Gamvik had access to the Nigerian stockfish market and Nigeria
> served as the entry point of distribution in West Africa. But the war meant
> there were no buyers. They couldn't sell the stockfish to Nigeria so the
> market folded.[1]

It seems ironic that Gamvik should survive the burning three times and then its fortunes would depend on the fluctuations of the market for dried fish. In the time we have spoken the museum has become quite busy, so I bid Torstein farewell and steer my borrowed Mitsubishi Galant up the hill to see the old gun battery from where there is a stunning view over the sea and surrounding coast. I pick my way through the blueberries and cloudberries growing plentifully in the mossy grass to get a better look at the concrete dugouts and circular depressions in the hills, where those 150 Germans and Austrians had scanned the horizon for enemy ships. Perhaps some of the people, who as children had watched them and perhaps cadged sweets from them, were now watching me.

It's peaceful and quiet and so far removed from war it doesn't seem possible. But here, less than a kilometre from the fish-drying nets, the cheerful colourful wooden houses, the fish processing factory and the kids playing on the beach are the decaying bunkers and concrete-rimmed scars in the landscape which confirm that, yes, war did come to Gamvik.

My luck changes on the journey back. It starts to slash down with rain as I drive along the single road through the mountains, which now look gloomy and ominous. I have 30km to cover to get back to Mehamn, where there is a small airstrip. It was very kind of my hotel owner to lend me his old Mitsubishi, but the brake warning light and oil light keep coming on and the tyres look pretty bald. I keep my fingers crossed and drive very gingerly.

Mehamn is a small fishing village clinging to the Arctic coast of Norway east of Hammerfest and Honningsvåg. It's a place for hardy souls, subject to gale force blasts and driving rain in summer and unimaginably low temperatures due to wind chill in winter. In summer the wind can blow so hard it's difficult to stand up. In winter, snow can form drifts a metre deep in minutes, which means a motorist heading for the mountainous roads in a snowstorm is taking something of a gamble with their life.

For some reason a community of expatriate Lithuanians has chosen to settle in Mehamn, working in local firms and hotels – including Renate, the receptionist at my hotel. When she goes off duty she's replaced by a guy from Sri Lanka who's brought his family here while he gets qualified in the hotel business. He speaks ruefully of clearing snowdrifts from his door so he can get back inside his house after late shifts in the winter. Sometimes he has to break the ice with a shovel: his dream is to work in a hotel in Bergen. I wish him luck.

When I reach Mehamn the deputy editor of the regional newspaper *Finnmarken*, Alf Helge Jensen, is waiting for me. He's had a call from Torstein and has volunteered to act as a translator for my meeting with Mette Mikalsen, the daughter of one of six fishermen murdered on the shores of a nearby fjord by German commandos seventy years ago. He offers to give me a tour of the remains of the German gun batteries on the coast.

We drive close to the edge of the cliff. There are shattered gun pits carved into the ground here, as in Gamvik. The field of fire of one battery is down onto the rocky beach at the bottom of these jagged, sharp cliffs; a second looks out to sea. Alongside the pits are subterranean concrete bunkers for the crews that would have manned the battery.

'These were anti-tank field guns, perhaps to fire on any landing craft in the event of an attack,' Alf Helge says:

> and over there were larger 14.5cm artillery cannon for shelling the convoys passing further out to sea.
>
> Many German tourists come here. My father was one of the civilians who was forced to build these gun pits. They didn't have any choice. We used to play here as children. When I was a kid of about 13 or 14 we used to come here a lot. All the kids did — of all ages. We had lots of fun.

He beckons to me and we peer over the edge of a steep, narrow cliff, with the sea crashing against the beach fifty metres below. 'Just down that cliff there,' he says:

> you could always find shells. I think they were dumped there by the Germans when they left. They were easy to find. I would carry a shell up the hillside in my arms [he puts both arms out straight in front of him, palms up, to demonstrate how he would carry the shells, like logs] and we'd put it on a fire and then hide behind rocks until it blew up. It was quite an explosion. Our parents would have been scared to death if they'd known — but in the 1960s everyone was working very hard and no one said anything.

Again I am a little shocked, but I know by now this is a more or less standard childhood in Finnmark in those days.

When the people of Mehamn were ordered to evacuate, Alf Helge's family decided against defiance in the hills and got on the boats heading south. 'My mother and father were sent south with the family, first to Hammerfest and then to Tromsø, where they were kept in a camp for everyone from Finnmark,' Alf Helge tells me as we scramble down to the beach below:

> There were many people in the camp and lots of people got head lice. If you had relatives nearby you could go and stay with them, so they went to stay with my grandmother in Vesterålen. If you didn't have any relatives in the area you were sent south to Oslo.
>
> Some people had a good experience and stayed friends for many years but many people had bad experiences. They were refugees in their own country. Many people wanted to come back as soon as possible, but the government wouldn't let them.

My mother and father secretly hitched a lift north on a cargo transporter ship that was bringing lots of materials to Finnmark. It wasn't allowed to take passengers but my father persuaded the captain. He said: 'OK, but you have to go in the hold and keep very quiet so no one knows you are there.'

In Tromsø they saw people they knew from Mehamn standing at the dock but they couldn't show themselves for fear of being discovered. When they got close to home they jumped off the cargo ship and hitched a ride on a fishing boat back to Mehamn. They started work rebuilding the place, first with a simple barracks that everyone lived in, then they built a barracks to use as a school. After that they built individual homes and rebuilt the town that way.

As we have been talking we have walked along the beach and round the side of one of the cliffs, where Alf Helge shows me a bunker blasted out of the bottom of the rocky hillside. The bunker entrance and passageway inside are made of smooth grey concrete, in strange contrast to the dark-grey layers of the slate and the grass growing green along the corridor leading inside the hill.

'I spent many happy hours in that bunker as a child,' he says. 'But then a man killed himself in there and it was blocked up. No one wanted to go in there after that.'

I decline his invitation to take a further look and we scramble back up the hill to the clifftop. As we walk, Alf Helge mentions something no-one I've talked to in Norway has touched on so far:

There were many Nazis in Mehamn, supporters of Quisling. One senior man – Karl Marthinsen, the security police chief – was killed by the Resistance at the end of the war. It was very stupid killing him because the Germans then executed a lot of civilians, maybe twenty or thirty. I've often wondered why there were so many Quislings in Mehamn but I've never been able to answer that. Many were from the same family and related in some way. There was one brother who was a Quisling and another who wasn't. The family was split.

It's time for me to go, so we walk back to the car. I ask Alf Helge how he feels about the gun batteries being a permanent reminder of the war. He says that recently efforts have been made to explain what that site is and what happened in Mehamn between 1940 and 1945.

'We must never forget the war,' he says:

It's part of our history and we should know it. Mehamn was totally burned. Lots of people went into the hills, some were sent to the south. Luckily the weather was mild so everyone survived. If it had been a normal winter it would have been very cold: many more would have died.[2]

When I get back to my hotel I look up Karl Marthinsen and Operation Buzzard, the Resistance operation to kill him ordered by the government-in-exile in London. I remember hearing about this when I was a kid, when *The Heroes of Telemark* was still being shown on TV and the films involving the Norwegian Resistance always had bitter-sweet endings.

From a tiny island near Tromsø, Marthinsen was one of the first members of the Norwegian Nazi party, joining in 1933. He acted as an intelligence officer in Finnmark during the Winter War between Finland and Russia in 1939–40, monitoring suspected communist sympathisers.[3]

In 1940 Quisling's police minister Jonas Lie, the man later appointed to oversee the evacuation of Finnmark, made him chief of the security police, a link man between the Quisling Cabinet and the Gestapo. He was also head of the Norwegian paramilitary organisation Hird, an equivalent of Hitler's SA: Nazi thugs, in plain language. He was a notorious brute who sanctioned the torture of his victims and played a key role in the deportation of Norwegian Jews, 700 of whom were murdered and many more mistreated. He was particularly disliked by the Resistance because he had been so effective against them.[4]

As the war drew to a close, the government-in-exile believed Marthinsen planned to step up security police attacks against the Resistance and use his Hird thugs to subvert the Nazi capitulation. Milorg was ordered to assassinate him in an ambush near his home in Oslo on 8 February 1945. The Resistance group known as the Oslo Gang prepared the attack, led by Gunnar Sonsteby, also known as Number 24 or Kjakan.[5]

That morning a team of Resistance gunmen waited behind a woodpile for Marthinsen's car to pass as he was driven to his office. As it did, they opened fire with automatic weapons, hitting Marthinsen in the passenger side, killing him instantly.

The reaction of Reichskommissar Terboven was one of fury, demanding that seventy-five Norwegian civilians be executed in reprisals for Marthinsen's death: fifty by the Germans, twenty-five by the Norwegians. Quisling, Lie and Justice Minister Sverre Riisnaes objected and eventually managed to get the number to be shot reduced.[6]

Terboven used the reprisals to take out Resistance activists he considered to be the 'brains' of the movement – all were found guilty and shot. Among those put on trial were high-ranking Oslo barrister Carl Gjerdrum, who supplied the Resistance with fake passports and helped identify informers working for the Germans.[7] Another was internationally respected neuropsychiatrist Haakon Saethre, who ran several clinics in Oslo. A Resistance sympathiser and financial supporter, Saethre helped Jews escape to Sweden after concealing them in his hospitals. He was arrested at his hospital the day Marthinsen was gunned down and shot the same night.[8]

Two other victims included engineer Kåre Sundby, a Milorg courier who was also found guilty of having listened to the news from London, and lawyer Jon Asbjorn Vislie, a Resistance sympathiser and financial supporter: both were executed at Akershus fortress on 9 February.[9] Twenty-eight people in total were executed in reprisals for the killing of Marthinsen. The condemned were taken to Oslo's Akerhus Fortress and shot over the next two nights by German and Norwegian firing squads overseen by Riisnaes, who even apparently joined in with a pistol, worse the wear for drink. As a result of the reprisals, the Norwegian government-in-exile suspended political assassinations.[10] The members of the court which sentenced the victims to their fate, and the firing squad which executed them, were given stiff prison sentences after the war.[11]

The summary execution of Resistance fighters and the cruel selection of victims by power-crazed Nazi brutes is sobering stuff. But the farther I travel down Norway's wartime roads, the worse it gets. These scorched-earth stories have already become a matter of life and death; but it's going to get a lot worse.

5

STILL MOURNING THE MEN OF HOPSEIDET

I meet Alf Helge Jensen for a second time at 8.30 a.m. on a Saturday morning at a snowplough-passing point in a remote mountain valley.

We are meeting on a bend on Road 888 between Mehamn and the rest of Norway. This is Hopseidet, scene of one of the most tragic incidents of the scorched-earth period: the killing of six local fishermen by German commandos in May 1945, two days before the war ended. I am here to talk to the daughter of one of the men killed and to her husband, who was first on the scene seventy years ago. Alf Helge will translate and also write a story about my visit for *Finnmarken*.

Gale-force winds whip the door of my borrowed Mitsubishi Galant out of my hands as I get out of the car in the slashing rain. We are at the base of some very steep-sided slate mountains. A narrow strip of land here separates two fjords: the Hopsfjord to the east and the Eidsfjord to the west. During the war the Germans tried to cut a channel between the two so their boats could use it as a Suez Canal-style alternative to running the gauntlet of Allied planes in the Barents Sea. With dark, foreboding clouds, gusting wind and driving rain this strikes me as a very lonely place.

We drive first to a solid column of black stone a short distance away, overlooking the grey-blue Hopsfjord, rippling stiffly in the wind. It's carved with the names of the three men and three teenagers who were gunned down here and stands in an area of marshy shoreline fenced off with chicken wire. A piece of twisted wire keeps the gate closed. Alf Helge wants to know what I think of the monument: his paper thinks the council should improve access to it and clean it up.

'The monument is fine,' I say, 'but there are no signs saying where it is, there's nowhere to park when you find it and there's no path down to it. And the chicken wire is a bit – disrespectful.' On a visit to the First World War graveyards of the Western Front in Belgium and France a few weeks previously, I had chanced upon a remote cemetery several kilometres off the beaten track to find it spotlessly maintained. I tell Alf Helge I think more could be done here to respect the memory of these unfortunate men – definitely. We take our photographs and move on.[1]

At 9 a.m. Alf Helge and I are sitting in the kitchen of a fisherman's cottage a few kilometres further east with an elderly man and woman who are offering us coffee and cakes. Mette Mikalson was 5 when this tragedy happened; her husband Øyvind was 20. It will turn out to be a very emotional and tearful morning.

Two U-boats, U-318 and U-992, broke surface in the waters near Hopseidet on the night of 5 May 1945. Thirty commandos were put ashore. They reached the coast 10km from the village and took prisoner a local fisherman, Ivar Oye, who was taken back to the U-boats as a guide.[2]

Hopseidet had been burned in November 1944 during the German withdrawal and Arne Dahl's men were monitoring the area. In his book *The Liberation of Finnmark* he says there was a garrison of six men at Hopseidet: regulars from the Norwegian Brigade and Norwegian 'police' trained in Sweden. Other accounts say there were three police. But, despite warnings of the German landing, Dahl's HQ did not send reinforcements immediately. The police were apparently told to use the local fishermen to help resist.[3]

The Germans were a special forces team from the Marine Einsatz Kommando 35 (MEK 35) unit based in Harstad, trained for action behind enemy lines. Captured Norwegian police had apparently revealed that the village was being used to transport supplies to the growing band of Norwegian soldiers spreading out across Finnmark. Special Forces Commander Kapitän-Leutnant Wolfgang Woedermann had drawn up plans in March for a U-boat to visit Hopseidet to destroy any landing piers and buildings being used by the enemy.

Although Hitler had committed suicide the day before, approval came from Berlin and the U-boats left their base in Narvik on 1 May, meeting up with a fishing boat carrying the special forces troops and Woedermann, overall leader of the operation. There is a photograph in German U-boat histories showing the MEK troops, the U-boat crew and Woedermann on the deck of a surfaced U-318, en route to Hopseidet.[4]

But the day before the U-boats broke surface in the Hopsfjord, the new commander of the Reich's forces, Admiral Donitz – successor to Hitler – had ordered all U-boats to return to their bases. Whether U-318 received that order is not known.

The Norwegians spotted the German subs on the night of 5 May and some of the fishermen prepared to engage them with the weapons they had: one machine gun, a revolver and two old guns. When the Germans came ashore the following morning the defenders opened fire but the commandos drove them back, leaving one man – Mathis Person, shot through the knee – stranded on the beach. Having overcome resistance, the Germans shot every animal they could find and destroyed every building. At this point they caught the six fishermen trying to escape into the mountains.[5]

Seventy years later I am talking to a woman who was 5 years old at the time and hiding in a cowshed with her mother and eight siblings. Her husband, now 89, lived a few kilometres away. They tell me three Norwegian military officers came to Hopseidet to investigate German submarine activity in the area. The six doomed fishermen, who were ordered to help by acting as look-outs, were Mette's 47-year-old father Einar, his 18-year-old son Johann and his friend Reidar Karlsen, 17, who had come to Hopseidet after being burned out of his home in a nearby fjord. He became friends with Johann; they were destined to die together. Mette's uncle Leonard Eriksen, 35, and cousin's husband Harald Kristiansen, 39, were there too, along with Harald's 16-year-old son Henry, who lived nearby. The fishermen were unarmed and wearing civilian clothes.

German soldiers came down from the hills and captured the group as they were trying to leave the area, Mette says. Two other fishermen managed to avoid being spotted. One, Odd Olsen, hit behind a rock, clenching his jaw from fear so hard he broke a tooth. Another – Juul Ferman – camouflaged himself with seaweed. Both witnessed what happened next.

Mette begins:

> My father and mother had eleven children but two were away when this happened. Our house had been burned down in November 1944 so we were living in the cowshed, which my father had cleaned up. He made a roof for it from the wreckage of a German ship which had been bombed by the Russians.
>
> A German soldier came to where we were and fired three shots through the roof. One bullet missed my brother by a metre. Then he raped my mother in front of all of us. I saw it happen. As he left he threw a hand grenade inside, but it landed in a pile of clothes and didn't explode. My mother threw it out of the window.
>
> There was a lot of shooting, for a long time. Even the Germans up in the hills were shooting. One civilian and one military man escaped into the hills and Germans on the submarine were firing at them as well but they escaped. My mother and all the children were lying in the cellar and we heard the shooting.[6]

Her husband Øyvind lived a short distance away to the east. The news of the killings reached him quickly and he went to the scene with his sister and cousin. He was shocked by the sight that greeted him.

'The Germans lined them up and shot them. It was an execution,' he says:

My sister Astrid, cousin Rudolf and I were first on the scene. The bodies were
not lying very close together so they had probably tried to run away when
the shooting started. The two military men and one civilian who had been in
the hills said that, when Einar was hit, he got up on his knees and said, 'You
wouldn't shoot civilians?'

They were his last words. He was shot again and fell dead. When the submarine left it didn't dive – they played 'Lili Marlene' over the loudspeakers. They
were so close to the end of the war, so near to being safe. These deaths were so
meaningless.[7]

Subsequent accounts of the murders described two German soldiers plac-
ing knives they found in a warehouse in the hands of the dead fishermen.[8] The
Germans also pinned printed notices to the bodies which read:

Norwegian Men and Women:

Point I: We fight and work for you and for a future European state.
Point II: We do not give away chocolate and tobacco as bait, but we have shown
a friendly attitude toward you during five years of our stay here.
Point III: We protect your homes against Bolshevik blood terror.
Point IV: We protect your homes from capitalistic plundering.
Point V: We grant you fishing grounds for your own personal use.
Point VI: We get you work and bread.

The one who opposes us, the one who supports the anti-European powers
with English, America, and Soviet Russia as leaders, the one who openly or
secretly places himself against us in this for Europe so difficult time, the one
who fleeing in fishing boats or escaping across the border opposes our arms, the
one who openly or secretly assists the enemy on this or on the other side of the
front, he is a traitor to Europe and to his Norwegian homeland, and he will be
found and destroyed regardless of where he is hiding.[9]

Mette's mother would prove to be a lifesaver the following morning when she
heard the cries of the wounded fisherman Mathis Person. She rowed across
the fjord to get him to medical help; without it he would have bled to death.
At 5 a.m. Norwegian troops from Arne Dahl's relief unit arrived on the scene
with a doctor. Two hours later Germany surrendered. The war was over.

I ask Mette what it has been like growing up without her father and brother
and so many close relatives. She has been in tears several times already during this

interview but cannot even get started on this answer. We pause while she regains her composure.

'I couldn't believe that my father was dead. I was 5 years old. I couldn't accept it, even after the funeral,' she says:

> I was sitting by the sea waiting many times, and all this has followed me through all these years. I had nightmares when I was a child. I saw German U-boats in my nightmares.
>
> The government in Finnmark gave us a new house and cowshed and a couple of cows and sheep as a sort of reward, so we had milk and meat but it was very hard all the time. We were quite poor. After a while my mother got a small pension every month but that was it. From when we were very young we had to help support the family. The oldest had to go away to work.
>
> The worst thing is that after the war all these Germans were arrested at their base in Harstad. There was a trial but the result was nothing. No one was punished in any way. They had every possibility to punish them but that didn't happen.

The deaths at Hopseidet were investigated by the Norwegian police at the end of the war. Kriegsmarine Leutnant Ewald Lubben admitted killing the men but said he had fired in self-defence because the Norwegians were armed with knives.[10]

The case was shelved by the Norwegian authorities in 1947. Further investigations took place in 1967 when six men were arrested in connection with the killings, again with Lubben as a suspect and also including Special Forces Commander Wolfgang Woedermann.

The six men claimed self-defence, saying the fishermen attacked them with knives. Despite evidence showing the fishermen were shot in the sides and back and ballistics tests showing more than one weapon was fired at them, the cases were dropped in 1969, perhaps because the Norwegians were conscious that civilians had been ordered to fire on soldiers.[11]

In 2005 an investigation by the Norwegian TV current affairs show *Brennpunkt* (Focal Point) interviewed some of the seventeen children orphaned at Hopseidet, highlighting their unhappiness that Norway had never properly explored the incident.

I ask Mette why she thinks no-one has ever been brought to justice.

'I have a theory,' she says:

> The big mistake the military made was in using civilians as guards with no uniforms or weapons. I think General Dahl wanted it covered up so there wouldn't be a big scandal on the military side. He was responsible, and afterwards he became a big hero.

In those days the telephone system was a switchboard so the operator could hear what people were talking about. The woman who was working there said she heard the conversations between General Dahl and one of the three Norwegian military officers. He said to them: 'You must not give up Hopseidet under any circumstances. Use the civilians to help you.' She is sure about that. We never had any apology from the Norwegian military either. That hurt as well. And General Dahl denied everything.

We finish our coffee and take some photographs for Alf Helge's newspaper. As we leave to go, Mette says:

Before you came I thought I would be OK talking about it. I thought I could talk about this without crying, but it's still so strong after so many years. But what would I have done without Øyvind? Not only a good husband but a great comfort to me.

6

THE WHITE CHURCH
OF HONNINGSVÅG

I'm sitting on the dockside of a picturesque fishing village at 6 a.m. on a Sunday morning, having just stepped off an enormous black, white and red Hurtigruten coastal steamer. My plane out of Mehamn yesterday lunchtime was cancelled because of unpredictable gale-force westerly winds that would have overcome the green and white Wideroe Airlines turboprop that should have taken me back to Hammerfest.

Instead, I was sent onto my next destination late that night by sea, grabbing an hour or two's sleep in a cabin as the huge Hurtigruten smashed through the buffeting waves and howling wind – arriving safely but a little earlier than intended in Honningsvåg.

Thankfully by the time the ship's ramp is lowered to the quayside the gale has blown out and the rain has stopped, so I while away a peaceful Sunday morning eating a breakfast bought on board ship of dried fruit, rolled-up sweet pancakes, yoghurt and fruit. After that I read a book until my eyes start to close and kill some more time walking along the coast out of town in one direction for a fair distance, sitting on a bench looking out to sea, and then walking back.

When Finnmark's most famous film director calls me at 9.30 a.m. to discuss the arrangements for meeting up, I'm snoozing gently on a bench in front of Honningsvåg's greatest and perhaps only landmark: the white wooden church that survived the scorched-earth burning in 1944 and inspired this book of scorched-earth stories.

Six years earlier I stood in the churchyard here looking at the horizon trying to imagine what this bleak landscape might have looked like after everything had been burned in the scorched-earth withdrawal – and wondering how people survived. Now I am here again hearing their stories.

An hour later Knut Erik Jensen meets me by the quayside and we slip into the Rica Hotel nearby. It is warm and has friendly staff who don't mind me conducting a full-blown interview at a table in the corner of the restaurant.

It's an absorbing encounter with a man immersed in culture, portrayal, symbolism, human nature and above all history. He is a ferocious researcher who spent several years gathering the material for the TV series *Finnmark – Between East and West*, which won him his first Oscar. Strangely, that hasn't been shown in Norway for three decades.

He's brought with him a book that accompanied the series. What's amazing is that he knows everyone in the pictures and has a story to go with each one. We sip coffee as he turns the pages: here's a guy who played the trombone in the town band, here's a fisherman who survived when the ammunition ship blew up in the harbour in 1942, this guy is still alive, and so on. Fascinating it may be, but the book has been out of print for decades and, curiously, the university press that published it destroyed all the negatives so it couldn't be reprinted. That's certainly a strange thing to do.

Knut Erik begins his story:

I was only 4 at the time of the burning. We went to live on the island of Måsøy from 1942 to 1944 because of all the bombings, the torpedo attacks and that sort of thing.

My mother was pregnant with my sister so she went where it was more peaceful. We were collected from there for the evacuation on my father's boat. It was 50–60ft long and full of people. There were two families – eight children and five or six adults, and maybe a few others that were working with my father.

We settled for the south and were set ashore on the island of Senya [on the tip of Norway's extreme north-west coast between Harstad and Tromsø] where we were collected by horse and carriage. My mother was pregnant, I was 4, my brother was 7 and my sister was 14. We settled on a farm for a few months where we had relatives – aunties – and then we moved on to another place called Gryllefjord, where the family was established on the top of a fisherman's warehouse, and my mother was still alone.

There was an old bachelor who said to my mother that if she cared for the house and helped him with some cooking while he was out fishing she could stay there for free for as long as she wanted. So we stayed there till May 1945. Then we heard her brothers and family had returned to Harstad so we stayed in the former German barracks in Trondenes. They were turned into a camp for evacuees which everyone called 'Little Finnmark'. We lived there till 1951.

We slept in German beds with the swastika stamped on them and all the things we were eating from, plates and cups, had the swastika stamp. This place had also been a prisoner camp for the Russians. There was a fortress at Harstad with one of those big Adolf cannons that could fire shells all the way to Narvik, 30–40km. That was built by the Russian prisoners: 800 of them died, more or less exterminated. At that time the prisoners were buried at the church with Russian Orthodox crosses. There's a memorial there now. [The fort, the cannon and the prison camp are still there, now a tourist attraction. In 1953 the remains of the Soviet prisoners were moved to a collective mass grave of 7,500 Soviet war dead at Tjøtta.][1]

It being a big fortress, we had all the things the Germans left behind. There were helmets, bayonets and signal pistols and also the flag with the skeleton on warning about mines. We had a good time playing with these things. It was in many ways an exciting time, until you learn what really happened.

Everyone was talking about going back [to the ruins of their homes] and starting again but it was forbidden to go back, for many reasons. The problem of the mines – yes, that was dangerous. Many Germans were used to clear the mines and a lot died, and so did a few civilians. So it was forbidden for us to return – but people just went back anyway.

Knut Erik speaks fondly of the north of Norway, and much less so about the south. Many of the northerners I've met have the same complaint: that Oslo had its war and its heroes – the Resistance 'boys in the forest' – while the north, being battered and burned and blown up, barely gets a mention. This sense of a country on different tracks didn't end after the war. Knut Erik is particularly critical of post-war authoritarian decisions when evacuees from Finnmark first weren't allowed to return home, and then were told the kind of houses they could have to replace their destroyed homes.

'The planners in London – we call it "The London Plan" – had already restored the area of Finnmark and northern Troms in their way,' he says:

Everything should be social democracy, equal – with a bathtub and a basin. Everybody should return to a certain type of uniformity. They tried to restore the whole area before the people came back because they thought they wouldn't return to these very primitive circumstances. I think it was the biggest civil protest in Norwegian history – a mass movement of 'civil disobedience'. Everybody just went back. Then the authorities realised they had to do something, so barracks went up everywhere while permanent rebuilding began.

The first people to go back to Honningsvåg stayed in the church. They lived there in primitive circumstances but in good spirits; they even had a bakery in the church. I talked to the man who was the first person to get a key for the church. He was completely alone in this place with the ruins and the church on the hill. He said it was utterly quiet, like being in a moon landscape.

The church is the only building that gives a reminder of the history of the town, and the church is a holy place in principle. The importance of this building in this small town is growing and growing. Knowing that it survived and knowing it was the only place that people could stay when they returned, it has both a religious history but is also the story of everyday people. The people have a spirit you can never kill.

I've been trying to say in my films that the scorched-earth period is a remarkable part of Norwegian history. It's a history where the nation could learn what war really is and what 'scorched earth' really means. It's knowledge, historical knowledge, and we could use that to understand ourselves better and to understand the world better.

There's a new conscience of what happened, like 'Oh, that's what the old town looked like'. There were a lot of buildings that would have been bigger than the church – the old school, the post office, the pharmacy, the telegraph house – beautiful houses at the time, and well built, made from good resources. The more young people see these old pictures the more they feel proud and take that out into the world with them. And there are still old people around who remember the way it was. It's not long ago.

We take a break to refill our coffee cups and Knut Erik points out the fish factory at the Bryggen that his father used to run, and where his father had been working when the ammunition boat was hit by Russian bombers in 1942:

You can still find remains from the boat around here, you know. There was a lot of bombing. One bomb fell right outside here and my father was working round the corner. That saved his life but he said there was a head rolling along the quayside. There are the remains of Russian planes still on the islands. I have found ammunition, pieces of bones, even a piece of skull. A few years ago a friend of mine found a foot in a boot on one of the islands.

After we have finished our conversation, Knut Erik has a family fishing trip to go to. There are a few things he wants to add. I start the tape recorder again to catch his closing thoughts. 'The occupation of Norway was the fight against Bolshevism,' he says:

Norway was just a marching area through to the Arctic, to stop the convoys going to Murmansk, to stop the Russians. After the capitulation Norway was a peaceful country. OK, there were a few sabotage operations in the south, the important one being the heavy water [at Norsk Hydro at Telemark in 1943], but the Germans went all the way up to Kirkenes to get into the Soviet Union. They attacked a few weeks too late.

I think it takes time to realise what really happened – generations even – and I don't think the nation has realised that. And once you have experienced war it will be a landmark in your life. For years [as a kid] I dreamt about German soldiers and I would wake up with the dogs barking, trying to get off the rope. It's an extreme experience and you experience it through what your parents say, what you remember. And when I meet people from Palestine and Afghanistan I recognise the symptoms of war, because it's the same. [2]

Before I leave, Knut Erik wants to show me the statue of himself in the hills overlooking the town. We drive up as far as we can talking about his plans for the future, and I take a picture of him alongside his bust.

He drops me off at the side of the white church and heads off for his fishing trip. I walk around to the Nordkapp Museum to see if I can catch it before it closes but as I get to the front door I realise it's Sunday and it's not open. Instead of hanging around in the town any longer I find a cab and head out to the airport a few kilometres from town to carry on with my book. The only other passenger in the terminal is a well-dressed man in his 20s who has a sports bag and a strong Latvian accent.

'Where are you heading, mate?' I ask as we pass through security.

'Back to Latvia for holiday,' he says. 'I work here. I am an engineer. Good money!'

I can feel the short night on the boat and the long day catching up with me. I open my book and try to read but can feel my eyes closing. Wideroe certainly looked after me when my plane was cancelled by paying for a cabin on the boat, but I am looking forward to a nice, comfortable bed when I get to my hotel in Hammerfest.

7

THE DESTRUCTION OF HAMMERFEST

My hotel in Hammerfest is on the far side of the bay, a short but expensive taxi ride down a steep hill from the airport, built on a plateau above the town. Next to the hotel several excavators and a team of engineers are cutting a very large hole through the rock cliff. As I arrive an alarm sounds; there is a powerful but muffled explosion and an enormous piece of what appears to be rubber matting bucks and twitches with the force of the detonation underneath it.

When the mat lies still again, the arm of one of the excavators swings over and pulls it from the bedrock it was covering then begins to scoop broken chunks of blasted stone from the area, loading them onto a procession of lorries which ferry them away from the building site. The level of the hole is at least 10m lower than my hotel next door, and at least double that wide. While I'm there, the work goes on night and day. Luxury apartments are being built.

Hammerfest is a curious mixture of architectural styles. Post-war wooden houses painted in traditional blues, reds and whites rub shoulders with blocky 1960s-era concrete shopping centres and flats. Depressing 1950s shops and galleries line the uneven, patchily surfaced harbour car park. The white fibreglass polar bear statues guarding an entrance arch to the council building offer some cheer to the eye. The main road is lined mostly with dreary shops, except for a colossal angular modern building facing onto the harbour which appears to be some kind of arts and culture centre. The side of it is raised on stilts with stone stairs leading up from the harbour, so if visitors are not able to find artistic solace within they can at least shelter from the rain. I make use of it to eat a lunch of cheese buns and blueberry yoghurt. Across the main road the architectural styles become more recent, if no less uninspiring. Squat apartments made of dark-grey bricks with balconies of chrome and black wood have sprung up in small clumps, decorated with a splash of gaudy yellow here or jaunty pink there. Hammerfest may be many things, but it is not blessed with beauty. There is a lot of building work going on and, judging by the fencing and the notices everywhere around town, a lot more planned.

Throughout the occupation Hammerfest was a major base for the Nazis. It was the main U-boat base for the Finnmark area and a supply centre for ships attacking Allied convoys to Russia. Three powerful coastal batteries were built to protect against attack from sea or air, more than 4,000 mines were laid and numerous anti-aircraft gun positions set up, whilst Luftwaffe seaplanes operated from Rypefjord, the next fjord along. Local people were evicted from their homes to accommodate the 400 to 500 Wehrmacht troops needing living quarters.[1]

A report on the scorched-earth demolition of Hammerfest was submitted to the Nuremberg war-crimes hearings after the war. It reads like a diary of destruction. On Sunday 29 October 1944 came the news that Hammerfest was doomed. The posters were pasted up around the town: by the harbour, in public spaces, in shops and offices. 'To the population,' they read. 'It has been decreed that the compulsory evacuation of the population of Finnmark will be carried out immediately.' The orders came from Lothar Rendulic, the Nazi general in charge of military operations in northern Norway, and the Reichskommissar for Norway, Josef Terboven.

Citizens were to report to the tax office on the second floor of the City Hall to be assigned transport out; those who failed to comply with the evacuation orders would be rounded up by the police and the army. Norwegians had been quietly ignoring NS orders to evacuate Finnmark for two weeks, but 'Hitler commands' were different. They could not be ignored. Defiance would be difficult and, if Terboven's ruthlessness in the past was any measure, might mean death. Evacuation 'immediately' was at noon the following day. Soon afterwards houses in a district a few minutes walk from the harbour were doused in petrol and set alight.

Over the next three days the population was rounded up and sent south on motorboats and fishing vessels. The cutter *Ethel May* was loaded with men, women and children and packed with stoves before setting sail[2], although several men were kept behind to operate the water and electricity works. The firemen were told they could go: as of 1 November there was no further need for a fire department. Two freighters took evacuees and sailed away. Rumours began to circulate that the entire town was to be burned to the ground.

Five days later those rumours started to come true. On 5 and 6 November three farms and some small buildings on the outskirts of town were burned down, as well as all the houses in the centre. One building contained important valves that stopped the water works mains freezing. A heavy frost would now put fresh water supplies out of action.

On 22 November fires were set in fifty houses in the hills facing the harbour, with one or two buildings being blasted to stop the flames spreading. During the following days all the foundations of the charred houses were blasted and on 16 December five houses along the main shore road were torched. On Christmas Eve it was the turn of Breilia, an area slightly inland, where a barracks, a nursery and some private houses were set ablaze. After Christmas the soldiers came back and destroyed the rest of the area, including the remaining buildings around the power plant and, on 28 December, a large naval barracks at Skansen Fuglenes, the tip of the claw forming the harbour of Hammerfest. The smoke from this fire would have been seen several kilometres away and from neighbouring islands.

Midway through January the fire squads came back, burning the district of Fuglenes and the Feddersen and Nissen fish factory, run by a family with roots in Hammerfest dating back to 1861. Feddersen and Nissen had been involved in fish production, trapping and export for decades and had run a fleet of fishing boats and a retail business stretching across Finnmark, including Gjevsvær, Honningsvåg, Mehamn and Berlevåg, all destined for destruction in the flames.[3]

Now the pace began to pick up. In the following days the remains of the eastern town were burned, the landing stages of the Finnmark Canning Factory and associated buildings were demolished, as was the Robertson coal depot. All the nearby houses were doused with petrol and set ablaze too.

A fresh southerly wind whipped up a fire started in the elementary school which spread to the centre of the city and burned all night. All the churches — initially earmarked to be saved — were engulfed. The west of Hammerfest was charred timbers. The hospital, refrigeration plant and the offices of the bus and boat company Finnmark Fylkesrederi (FFR) were blown up. The steamboat landing stage was dynamited and the two bridges into town were blown and mines laid on their approaches.

The Germans cut down every telegraph pole, rolled up all the cables, smashed all the ceramic conductors and dismantled all the transformers and apparatus at the power station. Then they loaded everything onto ships and took it all away.

At 9 a.m. on 5 February the power station was shut down and an hour later the transformer stations were blown. Depth charges were laid alongside the 9in main pipe to the water works running through the lake. Pipes further out were ruptured when the bridges were brought down.

On 6 February orders were issued for all remaining Norwegians, Germans and Soviet prisoners to leave the city. This left behind twenty engineers and a lieutenant to blast the rest of Hammerfest then escape in a tugboat. After each building was burnt, the engineers set explosives to blast the foundations, levelling smoke stacks, apartments and foundations.

By 6 February snow had started to fall. A white blanket covered the devastated town with its shattered buildings and charred timbers. On 10 February 1945 the Germans pulled out of Hammerfest. Only the white chapel in the cemetery remained standing.[4]

The white Hauen funeral chapel stands across the road from the architecturally striking Hammerfest church, one of the modern images of the town, built in 1961 to replace a predecessor engulfed by Nazi flames. Constructed from stone and concrete with beautiful stained-glass windows inside, the church has a dramatic triangular design, repeated in the tall steeple facing town. Next door is another of Hammerfest's modern buildings, but on a much less breathtaking scale. The Museum of Reconstruction is low, flat and square and painted a disconcerting salmon pink. It is instantly depressing. Thankfully the contents and the curator are as inspirational as the exterior architecture is not.

I climb a flight of metal stairs to the second floor where I meet curator Yaroslav Bogomilov, a Russian from the White Sea region. He's an expert on the war years in Finnmark and is a generous and very knowledgeable guide. He shows me around the museum's collection.

'The Germans had submarines at Hammerfest for two years and here was a staging post for supplies north,' he says:

> German ships would congregate at Honningsvåg to form a convoy to go to Kirkenes as a protection against the Russian bombing from the air. In the Alta region the battleships *Tirpitz* and *Scharnhorst* were hidden, and there was an airbase at Lakselv.
>
> Most of the soldiers here were mountain troops from Austria. The soldiers enjoyed the creature comforts of home and mingled with the locals. They lived side by side for several years, and the troops were boys barely out of their teens. Hammerfest too played its part in the yield of 10,000–12,000 babies born in Finnmark of German-Norwegian parentage during the war. Life was peaceful until the order to evacuate was given first on 17 October 1944 and then as a 'Hitler command' on the 27th. It was only those that came from the front line that were aggressive.

We stop in front of a display cabinet showing two armchairs and a 1930s period American barber's chair which had been buried by people forced to leave Hammerfest by the Germans.

'People didn't go at first. They didn't want to,' Yaroslav says:

> They buried their belongings because they thought they were coming back. We have armchairs and furniture on display in the museum, including this barber's chair. Some people even cleaned their houses before leaving, then locked the door. The Germans just burned the houses at first, then they started mining them and blew them up.

The Norwegian government-in-exile in London got messages to people here by radio telling them to go and hide in the hills rather than be evacuated. Some went over to Sørøya, the big island across the fjord from Hammerfest, and 1,000 people ended up spending the winter living in a cave. In the end they were all almost starving and the British had to send a destroyer to rescue them. The warship managed to avoid a German submarine waiting in the bay and took 500 people first to Murmansk and then back to Scotland.

Fifty thousand people were evacuated from Finnmark: first to Tromsø, then on to the south – Mosjøen, the Lofoten Islands, Trondheim, Oslo. Tromsø was so overcrowded the refugees had to sleep in the cathedral. Of course, families got separated and people lost touch with each other. The Lofoten newspaper was full of adverts from people looking for their relatives. In Oslo there was even a special paper carrying messages from displaced people trying to be reunited with their loved ones.

A cinema screen is showing black and white images of Hammerfest before the war, then scenes of the burning and the immediate post-scorched-earth period:

In summer 1945 Norwegian TV sent a camera crew to Finnmark to film the scenes of destruction so people in the south could see for themselves what had happened. Southerners couldn't imagine what happened here – that's why they sent the camera crew. People were living in tents, under boats and in makeshift cabins. They built barracks to provide provisional facilities, fitting planks from the wartime runways to use for the walls.

We have moved to an exhibition area dealing with the post-war reconstruction of Hammerfest and Finnmark. Here, alongside models of 'traditional' housing – turf huts with extremely basic facilities and fittings – are clean, spacious rooms with ample furniture, washbasins, hot and cold water, flush toilets and modern kitchens.

After the war the government wanted to improve living standards, Yaroslav explains, and the scorched-earth destruction offered the opportunity to do that, rather than return to the old, traditional housing.

The Norwegian Labour Party [Arbeiderpartiet, aka Social Democrats] imposed a new type of life here after the war. First people weren't allowed to go back to Hammerfest as the government wanted to develop Alta as the main city instead. Then – after people returned to Hammerfest anyway – they weren't allowed to decide what kind of homes they could have. There was a Minister for Reconstruction who decided all this. People had to choose from designs made by architects sent by Oslo to build uniform houses to certain standards. Of course, that caused resentment.

And then there was prejudice. Southerners believed people from Finnmark were 'not Norwegians like we are'. That prejudice continued for several decades after the war. Until the 1970s adverts offering accommodation to rent in Oslo specified that the rooms would not be rented to people from Finnmark.[5]

I'm a little surprised at this, but I can believe it, as prejudice like this was similar in 1950s and 1960s Britain, with landlords and B&Bs specifying 'No blacks, no Irish, no dogs'. But Norway?

Knut Iversen is a friendly 73 year old who laughs readily and regularly as he tells stories of his wartime childhood in Finnmark. We are sitting at a table opposite a stuffed polar bear standing on its hind legs at the back of Hammerfest's tourist office, which is run by Knut's son, Knut Arne. Knut tells me he was born in Svolvaer in the Lofoften Islands in 1940 and settled in Hammerfest two years later before being evacuated when the town was burned down.

'My family went by boat to Tromsø – me, my brother, Mama and Papa, my aunt and uncle and their children, two boys and one girl,' he says:

We were all living together with one family in Mo i Rana [quite a long way south down the coast towards Trondheim]. We didn't know them. One of my cousins played a trick on me. We found a hole in the ground and he said: 'Jump in there.' So I did. But it was the outside toilet and suddenly I was up to my neck in poo. My mother went crazy. She dragged me to the river and cleaned me up.

I think 3,500 people went from Hammerfest all over Norway during the evacuation. Some were living in caves – 500 of them on the island of Sørøya, all through the winter. When the war ended people just wanted to come back. They turned boats upside down and lived under them.

We came back in 1946–47 on the coastal steamer. Many people came back to nothing, with nothing. The Germans took everything and burned everything, except the small church. I don't know why they left that. I think it was because there had been funerals for German seamen held in that church.

From 1946 to 1947 work started rebuilding Hammerfest. As we say in Norway, they built it rock by rock. The government said Hammerfest won't be rebuilt because they thought the town should have been in the Alta area but the people of Hammerfest ignored them.

There was ammunition everywhere. The harbour was full of mines. The government said: 'No Norwegian can go back to Hammerfest before the army has taken up all the landmines in the street,' but the people didn't listen – they just went home. For the first 17 May National Day parade after the war, in 1946, there were two accordions, one trumpet and one drum, but they were all singing: 'Yes, we love our country.'

Knut is warming to his theme. The memories are coming thick and fast and he clearly has a 'glass half full' outlook on life:

> We started building houses in 1950. Many of the houses you can see today were built then. We were sent barracks from Sweden and these were all over the city until 1960, until the rebuilding was complete. The barracks were very cold in the winter, but we had a roof over our heads and something to eat. Everyone was working, fixing the houses. We all helped each other. Most people came back.
>
> I had a great childhood: outside all the time, fights between the different gangs in the town. There were only 5,000 people living in Hammerfest. We had food, my parents were working, everything seemed fine. After the war five boys and one girl got polio; I was one of them. That's the only illness I can remember having.
>
> Of course there are bad stories from the war but when you're young you don't notice it. My mother and father didn't talk about it. Everyone was working so hard to build the town, get some fishing boats, to work, to get money.
>
> The Germans blew up the fish factory when they left. I think 80 per cent of people were involved in the fishing industry, so it was important to get that working again. Lots of teachers came here from the south as volunteers. We had 'Swedish police' in Hammerfest [Norwegian exiles trained for military in Sweden, categorised as 'police' so as not to break Sweden's neutral status]. We got a new hospital in 1955.
>
> When they burned the town, the Germans set fire to the Catholic Church but after the war German Catholics sent money for a new one to be built – and it was, in 1956.
>
> We had a good relationship with the Germans. We all spoke German – they lived here alongside us. There had been lots of people here aged 18 or 19 and the German soldiers were the same age and they were talking, not fighting. It was a peaceful occupation. I never heard anyone say, 'I hate the Germans.'[6]

When the younger Iversen, Knut Arne, sits down to talk it's not hard to see why he's the manager of the tourist office. He left Hammerfest in his 20s but has been back in town since 2006. He delivers facts and figures at terrific speed and paints a very positive picture of Hammerfest's future. He describes the latest twist in the fortunes of the town as 'a money shower':

> Fishing was Hammerfest's main industry in the past. We have the Gulfstream along the Norwegian coast. That's why people settled here in the sixteenth and seventeenth centuries – that was Hammerfest's main business. The fishing is still important but not as important nowadays as gas, which has become the main industry.

Gas was discovered in the 1980s. There's a gas field called Snow White [Šnøhvit] about 140km offshore. There's a pipeline along the seabed and here in Hammerfest there's a big gas factory which liquefies the gas and ships it out, mainly to Spain and the United States.

They are producing gas worth between 2–3 million euros a day. That's quite an important contribution for Norway as a country and the estimates are that there are enough resources for the next forty years. We say here we have won the lottery since 2002.

Hammerfest gets tax income from this gas plant – about 20 million euros a year. There are 10,000 people here, so that's quite a lot of money for such a small town. Since 2009 they have renovated the whole of the city centre and from next winter the sidewalks will be heated, so we can do shopping almost without wearing shoes. We don't have unemployment – only about 2 per cent, or 150 people – and we have a lot of foreigners here, about 10 per cent, which is quite a big number.

To live so far north is not for everyone. You need some courage to live here and to stay here. For some people it's an adventure for 2 to 3 years. Some people in Norway don't want to live here because of the climate and the distance to other parts of Europe, but we see that people from outside Norway want to try it.

If you are an engineer on the gas plant, you can earn a lot of money: 120,000 euros a year [nearly four times the average wage in Britain], paying 30 per cent tax. But houses are expensive – about 300,000 euros [£250,000] – and about the same for an apartment in the city centre. That's quite a lot of money and it's not so easy for young people to settle down. There's a lot of competition for those jobs in the gas industry but the best engineers can earn a lot.

We had a big fire in 1890 and two-thirds of the city was burned down, and then in autumn 1944 the town was burned down for a second time, but people struggled and fought each time to build up the town and stay here. The fishing industry had its ups and downs and people were leaving and there wasn't much work. It wasn't a rich town.

But since 2002 everything has changed and now it's a really good place to be. And there's more to come. People have been moving back: they want to stay here and create a future, especially young people. There are 10,000 people living here and we have people from 50 different nations.

There are building sites all round the town: new offices for the oil companies setting up here, luxury flats, hotels, even more houses. You can see the activity everywhere, and the wider town is spreading, There's lot of space to build on so I think the next ten to twenty years will be exciting. You can see people are in a good mood, feeling positive, and there are lots of young people. There's a definite feelgood factor.

After the Second World War people hated the Nazis because of what they did here. I say 'Nazis' because it wasn't just Germans, there were a lot of Austrians here. My feeling is that all those young Nazis had no choice. They either did what they were told to or they were shot. It was war, but here it was quite peaceful. There was no bombing, there were no battles. I think the Germans wanted to occupy Norway but not to fight the population. The Norwegians didn't resist. They did what the Germans wanted them to do.

There was a fish factory here, so Hammerfest was more or less a support town for food and also there was a submarine base. In Alta nearby they kept the *Tirpitz*. Hammerfest was a place for soldiers to rest and take some leave from the front. They took part in life here, in a way.

Nowadays we have a lot of tourists here, especially Germans. A lot of them say their fathers or grandparents were here in the north in the war but never talked too much about it. It can't have been a good story or an easy story to tell; they can't have been proud of it. But some certainly did tell their children or their grandchildren because they come here and want to get a feeling of what it was like for Grandpa.

Personally I feel proud that my grandparents came back and helped rebuild the place. That showed a lot of courage and I feel good about that.[7]

I thank Iversen Senior and Junior for their trouble. They turn out to be the only people in Hammerfest I can persuade to talk about the scorched-earth burning. I make a dozen phone calls to people with stories or who have been interviewed before or recommended, but all are busy or out of town. Yaroslav suggests I come early on my last morning and speak to a group of older men who meet every morning in the café of the Museum of Reconstruction, but, strangely, the older generation refuse to talk to me – or even to write to me. I explain that I'm interested in hearing their stories in English but I am met with frowns and grumpy expressions.

'Do you know the trouble you're asking us to go to?' one veteran of the war years complained – in perfect English – when I suggested he might share a tale or two from Hammerfest's darkest days. Another suggested I translate stories from some of the excellent books about this time written in Norwegian, which rather misses the point of what I am trying to do: to tell these scorched-earth stories in English. Others who had initially seemed positive didn't return my calls.

Eventually I give up on Hammerfest's older generation and instead walk along the main street, Strandgata, to St Michael's, the Catholic church rebuilt with money sent from Germany after the war, which has a full-length mosaic of the saint on the outside wall. The door is open, so I go inside. It's simple but all the better for that: two rows of pews fill the hall, with light streaming in through stained glass windows. There are occasional photographs of sailing ships from bygone days in the harbour and a notice explaining how the nuns who run the church, the 'grey nuns' of Sister Elisabeth from Silesia, have been working in Hammerfest since 1880. There's a sense of peace and yet purpose in the church. I'm glad I came.

Later in my trip I am in a taxi on the way to an airport when the driver says: 'Hammerfest? Oh yes, it was totally destroyed. Everything except the church. My grandfather went there after the war to help with the reconstruction. He drove a lorry – he was a volunteer.'

'How long did he stay?' I ask.

'The rest of his life,' says the driver. 'He met a girl and, you know, he stayed. Without the burning, there'd be no me!' [8]

8

REFUGEES, RESCUES AND RESISTANCE

As an historian in his early 30s, Kristian Husvik Skancke is relatively young. His Masters thesis was about the humanitarian crisis on the island of Sørøya, which led to the dramatic rescue of 500 people by the Royal Navy. He had family on the island during the war – it's a topic he knows about.

A former curator at the Museum of Reconstruction in his hometown of Hammerfest, Kristian now runs a folk museum at Deiarn in the countryside further south down the coast near to Bodø. He has conducted extensive archival research into northern Norway's war years.

We sit in armchairs in my hotel room, sipping lemon tea and occasionally leaning over a large map of Finnmark spread out on the bed. Kristian's contribution is definitely thought-provoking.

'Finnmark became a no-man's-land, a security buffer between the Red Army and the Wehrmacht,' he says:

I've seen documents that show the Germans actually planned to pull back as far south as Trondheim and level everything north of there, but, because the Russians halted, the Germans built defences at the Lyngen Line.

The Lyngen Line was only a temporary line of defence because the Germans believed the Russians might continue and there might be a British landing too. It was only the Russians stopping their advance and the war ending that prevented the rest of northern Norway being destroyed as well.

Initially the German army only wanted to destroy the infrastructure and the military installations [in the north] and not waste time evacuating the civilian population but the National Samling [NS] collaborationist regime of Quisling wanted the civilian population removed. Their aim was to prevent the exiled Norwegian government in London returning and having proper towns to operate from and a population to govern in Norway proper.

There were no real plans by the government-in-exile to return but the Quislings didn't know that. They put stories round that the Russians were going to massacre everyone and that the population was fleeing south voluntarily. That created problems for the evacuees because the people in the south believed the northerners were leaving their homes voluntarily and were in effect collaborators with the NS regime. In fact only a few hundred people packed up voluntarily and moved south and they were mostly members of the Norwegian fascist party. In the end the Germans had to force almost everyone to leave.

Quite a few people were allowed to use their own boats. Those were the fortunate ones. The unfortunate ones went on the big German cargo ships *Carl Arp* and *Adolf Binder*: they were forced on board in unhealthy conditions and people died. In inland areas some people were ordered to march. In the case of the Samis in the inland areas the Germans ordered them to leave their homes and move down to the area of the Lyngen Line with their reindeer [which were to be used] to feed the German army. Well, those reindeer never arrived. The Germans trusted the Sami to do what they had ordered but the Sami snuck away and went into Finland and Sweden with the reindeer. The Germans got almost no reindeer. Local dignitaries in the Sami towns of Kautokeino and Karasjok arranged the escape of the reindeer with the local police, moving them and the population away. So when the Germans arrived, they found only a couple of elderly people who couldn't move: there were no people, and no reindeer. They basically got away.

We drain our cups of lemon tea, open a window and stretch our legs. I put the kettle on again for our next topic, the story of 1,000 refugees who fled the German evacuation by hiding in huts and caves on the remote island of Sørøya off the coast of Hammerfest. They fled believing the war was only weeks from ending but found themselves without proper shelter or food trying to survive an Arctic winter.

'Around a thousand people hid out on Sørøya,' Kristian begins:

People from Hammerfest and the surrounding islands went there. There are many caves and inaccessible locations and few roads. In many places you have to know where you are going, and some you can reach only by boat. On the island of Kamøya for example [a tiny island to the north of Sørøya] you have to know where to land, and people stayed there undisturbed in their houses throughout the winter of 1944–45. The Germans didn't get there, and perhaps didn't even know people were living there. Going into the caves was a short-term plan – eventually things started getting critical with food.

At the same time as German patrols were searching for civilians who had escaped the evacuation, soldiers from Colonel Arne Dahl's Norwegian mission were pushing west, rescuing people who had evaded the evacuation and were living in caves and makeshift huts. The operation leader, Gunnar Johnson, another veteran of the 1940 campaign and medical director for the government-in-exile, evacuated 1,000 people from the Nordkyn peninsula in fishing boats to the liberated east, from villages like Gamvik, Mehamn and Finnkonckeila.[1]

Local men who stayed were organised into militia to repel any future German raids. Dahl ordered that the Germans should meet resistance at every point and where possible the burning patrols should be stopped, by force.

Eventually the situation on Sørøya became so desperate a boat was sent east to make contact with the liberated areas to ask for help. Fishing boats sneaked into Sørøya to take a few hundred sick and elderly out but Johnson knew a full-scale rescue was required. So he went to the Norwegian government in London and the military authorities and eventually the British Admiralty and requested an evacuation. In February 1945 four destroyers escorting one of the Allied convoys to Russia were diverted to Sørøya for a rescue.

'It's quite extraordinary: all the other Norwegian requests for support for Finnmark were refused,' Kristian says:

> There were suggestions made by the exiled Norwegian authorities like sending supplies for liberated areas, landings at various areas in the north and even in the south, to cut off the Germans at the Lyngen Line and starve them out. There was also a suggestion to land on Sørøya and move from there to liberate Finnmark. The rescue at Sørøya was the only request that was approved.
>
> The first operation was called off because of a misunderstanding that the population had already been evacuated. At the time the Allied convoy was subject to intense air and U-boat attacks, which the crews on the ships believed was the reason for the cancellation. Once the convoy reached Russia and was unloading, the misunderstanding was cleared up and the destroyers went to Sørøya – despite the U-boats in the area, despite the uncharted minefields, German bombers a short distance away, the German patrol boats. They landed at three different spots: at Storelv and in the general area of Borstrand [two small settlements on Sørøya].
>
> For several days prior to the operation people had been moving from their hiding places to gathering points. There were a few Norwegian military that had made their way to Sørøya from eastern Finnmark and they had radio contact with the British and Norwegian authorities. Luckily the operation went well. It was very risky: the destroyers were stationary for quite a while as people rowed out and boarded them and they had little room to manoeuvre, but it worked out well.

They unloaded weapons for the Norwegian forces on the island and then headed back to Murmansk, attacked by bombers and U-boats on the way.

There, the refugees from Sørøya were transferred to the returning convoy boats for the return leg to Scotland, but two Liberty ships with refugees on board were sunk. One - the *Henry Bacon* - was separated from the convoy and was sailing alone when German bombers discovered her, and, after a fierce battle between the anti-aircraft gunners and the bombers, eventually managed to sink her. Several of the lifeboats were damaged but the refugees were put in the boats first with a few crew members to steer them, but the rest of the crew basically sacrificed themselves so the refugees could survive. They had to jump into the ocean and when you do that in the Arctic, you're dead.

The refugees survived. They were rescued by a destroyer which had received a radio signal from *Henry Bacon* before it was sunk, and they were taken to Scotland. All of them made it to Scotland and one child was even born on the way. They stayed in a camp near Glasgow until the autumn of 1945.

That's the evacuation – but it doesn't end there, because there are still a few hundred people on the island, though now with more supplies and guns, led by the Norwegian officers. They organised the young men and some of the young women into military units, about 100 strong, to carry out ambushes of German units moving into Sørøya and raiding. The senior Norwegian officer was a coastal artillery officer, so they were all enrolled into the coastal artillery and set up to defend Sørøya, including one of my mother's uncles, who was made a machine gunner. He was a fisherman, used to the harsh conditions on Sørøya. They set up defensive positions around the island and even sent patrols to neighbouring islands to look for the Germans.

I found some documents relating to the plans for Sørøya at that point in the war – for an ancient submarine to provide power for a base there, with artillery, flying boats and so on and for Sørøya to be used as a base; sending motor torpedo boats down to Tromsø to attack the German shipping there in the harbour and really stir things up – this is completely in the spirit of the offensive-minded Colonel Dahl. But the Allies were in charge and refused to allow it. The Norwegian military couldn't carry out independent operations so it ended up being 100 men and women with submachine guns, rifles and machine guns.

What the Germans sometimes did was leave a structure intact to lure people to live there and then they would come back and catch them. When they came back to Hasvik where they'd left the lighthouse still standing they were fired upon. At least one German was killed, so was a Norwegian. The Germans feared the Russians had arrived and set up a base on Sørøya, so over several days in March 1945 they attacked from several directions.

Initially they steamed into a fjord with gunboats to destroy houses and look for people; they were ambushed and fired upon by the militia, including my mother's uncle, who was described in a post-war report as 'a God-given machine gunner' despite never having had anything to do with the military until the month before. They shot them up and the Germans retreated, but regrouped and came back, this time from several directions with air support and everything, and they had a proper battle.

The Norwegians gave as good as they got with everything they had: ancient Norwegian rifles, British submachine guns, Russian machine guns, German rifles, everything. But with naval artillery and air support, the Germans over-powered the Norwegians on Sørøya capturing a good number and killing six or seven soldiers, including my mother's uncle. He was hit by shrapnel from a shell and mortally wounded, and though he was brought back by his comrades he died of his wounds the following morning. He was only in his early 20s. Another guy – from Hammerfest – was wounded and as he was being helped away by two comrades, a shell killed all three. It was quite rough. The youngest soldier was 15 – he's still alive.

There were women too, at least four of them, in their late teens or early 20s in snow camouflage outfits with Russian submachine guns. I have a picture of them. All the fighters wore uniform so the ones who were captured would be treated as soldiers. Some were put in rather nasty conditions in prison camps but they would have been shot if they hadn't been in uniform.

Colonel Dahl wanted to reoccupy Sørøya but that didn't happen. Some soldiers escaped and came back later to set up observation posts, but it was nothing major. Some people just hid away and had to be found after the war ended, and they had hidden very, very well. Some were discovered when people basically stumbled over them; others fled when Norwegian fishing vessels came and sought them out, even when they were flying big Norwegian flags and the war had been over for several weeks.

In a way the scorched-earth policy worked. It was almost impossible to carry out offensive operations against the Germans when you have to move through a devastated landscape where all the roads have been destroyed without anything to sustain yourself on. It took a long time to move anything involving more than a few people any distance to carry out an attack so – I'd have to say – it worked.[2]

In a four-year period between 1941 and 1945, around 1,400 Allied merchant ships delivered 4.5 million metric tons of vital supplies to Russia, under constant threat of attack by German U-boats and aircraft and braving severe cold, storms, fog and ice floes.

Thousands of Allied seamen lost their lives as 16 Royal Navy warships and some 100 merchant ships from Britain, the USA and the Soviet Union were sunk in four years of running the gauntlet of attacks by U-boats, bombers and destroyers. One convoy – PQ17 – was almost wiped out.[3] Winston Churchill called the Arctic convoy route 'the worst journey in the world'. Veterans told of salt spray that froze as it fell, waves so huge they tore at ships' armour plating, and pilots so numb with cold they had to be lifted out of their cockpits.[4]

More than 7,000 airplanes and some 5,000 tanks, cars, fuel, medicines, food, metals and other raw materials were shipped to Murmansk and Archangelsk, about a quarter of the total aid sent by the Western Allies to Stalin.[5] The convoys continued until the end of the war, even though they were less important to the Soviet Union after the Russians had gained the upper hand in the land offensive in the East.

The bravery of the British sailors who manned the Arctic convoy ships has been consistently ignored over the past six decades. It's only recently in the UK that they have been recognised with medals.

One of those sailors is John Fearn, a Londoner who joined the Royal Navy in 1943 and sailed his one and only Arctic convoy at the age of 17 with the battleship HMS *Rodney*. Later *Rodney* supported the D-Day landings of June 1944. John was awarded a medal for his service in 2013, long after he had retired to South Wales. John was a gunnery support rating on HMS *Rodney*, which acted as escort to Convoy JW60 from Shetland to Murmansk in mid-September 1944, made up of thirty British and American supply ships escorted by a guard of destroyers, battleships, cruisers and corvettes.[6]

Although he only did one convoy run, John's memories are no less intense for that:

> We left Scapa Flow on a very dark night and it took us about three weeks to get back. We were escorting a hospital ship so we had to go at the same speed. We were covering about 5 knots but we had no choice.
>
> The German bombers only flew certain days. We arrived on the Monday and had to get out again on the Thursday to miss them. Everything was quiet on the convoy I did but we were always on guard. We knew the subs were there.
>
> The weather conditions were terrible. It was so cold. We kept the guns moving 24 hours a day. If we stopped, the guns would freeze. If you touched a guardrail without having your gloves on, your skin would freeze to it. The fear was there but I was young. We were all young. We didn't feel it like the older men might.[7]

John made it safely to Murmansk but *Rodney* was soon on her return journey to Shetland as part of the ocean escort convoy for RA60. This crossing would be less fortunate. 'We were on a three-day turnround in Murmansk so we didn't leave the boat,' he says. 'We saw Russians on horses and German prisoners [on the quayside] but, apart from that, nothing. When we left Murmansk we went hell for leather back – about 25 knots.'

Convoy RA60 left Murmansk on 28 September and *Rodney* and the escort ships joined up outside the Kola Inlet for the run across to Shetland. But the next afternoon U-boat 310 spotted the thirty-two-strong convoy just off the North Cape [Nordkapp] and fired torpedoes at them, sinking the American 'Liberty' ship, the *Edward H. Crockett*, and the British freighter *Samsuva*.[8]

The *Edward H. Crockett* was named after Associated Press reporter Edward 'Harry' Crockett, who was killed in a torpedo attack in the Mediterranean in 1943. It had only been launched – christened by his widow, Sally – in January 1944.[9] The torpedo wrecked the engine, caused serious damage and killed the first assistant engineer. Captain Albert Baldi gave the order to abandon ship and the crew of eight officers, thirty-three men and twenty-seven armed guards were picked up from lifeboats by the convoy's rescue ship *Zamalek*.[10]

The *Samsuva* broke in half after being hit but remained afloat until the crew of thirty-seven and twenty gunners could be taken off by the rescue ship *Rathlin*. Three men died in the attack. The convoy arrived in Scotland on 5 October 1944.[11]

9

THE DEATH OF ERIKA SCHÖNE AND OTHER SECRET TRAGEDIES

Much of the observation and reconnaissance work for German military forces in the Arctic region was directed from the Porsangerfjorden, the next but one fjord west from Hopseidet. Midway between Kirkenes and Alta – within easy reach of the harbour at Honningsvåg, the U-boat base at Hammerfest and the coastal batteries at Mehamn, Gamvik and Vadsø – Porsangerfjorden was an important nerve centre for German military operations.

Streams of bombers set out to attack the Allied convoys to Murmansk from the airstrip at Banak, which was developed to become the main base for Nazi air operations in the north of Norway. The airfield was upgraded during the occupation with hangars and storage dumps for fuel and bombs, with a British intelligence report of 1943 identifying two runways in parallel 1,800m long and 200m wide covered in wooden planking to allow all-weather operation.[1]

When Hitler gave his order to withdraw from Finnmark in October 1944, the German forces destroyed their bases, installations and camps as soon as the last Wehrmacht soldier passed through the main town, Lakselv, and the runways at Banak were dynamited. However tantalising fragments of everyday life during wartime were left behind, and a group of war historian enthusiasts in Finnmark is attempting to establish exactly what did happen here between 1940 and 1944.

Roger Albrigtsen is one of these enthusiasts, who call themselves Foreningen Krigshistorisk Landskap Finnmark, or FKLF for short, which means 'War Historical Landscapes of Finnmark'.

In quiet corners of Finnmark they find clusters of barbed wire around what were machine-gun positions, silent now for seventy years but still surrounded by the debris of hate: live cartridges, bits of guns, tools; even rusted jerrycans that once carried the petrol that fuelled Hitler's armies and reduced Finnmark to charred timbers. In one remote place a German tank remains where it was abandoned, slowly being stripped of its parts by war collectors. In another Roger and his colleagues are piecing together what's left of a German field hospital.

There are still scraps of old German newspapers to be found in some locations; in others rusty barbed wire curls round the trunks of birch trees like some evil snake. The finds are documented and photographed and displayed on the FKLF website alongside photographs showing Germans occupying this area. In one wartime picture a German sergeant mans a machine gun in a pit shored up with wooden beams – now, where he once stood is overgrown with silver birch trees, almost reclaimed by nature.

FKLF's work is entirely self-funded, but their network of contributors stretches from Finland and Russia to Germany and the United States. It's a window on a war I've never seen. The pictures show Luftwaffe men playing football, Soviet prisoners on a break from their labour and German soldiers boating on a lake with Norwegian girls, both groups clearly enjoying their afternoon. Looking at these photographs you wouldn't believe there was a war on, and there are certainly no hints of the wickedness we know was present.

In a way history has passed Lakselv by. It has not registered on my previous encounters with the war in Norway but now its significance is clear.

Roger agrees:

Lakselv was a strategically important place during the war. It was more strategic than Hammerfest and Alta but not as important as Kirkenes.

The bombers went out to attack the Allied convoys from here: the weather observations came from here. There's the Billefjord seaplane harbour and Banak airport with its wooden runway [making it] the best place to land in this part of Norway. Fortresses were built around the Porsangerfjord, on each side, and along every road. Really it was in the middle of everything. There were 5,000–6,000 German soldiers at the airport, another 1,000 at Billefjord and 25 minutes away another 1,000 troops at Skoganvarre – so with 3,600 people living in Lakselv and 3,000 prisoners of war too there are lots of people living in this region.

There were many dramatic events here. There was a catapult ship based here – *Friesen Land* [one of seven used by the Luftwaffe] – which launched Blohm und Voss BV138 seaplanes for weather observation flights. That was hit by a Russian torpedo bomber in September 1944. Then there's the terrible fire aboard the DS *Blenheim* in 1941 in the Porsangerfjord in which 103 SS men and 8 Norwegian crew, including 4 girls and 2 pilots, were burned to death or drowned. In August 1943 when the ammunition ship D/S *Argus* caught fire and exploded, 44 people were blown to pieces [even now people are still finding bits of the ship in the surrounding area].

Then there was a really notorious incident in the evacuation when the German freighter *Carl Arp* docked here to take 1,800 people from Finnmark south to Narvik, packed in like sardines on a boat with only two toilets. Many people got sick with dysentery and typhoid and 29 people died, mostly children and the elderly [a memorial park for those who died on the *Carl Arp* was opened in Narvik only in 2012].

Lakselv was a significant town not only during the occupation but also in the Operation Nordlicht evacuation. Troops falling back from Kirkenes and all the coastal fortifications in the north-east of Norway went through the town, as did vast numbers of soldiers retreating from Ivalo in Finland. Not only men but a mountain of supplies went through Lakselv, as the German rearguard tried to hold back the relentless Soviet pressure as long as possible. Supplies were dumped along the road to keep the withdrawal moving: roads and bridges leading into Ivalo were destroyed and defensive positions constructed. With German forces withdrawing from Kirkenes and also through Ivalo to Lakselv, the Soviets split their pursuit. When the Soviet commander General Meretskov requested permission to cross into Norwegian territory, Stalin gave him a short answer: 'That'll be good.'[2]

The Soviets did not pursue the Germans far into Norway, liberating Kirkenes and then halting at the Tana River, but this phase of the operation alone cost them the lives of 2,900 soldiers.[3]

Free of the dangers of Soviet attack, streams of German soldiers and supplies poured through Lakselv in November and December, heading for Skibotn and the Lyngen Line defences. Tens of thousands went further south, to Oslo and Denmark and onward to shore up the defence of the Reich. In November alone, 50,000 soldiers and 6,000 vehicles were ferried across the Lyngenfjord.[4]

Many people in the Porsangerfjord area remembered those scenes or took part in them, Roger says:

My mother-in-law saw the Germans march through here first going to the front and then later on coming back. There was a man whose job was just to regulate traffic through Lakselv. After the withdrawal the seaplane harbour was blown up on 11 December 1944. Of course the Soviets stopped at Tana but I'd say militarily it was important for the Germans to destroy Finnmark.

Against this enormous movement of men and materials – an entire war machine and its supplies of ammunition, weapons, fuel and food – Roger finds traces of the human dimension. The FKLF has valuable friends among the curators of archives, who release documents to help them piece together personal pictures in a wider war.

'I would love to open a documentation centre in Lakselv where researchers could work and where we could showcase our knowledge and our finds,' says Roger:

For instance, I have a report from 1942 from Skoganvarre. On 15 July, Peter Mäder, a 30-year-old German soldier, shot a Russian POW in Skoganvarre. The report tells the story of prisoners clearing trees that had fallen down in the winter. One prisoner was reluctant to work and when the German told him he had to, he pushed him with the palm of his hand. The German soldier was pushed back a couple of metres, so he pulled his gun and shot the prisoner. And then [in a collection of prisoner identity cards] I found the prison card of the same man, and the story of his shoes being brought to Lakselv because they were still usable. We can put together the whole story of a little incident in Lakselv, and Lakselv isn't the capital of the world, it's a pinpoint small place.

Maps are great for us because they show where the prison camps were, the barracks, the minefields and so on. We send our people to these areas with metal detectors to see what they can find – spoons, tools, bullets for a Mauser, that kind of thing. For me, every time I see this stuff it's fantastic. It's history in your hand. You can talk about it to your children, to kids at school: 'This is the real thing – a glass from 1945, a bullet, a German jerrycan that they used to burn Finnmark.' It's really important. Trying to collect all this material together and present it to tell stories is hard work but it's worth it. But where can I get money from to fund it? There is so much to do.

Roger is an author and his book *Sepals* details a network of secret agents which operated in the mountains of northern Norway from bases across the border in Sweden. His grandfather was part of this group, guiding agents in and out of the safety of Sweden, sending intelligence on German troop movements and progress reports on the construction of the Lyngen Line defences. Weather reports sent by Sepals agents were used notably during the bombing of the battleship *Tirpitz*.

'My family is from Bogen, between Narvik and Harstad,' Roger says:

and the story of Sepals is really from the Narvik and Troms area [close to the Swedish border]. It's the story of co-operation between the Swedes and the American OSS, special agents, the Norwegian XU organisation [a separate Resistance organisation from Milorg, but prolific], the British Special Operations Executive [SOE] and the OSS [later the CIA], the Norwegian police troops and the Norwegian Independent Company 1 [the legendary Linge Company commandos, based originally in Banff, Scotland, and named after their founder Martin Linge, who was killed during an early operation]. And then Sepals came around in the summer of 1944, around August, when they started to set up these bases.

My grandfather was working as a courier between Narvik and Sweden, helping Resistance agents get to Sweden. He was in the XU movement but then
had to flee to Sweden in the fall of 1944 and ended up at one of the Sepals bases
as a guide. He knew everywhere like the back of his hand. Sepals sent people
from these bases into Narvik to train the Resistance in basements just inside the
town; they helped get refugees over the border, they even brought post across
on the railway from Sweden hidden in casts for broken legs. They had a network of reliable people on the railway and in Narvik helping people get across
the border. Had the war lasted a month or two longer the importance of Sepals
would have been much more high profile – they did a lot of important work.

The focus [of Resistance stories in the war] has been on the south and the
guys in the south did not see Sepals as important. In my opinion the war was
in Finnmark and there were only sabotage acts in Oslo. Really they did more
harm than good, because of the reprisals. When the Resistance assassinated Karl
Marthinsen, the Quisling security police chief, the Germans shot twenty-eight
people for that. In my opinion the Resistance did more harm than good.

I ask Roger what he makes of the Norwegian soldiers under the command of
Colonel Dahl, who turned on the women of Kirkenes after the liberation for
fraternising with the Germans, relationships which in some cases left lasting
reminders in the form of children.

'These guys from the 2 Bergkompani were all from the south,' he replies:

They were trained in Britain before they went to Finnmark. When they got there
they found the people had been living in peace with the Germans and working
for them. This was quite a different world to the one they expected. In January,
February, March 1945, those Norwegian troops must have been met with terrible
sights. The whole place was burned down and there were mines everywhere. They
were even having fights with German patrols until April, May 1945. But more
and more is being discovered about Dahl's troops and what they did, especially to
Norwegian girls who were pregnant or who had been with German soldiers.

Dahl is really a bad word – like swearing – in some parts of Finnmark. If you
are a community of 300 and you put in 3,000 soldiers you have to work with
them, work for them, live alongside them. You have to deal with them to get
food. Then these southerners come to the north not knowing what life was like
there, and their rage against the Germans made some of them – unbalanced.
And, even though the Russians were the ones who had been bombing Kirkenes,
they were still the liberators. They were the heroes – not the Norwegians.

Roger's research is driven by the desire for facts to build a true picture of what
happened here in the war and, where possible, put faces to some of the people in

these graves. With 3,000 Soviet prisoners in the area and many German casualties during four years of occupation, he's a little surprised that more people haven't come in search of their family history:

> It's strange that no Russians are coming to Lakselv looking for where their relatives died. There are no Germans looking for where the *Argus* blew up or the *Blenheim* blazed with the 103 SS soldiers killed. There are no memorials, no signs. The Germans probably got a card in the post saying they died on the Northern Front – no more, and no grave, no nothing. Are there any Germans or Russians wondering what happened to their fathers or grandfathers who were here?

'Do any Austrians contact you?' I ask.
'No,' Roger says. 'We don't hear from any Austrians at all.'

But sometimes a chance message can open an unexpected and astonishing window onto lives that were changed forever in Finnmark. The story of Erika Schöne, a 23-year-old Luftwaffe Stabshelferin [clerical auxiliary] who died in a plane crash in October 1944, is an exceptional example. Roger says:

> I knew of the crash of a Focke Wulf Condor transport plane in October 1944 into the Lavangsfjord near Troms because a man who was just 3 at the time saw it happen.
> He was standing in the garden eating a stick of rhubarb dipped in sugar when he saw the plane making a steep turn over the fjord. As it did the wing broke off. He saw bodies falling out of it and fuel pouring onto the fjord as it caught fire and went into a spin. When it hit the water the fuel caught fire. There were no survivors. His sister is still so traumatised she can't talk about it.

The Condor was significantly overloaded for its final and fatal flight, carrying fifty-one passengers instead of a maximum thirty. Among those on board were two wounded soldiers, two officers and a crew of six, as well as forty-one women, mostly in their 20s and listed as 'Helferin' – nurses and female Wehrmacht and Luftwaffe staff assistants. The Condor took off from Banak airport and flew to Finland to pick up thirty nurses, then returned to Banak where another eleven women auxiliaries climbed aboard, including Erika Schöne. The plane was so full by this stage the last passengers loaded had to sit on the floor. And forty-five minutes after take-off, everyone on board was dead.[5]

It seems the overloading of the plane put unbearable stress on the wing joint, possibly damaged in an earlier accident during landing. Passing over the fjord, where turbulence would have been greater because of the high mountains on either side, could have caused the wing failure. Although there are few details recorded officially about it, the Condor crash remains the worst aircrash on Norwegian soil.[6]

'This is a tragedy and it seems like it was edited out of history,' Roger says:

When I was doing research for my book *Last Letters* I got an email from a man who said one of his family members was buried in the German cemetery at Narvik. The family member was Erika Schöne. He wondered if I might take a picture of her grave so he could show it to her brother and sister who were still alive but too elderly to travel. I agreed to get a picture taken and in return he showed me her personal effects. From this I could build up a picture of her life not only in Norway but also in Germany, before and after her death.

Erika came from Wismar on Germany's Baltic coast and worked as a maid and in a baker's before joining the Luftwaffe in 1942. She was posted first to Rimini in Italy and then in April 1943 to Banak in Norway, where she worked as a secretary. In January 1944 her sister Eva had a baby, Peta, and Erika wrote a number of letters to her, addressing her as 'my beautiful ray of sun'. She sent presents home: Sami shoes, a sheepskin jacket, an ornamental knife. In her last letter she tells Peta that she is excited about coming home but has grown to love the part of Norway where she is stationed.

'After the war has ended I will go back to Norway, because it is so beautiful,' she writes. 'If I do not survive, I will be buried there.' It's as if she knew.

Her family took her death very badly. For years afterwards her father would stare at the sky, as if looking for his daughter. Her elder brother and sister are still alive and say she was a very happy and generous girl. Her name is on a grave in Germany. But of course, she's not there.[7]

Roger tells me he arranged for a rose to be laid on Erika's grave at Narvik cemetery when the photograph was taken and wrote to her brother and sister to let them know when his collection of letters from wartime Norway was to be published.

'How does it make you feel, being able to roll back history like this?' I ask.

'Quite strange,' he admits. 'There have been tears, at times.'[8]

10

'YOU MUST NOT THINK WE DESTROYED WANTONLY OR SENSELESSLY'

The transcripts of the trial of the commander of the 20th Mountain Army in Norway, Lothar Rendulic, offer a fascinating insight into how the scorched-earth destruction unfolded and the thinking of the man giving the orders.

Rendulic stood trial on war-crimes charges at the Nuremberg hearings in 1947 as part of the 'hostages trial'. This trial was of a group of German commanders in the Balkans alleged to have committed crimes against civilians and partisans in the form of executions and hostage-taking as reprisals for the deaths or wounding of German soldiers.

In 1941 the German Army High Command had issued an infamous 'ratio' directive ordering that for every German soldier wounded, fifty civilians were to be shot, while 100 civilians would be executed for every German soldier killed.[1]

As well as crimes against civilians, committed when he commanded the 2nd Panzer Army in Yugoslavia, Rendulic was prosecuted for wanton destruction of property in the scorched-earth withdrawal through Finnmark.

Rendulic was convicted of the three other charges he faced but was acquitted of the scorched-earth destruction charge on the grounds of 'perceived military necessity' – that in ordering the burning of Finnmark to stop a Soviet pursuit his actions were not criminal because of the demands of the situation as he saw it at the time.

The decision of the court caused outrage in Norway and earned Rendulic a place in the international laws of war in defining the principle of 'military necessity'.

The 'Rendulic Rule' states that:

Civilian objects are protected from intentional attack or destruction so long as they are not being used for military purposes or there is no military necessity for their destruction or seizure. The law of war permits destruction of civilian objects if military circumstances necessitate such destruction or if the civilian object has become a military objective. The circumstances justifying destruction of civilian objects are those of military necessity, based upon information reasonably available to the commander at the time of his decision.[2]

The findings and comments of the court will be covered in more detail later, but the Nuremberg hearings offer an opportunity to hear the thoughts of Rendulic himself and also of his colleague-in-arms, the commander of the 19th Mountain Army, General Ferdinand Jodl, whose units bore the brunt of the Petsamo–Kirkenes offensive in October 1944. Jodl appeared as a witness for the prosecution against Rendulic.

The brother of Alfred Jodl – chief of the operations staff of Germany's Armed Forces High Command – 18-year-old Ferdinand joined the Bavarian Artillery in 1914 as an NCO and served at the front throughout the First World War. During the interwar years he rose through the ranks as a staff officer, tactical commander and trainer. At the outbreak of the Second World War he served in France, Yugoslavia, Poland and Slovakia before taking part in the attack on the USSR. In 1942 he was appointed Chief of the General Staff of the Army High Command, Lappland; later the 20th Mountain Army. In October 1944 he became commander of the 19th Mountain Army, against which the Soviet Petsamo–Kirkenes offensive was directed.

At the time of his appearance at Nuremberg, Jodl was living freely in his hometown of Wiesbaden, in the Rhineland. He told the court that he had never been a member of the Nazi Party. In his evidence, Jodl said that before he received the Hitler Command for the scorched-earth destruction of Finnmark and evacuation of its civilians, he had a phone conversation with the Chief of General Staff of the 20th Mountain Army, General Hoelter, a subordinate of General Rendulic. Jodl told Hoelter he intended to protest in writing about having to evacuate and destroy Finnmark after his men had been battered into retreat by the Soviets, suffering 5,000 wounded. This intended letter would lay out three reasons for his objections, he said:

First, my unit which is absolutely exhausted by the various attacks and offensives has something else to do than to deal with evacuations and destruction. We are glad if we can bring our 5,000 wounded into safety to the West and can get supplies of the most necessary things, materials, etc. We have no columns in order to transport population.

Second, I do not believe that the Russians will proceed to the West and will cross the Tana. We are not in touch with them any longer. We know for certain that the bulk of the Russian units have been transported to the East and even if the Russians should want to pursue us, they would be acting differently.

Third, if we force the population to evacuate and if we burn their houses we therewith create misgivings and ill-will amongst the Norwegian population and embitterment and this embitterment can be of no practical use to us. We even have to reckon with the springing into life of a partisan involvement.

When I told General Hoelter, he answered: 'The AOK [Army Command] is roughly of the same opinion as you but just now the order' – I do not know exactly what he said it was, a Fuehrer Order or whatever it was – 'has arrived, according to which destruction [and evacuation] has to be carried out and nothing can be done now. The submission of an application in writing is therefore no longer of any use.'

The destruction and evacuation – this is what I say today and I said it before – was for me a highly unpleasant and awkward matter, but on the basis of this order, and because I could not guarantee for certain that the Russians would not follow us, I carried out this order.

The evacuation and destruction of the territories of north Finnmark would have been considered a military necessity for those who had to expect the possibility of a Russian invasion of the territory beyond the Tana. I did not understand how the population of north Finnmark could have been fed if all bridges and other military installations had been destroyed [and] we had left the population in this no-man's-land.

A part of the population – that part which carries on agriculture – would have been able to live through the winter on their products, but the great bulk of the population was depending on imports of food, and these imports could not have been secured.[3]

Jodl was asked by chief prosecutor Stephen Rapp whether he had ever heard discussions that territories to the west and later to the south should be destroyed; and later also to the south of Finnmark, to Narvik and beyond. This is their exchange from the trial:

Jodl: No, it was never said. I myself, when I was present in Germany, had discussed these questions with my brother. I can almost repeat the exact wording which I used when I told him, and that was in the course of a discussion of the general military position. 'For God's sake don't send me such an order for scorched earth again, because I could not take part in anything like that a second time. If it should be decided to withdraw from the north of Norway into this space south of Narvik, I would not be prepared to lay waste once more flourishing villages and houses and to destroy everything.' My brother's reply to that was: 'I didn't think you would; I didn't expect you to say anything else, and it's quite out of the question.' So, it's only in this very personal connection that we considered the possibility of a further laying waste of the territory to Narvik.

Rapp: After this discussion or on the basis of this discussion with your brother, do I understand you correctly if I draw the conclusion that you discussed the whole point with your brother because you were of the opinion that this destruction was unnecessary or for what other reasons?

Jodl: I think I'd rather say for humane considerations. This destruction of the north of Finnmark was one of the hardest tasks I had ever been given throughout the war.

Rapp: Did you have any military considerations in that respect or were you only moved by the humane idea?

Jodl: I have already, at the beginning of my statements, expressed that I personally, right from the beginning, did not believe that the Russians would progress beyond the River Tana.

Rapp: Witness, when did you discuss these points with your brother?

Jodl: That was at the end of March, 1945.

Rapp: So that was at a time when there was no invasion from the Russians. Is that correct?

Jodl: Yes.

Rapp: So if the scorched-earth policy had been ordered for Narvik, you not only instinctively but also from a military point of view would have protested against it. Is that right?

Jodl: It's very difficult to answer this question because one doesn't know how the conditions had developed; but what I said to my brother and expressed to him was that for absolutely humane principles I would be quite incapable of carrying [it] out against a country in which I had lived, whose people I had come to value and to respect. And that had no bearing on the fact whether it was military necessity or not.[4]

Jodl was cross-examined by the defence counsel for General Rendulic, Dr Fritsch, who asked him to describe the preparations that were made for the withdrawal:

Jodl: The disposal of the heavy snow was of great importance. A large organisation for the traffic control was necessary and special arrangement had been made to secure the tunnels. Accommodation barracks had been built in the retreat area, military installations had been put up, and medical supplies were ready, and collection and transfer camps had been built.

Dr Fritsch asked whether the demands during the evacuation of the civilian population took preference over the demands of the troops:

Jodl: The position was such that we had to unload munitions and similar materials from our trucks in order to transport the civilian population instead. In some instances we put Red Cross ambulances at the disposal of the civilian population although we ourselves had thousands of wounded whom we had to transport into hospitals which lay hundreds of kilometres to the rear. I know of another case where we had a transit camp for wounded which we put at the disposal of the civilian population. This we did although the accommodation for our own troops along the main Route 50 was very limited. The food which we distributed to the civilian population in the area of Tana – this food did not really mean a sacrifice because these food reserves we could not have taken along with us anyway.[5]

Jodl left the area around Kirkenes on 12 October and arrived at the Lyngenfjord around six weeks later, on 20 November. His 800km retreat was along the Reichstrassse 50 and after his forces crossed a bridge they destroyed it. German troops and the Organisation Todt construction battalions had improved and extended this road through Norway during the occupation, he said. Before being released from the witness stand, Jodl was cross-examined again briefly by chief prosecutor Stephen Rapp:

Rapp: Witness, do you mean to say that on the basis of the fact that this order was a Fuehrer Order you were bound to carry out this order?
 Jodl: Yes.
 Rapp: Would you have carried out a repetition of this order in the sense of this discussion with your brother?
 Jodl: I expected this question, and I accept all consequences too. Secondly, then I would not have agreed to the destruction of things and villages probably after I did not see the necessity of them, and I would have taken all consequences in general.
 Rapp: General, what would the consequences have been?
 Jodl: I would have been shot immediately.[6]

Rendulic had denied the four charges against him, which were, in short:

1. The mass murder of hundreds of thousands of civilians in Greece, Albania and Yugoslavia by ordering hostage taking and reprisal killings.
2. The plundering and wanton destruction of villages and towns in Greece, Albania, Yugoslavia and Norway.
3. The murder and ill-treatment of thousands of soldiers, prisoners of war and their non-combatant relatives and the designation of combatants as 'partisans', the denial of their status of prisoners of war, and their execution.

4. The murder, torture, deportation and sending to concentration camps of
   Greek, Albanian and Yugoslav civilians.[7]

In October 1947, at the age of 60, Rendulic took the stand. Rendulic was an
Austrian of Croatian origin who had served in the First World War on the general
staff of the Austro-Hungarian army. After the war he studied law and joined the
army of the Austrian Republic. In 1932 he joined the then-banned Austrian Nazi
Party and served in the diplomatic corps from 1934, becoming military attaché
for France and England with an office in Paris. His Nazi membership was considered undesirable for a diplomat and he was pensioned off in 1936 because of his
Nazi views.[8]

After Germany's annexation of Austria, Rendulic joined the Wehrmacht and
commanded the 14th Infanterie Division in the invasion of France in 1940, then
the 52nd Division, a training unit in Poland. From 1943 to 1944 he headed the
2nd Panzer Army in Yugoslavia and led a mission personally ordered by Hitler to
capture the Yugoslav partisan leader Tito. Nearly 850 SS paratroopers parachuted
into the mountains near Tito's base at Drvar in a huge operation in May 1944 to
destroy Tito's partisan headquarters and military missions. Tito escaped – 600 SS
paratroopers were killed or injured in fighting, accidents and glider crashes.[9]

From Yugoslavia, Rendulic was appointed to replace the commander of the
20th Mountain Army, General Eduard Dietl, following his death in June 1944 in a
plane crash. Rendulic oversaw the scorched-earth retreat from the Litsa Front and
Finland west through Norway, then in January 1945 he was sent to command the
200,000-strong Nazi force isolated by the Soviets in the 'Courland pocket' in the
Baltics. In April 1945 he led the 450,000-strong remaining German force in Army
Group Ostmark which with Army Group Centre remained the final resistance
to the Soviets in the Prague Offensive of May 1945. Rendulic surrendered Army
Group Ostmark, to American forces in St Martin, Upper Austria, on 7 May.[10]

In his evidence at the trials Rendulic said he had fully expected Soviet attacks
by sea and air during the withdrawal from the Litsa Front. He had been concerned about the morale of his troops and fearful that they would be caught in a
freezing winter:

> Everybody was aware of the difficulty of the position. From censorship of
> soldiers' mail we learned that the morale of the soldiers sometimes bordered
> on panic. We found letters written by soldiers in which they said: 'A second
> Stalingrad is in preparation,' 'The army is doomed,' and 'When we freeze in the
> Arctic winter we will freeze as Russian prisoners.'
>
> The Russian propaganda made very clever use of this situation. Above all they
> tried to make the men distrust their leaders. Very soon after Finland left the Allies
> – by radio as well as by leaflets – spread the news that the Commander-in-Chief

of the Mountain Army was an Austrian and he wanted this army to fall into the hands of the Russians but this fact was discovered and his withdrawal and dismissal was to be expected.

In connection with the events of 20 July 1944 [the von Stauffenberg assassination attempt on Hitler at his Wolf's Lair] and the consequences of this event, which had only happened a short time before, this propaganda found fertile soil. There was a very dangerous crisis amongst the soldiers especially with regard to confidence in their leaders which could have led to a catastrophe if the army, or parts of it, came into difficult situations.

In order to counteract the effects of the Russian propaganda, Hitler, on the 17 September, decorated me with the Golden Cross of Honour, and thus the effect of the propaganda was counteracted immediately.[11]

On the need to destroy Hammerfest, Rendulic offered this justification:

We worked through all the possibilities which the enemy had concerning landings. On that occasion we again and again were confronted with the fact that Hammerfest would be the best point for supply for troops which had already landed. It would be a good starting point and would be a good place for distribution for the more detailed supplies to other landing points in the fjords. Further, Hammerfest was situated in the vicinity of Highway 50. In order to get there all one had to do was to cross the narrow Kvaenangen fjord and then one had an excellent road. The place itself could accommodate a strong regiment or even a division if necessary. This double significance of Hammerfest was a fact for an enemy in pursuit. You must not think that we destroyed wantonly or senselessly. Everything we did was dictated by the needs of the enemy. That was its necessity.

I was fully aware of the facts of this evacuation order on the population [and] I also knew that the execution of the evacuation would mean a considerable burden to the army. In spite of this I had to obey the order. Concerning the necessity of carrying out destructions, my opinions coincided with the opinions of the Supreme Command of the Armed Forces – Oberkommando der Wehrmacht (OKW). It was a matter of course to me and everybody else that the destructions had to be carried out.

My opinion deviated from Hitler's opinion in the beginning only in the one factor. I did not think it was absolutely necessary to transfer the population to other areas but I could not close my eyes to Hitler's reasons of military necessity. I could deny that they were justified.

Jodl warned me too. He said this time I had better follow the evacuation order since Hitler insisted under all circumstances that this order be carried out. Furthermore, I knew – and this is also contained in the OKW order – that the most decisive factor in this whole affair was the Reichskommissar in Norway.

It was well known that he, this man, was very angry because the first evacuation order had not been carried out and how he would closely supervise all activities of the army. It was therefore quite impossible not to obey this evacuation order.

Finally, I had to tell myself that it would possibly be better for the population to be transferred to other areas rather than spend the hard winter in the destroyed country. I participated in other winter battles in Russia. Therefore, I know what flight from cold means. I had to realise that the Russians, if they pushed up on us and if confronted with the choice of either saving themselves by using what remained in the way of shelter or sparing the population, it was certain that they would not spare the population. Therefore, in the final analysis, it was the best thing for the population that they were removed.[12]

Rendulic told the court the retreat through Norway was complex and demanding, but he insisted that his men treat the population well:

The operation which had to be carried out by the army was possibly the most difficult land operation of the whole war. During those days I said to my Chief of Staff: 'If sometime after this war you have to train general staff officers, then you will have to make this operation a basis of the training because it's impossible to think of anything more difficult.'

The army was spread over an area of 500km. That is, it was spread over a wider area than, for instance, the Allied forces in France and these forces were more than a million men strong. The problem was to relieve this army out of an encirclement from three sides and in battle with a superior enemy. Then this army would have to be concentrated on two highways and, finally, it would have to march along only one highway. All that would have to be done on foot and in the Arctic winter. That meant an enormous task for my staff: a more difficult task cannot be imagined. I could not burden it further with the extensive work concerning the evacuation. Therefore, I formed a special staff for this evacuation operation.[13]

I emphasized particularly that the evacuation had to be carried out with all the consideration for the population. Around that time I had learned unofficially for some time that after the army had gone back to Norway I was to take over the post of Commander-in-Chief over Norway. Immediately after the evacuation order I received the official order for this transfer.

I attached the greatest importance to good relations between myself and the Norwegian population. For this reason alone I insisted that the evacuation would not give any cause for misgivings amongst the population. You may also rest assured that if any kind of excuses became known to me, any unnecessary

harshness or any inconsideration, I would have taken counter-measures immediately. I was not a man who would let himself be prevented from carrying out
his intentions by some action of a subordinate agency.[14]

Rendulic was asked by his defence counsel to consider and comment on the
so-called 'Führer Order' given by Hitler for the scorched-earth destruction and
evacuation. 'The Reichskommissar was the man mainly responsible for this order':

> The military necessities are emphasised, the necessity for the evacuation, as
> well as the destruction. There is one sentence which I would like to draw to
> your attention. It is the last sentence in the second paragraph, and it reads:
> 'Compassion for the civilian population is uncalled for.'
>
> This sentence should not be regarded as an invitation to take harsh mea-
> sures. It is to be understood in connection with the next sentence, which is the
> first sentence of the next passage, where it says: 'The troops carrying out this
> order must be made to understand that within a few months the Norwegians
> will be thankful for having been saved from Bolshevism, etc., and that the whole
> operation is in the interest of the Norwegians.' ... There was an oral explana-
> tion of this order to the effect that Hitler attached particular importance to the
> measures ordered for Finnmark because he counted on the Exile Government's
> landing and settling in Finnmark if this area was left completely intact.
>
> At this occasion I received the warning from Jodl ... to the effect that this
> time I had better carry out the evacuation, and it was pointed out to me that the
> Reichskommissar played an important part in this affair.[15]

Rendulic was then questioned about his own order issued the following day, in
which he detailed how the operation would be carried out:

Top Secret
29 October 1944
Subject: Evacuation of North Norway:

> 1) Because of the lack of willingness of the north Norwegian population to
> evacuate the country *voluntarily* the Führer has ordered the compulsory evacu-
> ation of the population east of the Lyngenfjords in the interest of the security
> of the population, which is to be preserved from Bolshevism and that all houses
> be burned down or be destroyed. It is the responsibility of the Commander-in-
> Chief of Northern Finland that this order is carried out ruthlessly so that the
> Soviets supported by dwelling places and a population which knows the coun-
> try will be prevented from following our withdrawal with strong forces. Pity for
> the civilian population is out of place.

2) The man will understand the measures to be taken if it is explained that the barbarian methods of the air war against the German homeland and its cultural places have brought a misery on our people surpassing by far that which will follow in the wake of the measures which must be taken now in north Norway in order to prevent an early thrust by the Russians, according to plan.

3) *'The evacuation staff north Norway'* subordinate to the o.Qu. in his capacity as evacuation commissar is formed as the competent authority. Leader: Colonel Herrmann, Commanding Officer of the Grenadier Regiment 310.Corps Headquarters XXXVI Mountain Corps is to detach Colonel Herrmann immediately to Army/o.Qu. SS-Obersturmbannfuhrer Neumann joins the evacuation staff as representative of the Reichskommissar for occupied Norwegian territory.

4) The Commanding Generals of the XIX Mountain Corps and of the LXXI Infantry Corps are charged by me with the *responsibility of the carrying out of the evacuation*. Corps Headquarters XIX Mountain Corps will evacuate the territory east of the east coast of the Porsangerfjord (excluding the fjord). Corps Headquarters LXXI Infantry Corps will evacuate the area Porsangerfjord (inclusive) – Lyngenfjord (inclusive)

5) *Execution of the Evacuation*:

a) The entire evacuation area is to be emptied of people.

b) Evacuated settlements are to be used by troop marching through (that is, at the latest by the rear guard)

c) The operation must be a sudden one and the officers of the Reichskommissar of Norway must participate and Norwegian authorities must be harnessed for it: the latter, however, only from the beginning of the operation.

d) The seized population is to be led to the nearest ports under military guard (also small ports with docks suitable for cutters).

e) Local and district commanders are to erect reception camps in or near these ports.

f) Men capable of working and marching and in the western districts women capable of marching also, are to be coupled to the marching units furthest in front and to be taken along.

g) In as far as the population still has small ships available they are to be used for the deportation of the evacuees. Military cover!

h) All ships used by the Wehrmacht (freighters and army transports) are to be loaded additionally with as many evacuees as possible.

i) Columns on Reichsstrasse 50 to be formed only to an unavoidable degree; invalids, women and children to be assisted by loading them on trucks. Only men capable of marching to join the march columns!

k) Transportation of all evacuees first into the area west of the Lyngenfjordes, from there further control by Corp Headquarters, LXXI Infantry Corps in direct agreement with the Reichskommissar Norway.

l) In the area of the Corps Headquarters XIX Mountain Corps the operations will start immediately; in the area of Corps Headquarters LXXI Infantry
Corps on 1.11.44.

m) Mission to be accomplished:

i) By 9.11.44. in the area eastward of the line Kistrand – Billefjord – Lakselv-
Skoganvarre – Karasjok (including these villages).

ii) By 12.11.44. in the area east of the line Ialvik – Kautokeino (including these
villages).

iii) By 15.11.44. in the remaining area.

Norwegians found in the respective areas after that period are to be arrested
and to be brought to the nearest town headquarters. Directives will be issued
concerning their further treatment.

6) It is requested that the Reichskommissar Norway will make available as
much shipping space as possible as otherwise numerous casualties among the
Norwegians will be unavoidable during the evacuation.

7) I request all offices concerned to carry out this evacuation in the sense
of a relief action for the Norwegian population. Though it will be necessary
here and there to be severe, all of us must attempt to save the Norwegians from
Bolshevism and to keep them alive.

(Signed) RENDULIC
(Rendulic) Colonel General
  Roman Ia/Op. No. 1682/44 top secret.[16]

'This is my order, issued by me for the evacuation,' he said:

This order was composed on the basis of Hitler's order, and, of course, it is in
the nature of things that it contains more details that Hitler's order did. The
order contains general directives for the carrying out of the evacuation.

There are a few details here which I would like to point out as, for instance,
that only people able to carry out the marches are to be put on treks. People
were [not] herded together and just driven down Highway 50. But instead it
gives here quite a number of welfare measures for the benefit of the population.

There is something I would like to point out from passage six, and that is
that the ships which were used for the evacuation were property of the
Reichskommissar. There were quite a few disagreeable matters there, but the
army had no influence on these ships. [This refers to the twenty-nine deaths
due to terrible conditions on the cargo ships *Carl Arp* and *Adolf Binder*.]

I would particularly like to emphasise passage seven. This point states my
intention and my wish for the evacuation to be carried out. It says here: 'I request
all offices concerned to carry out this evacuation in a sense of relief action for

the Norwegian population. Though there be necessities here and there to be severe all of us must attempt to save the Norwegians from Bolshevism and to keep them alive.'

A person who orders something like this cannot desire cruelty and ruthlessness, but I am not in a position to put a general next to every lance corporal to make sure that the orders are carried out in a proper way.[17]

Rendulic was also asked to give his thoughts on a number of incidents reported in the Allied media alleging German brutality during the evacuation.

'The British radio, the Russian radio, the Swedish radio and the Swedish press did bring certain incidents to my attention,' he replied:

I had every single assertion followed up. I intended to take a large-scale counter measure against such excesses if they really had occurred, but all these assertions turned out to be mere inventions, or else they were matters in which neither the army nor the troops had been guilty. The Russian radio reported when the Russian troops came into the neighbourhood of Kirkenes they found Norwegians living in cases, Norwegians who were sick and had no medications, etc., and they added that [it was] the Germans left the Norwegians behind in such a condition. To this I could only say that the people concerned were people who had resisted being evacuated and they had arrived in this condition through their own fault.

Another report was in the Swedish press. Some Norwegians were found frozen to death in the Swedish–Norwegian frontier area. They had insufficient clothing and had marched through the mountains and so were frozen to death. These were clearly people who did not want to be evacuated and had resolved by themselves to find their way to Sweden and against this too the army was powerless.

Then the Swedish press carried a report that during the evacuation the Germans carried out such ruthless destruction that they set a house on fire in which there [were] old men and the name of locality was also given. In order to get this straight I ordered an investigation under military law. This was carried out by the XIX Corps and, in all details, it was shown clearly that no house had been set on fire unless it had been previously searched in all corners. In this way the propaganda accusations went on, but not in one single case did I find any justified reason.[18]

The cost of the scorched-earth destruction by Rendulic's men across the north of Norway is difficult to assess accurately. An estimate at 1940 prices of the total war damage across Norway from the occupation onwards was submitted to the Nuremberg trial, which reached a figure of 3 billion Norwegian kroner. This was a rough assessment for the court's purposes of the cost of the damage to roads, bridges, harbours, factories, ships and so on, and stocks of food and supplies that were also destroyed. That report from February 1945 was later amended upwards, with various attempts made to quantify damage before and as a result of the scorched-earth destruction. It is safe to say that the area was devastated and the costs were significant. The full damage report from Nuremberg can be found in Appendix 1.[19]

11

'OH, I KNOW OF A LAND FAR UP NORTH...'

After a week in beautiful, sunny weather in Kirkenes I have hit rain – due to the mountains and the fjords, they tell me. I walk from my hotel by the harbour in Tromsø up to the car-hire company at the top of the town. It's raining quite heavily and the clouds are grey. I'm glad I brought wet-weather gear as the next two days will be spent outside. I would have preferred it to be dry.

I gingerly steer the rental car over the skeletal humpback bridge that is Tromsø's signature but looks too rickety to support all those cars. I turn right at the stunning triangular cathedral on the other side of the fjord and head south for an hour, skipping the ferry crossings through the Lyngen mountains and instead skirting the shores of the Lyngenfjord for the next two hours heading for the north-east.

I am at the start of a dark episode playing out in Troms, the next county south from Finnmark. I have been transported by Wideroe's propeller-driven planes from the modern brutalism of Hammerfest to a place where the scenery is less harsh: softer, more lush; with fjords rather than rugged, rocky coast. Just open any tourist brochure for Norway and you're as good as there.

Perfectly flat turquoise lakes lap sandy shores, with small white motor boats nodding alongside orange buoys. Impossibly steep rugged mountains like shark's teeth rise almost vertically upwards to higher unfriendly dark-grey angular shapes, sliced by ice millions of years ago. Forests of deep-green pine trees cling to the lower slopes, with glaciers of white and grey nestling above and waterfalls like white necklaces tumbling from their slopes.

But in this natural paradise strode an evil capable of such wicked things that those who saw it still cannot shut it out of their mind. The death's head symbol was a sign that bad things would not be very far away: houses were burned, animals slaughtered; weakened, helpless men shot dead or hanged. A landscape of peace was transformed by checkpoints, barbed wire, machine guns and minefields into a world of hate and horror – and all this in a community of two dozen houses along a single road leading to a hilly headland overlooking a fjord.

My guide through this paradise turned hell is an artist called Grethe Gunneng. Her family come from a small village called Djupvik which lies on up the upper regions of the Lyngenfjord, its flat sandy shores making it the ideal place for paddling, or stepping into a rowing boat for an afternoon's fishing on the fjord – or, if you are a Nazi military strategist, a seaborne invasion.

By an unfortunate twist of fate, in the Second World War Djupvik became strategically important. Retreating back to their mountainous defensive positions in the Lyngen Alps, the Nazis imagined hordes of crack Russian troops leaping out of landing craft onto these sandy beaches, so they mined the mouth of the fjord. If that didn't stop them – or the British, or the Norwegians training in England – then the rows of anti-personnel mines on the grassy slopes leading up from the shore surely would. Behind the machine-gun positions on the top of the hill were a garrison of troops manning field guns and anti-aircraft cannon pointing out to sea and searching the skies for invasion forces. The binoculars of the Germans officers scanned the mountains and the skies constantly for any possible attackers.

Barbed wire channelled all approaches to the village through checkpoints. The Germans turfed some of the local people out of their homes and billeted themselves there instead. Russian prisoners of war were marched into the area to build enormous concrete bunkers so that massive coastal guns could fire shells at any boats or warships that might approach. This was the western flank of a line of defensive fortifications across a narrow strip of northern Norway called the Lyngen Line that was designed to keep Stalin's soldiers out.

Grethe grew up hearing stories of two completely different worlds in Djupvik: in one, a community at peace and living in harmony with nature and animals, and, in the other, at war and brutalising humans with machines and fear. She was inspired to create an art project called 'Compassion' using textiles, photographs, bits of barbed wire and a soldier's helmet she found in a field to contrast the peace of her family's simple life farming in the fields surrounded by such natural beauty with the violence of the Nazi war machine.

Grethe climbs into the passenger side of my rented car and we drive to the end of the headland, wisps of mist drifting by on the fjord, the rain still heavy on the grass.

'As a child I played by the seaside and up on the hills and in the trees. There was a checkpoint along this road here and fences and barbed wire all over, with mines from the sea all over the fields up to the mountains,' she says:

I wondered what it was like to grow up with the Germans so close and the prisoners of war where the people were living. There were 200 people and 2,000 soldiers here for four and a half years with 150 prisoners in the camp.

I also wondered why no one ever talked about this. My mother was thirteen when the war started and 18 when it finished. That was her whole youth. About 15 years ago I began to interview people I knew for my project: my mother, her siblings, other people in the area. At first they didn't want to talk. 'No, it's over,' they said. 'Let's just have a nice life.'

They were scared I might say something bad about someone. Perhaps some relationships with the Germans were closer than they should have been, I don't know – but that's not what I was interested in.[1]

As if to emphasise what she's saying, every now and then the windscreen wipers move across the screen and clear away the drizzle. Every so often a heavy lorry powers up the hill along the wet road, the E6, heading the 800km north to Kirkenes. Apart from being resurfaced and improved, it's the old German supply road, the one they used to enter Djupvik back in 1940. It's the road those combat-crazy veterans came into town on four years later when they were pulling back from the Litsa Front.

Grethe's family have lived here for generations, she says:

My mother was one of nine children: eight sisters and one brother. When the Germans were here my grandfather hushed them all up in the second floor. My mother was 13 and she had two older sisters and five younger sisters. They had to work and be inside: spinning, sewing, weaving, milking the cows. They couldn't go out at night. They had to close the curtains and keep the light darkened, especially in the winter when there was no daylight.

My grandfather was the postman in the village and he ran the postal service from his kitchen during the war so Germans and everyone came in the kitchen and were talking and fetching the post. My mother and the children were told not to speak to them or say anything but to run upstairs.

For my art project I collected memorabilia from the war and materials people here would have used, like yarn to make fishing lines, fishing hooks, bridles for the horses. As a contrast I used war materials like barbed wire and a German helmet I found. I put all these things together and made an exhibition which I've been showing at museums and schools across the region.

The children are very interested. They like the German helmet very much. I say: 'This is real. This was here in Norway and we must never forget and we must learn from it.' Sometimes the children come with their own stories about the war, usually their grandfather. Sometimes one says: 'My grandfather was a Nazi. He was a German.'

I ask Grethe whether she feels she's lifting the lid on dark secrets.

Yes, but now the people who didn't want me to start this say they're glad I've done it. It's part of their youth and childhood, like collecting peat to burn on the fire or looking after the animals. I have documented their lifestyle in a time of war.

The Germans believed the English would come here and they expected to stop them here, with mines across the fjord and landmines in the fields. There were signs saying 'Achtung Minen' everywhere. People got used to the minefields and went through them to collect peat at the top of the hill. They showed their identification at the checkpoint: 'Halt! Wer da?' [Stop! Who's there?] they said.

But the occupation had a more sinister side, with Russian prisoners of war forced to build fortifications, roads, canals and camps. They were kept near to the village in camps ringed with barbed wire. Fed meagre rations, they were worked like slaves and treated brutally, poorly clothed in freezing conditions, living in huts without heating. They became weak and unable to work and, when they could no longer lift a spade, they were killed. Local dignitaries – like Grethe's postmaster grandfather – would be invited to the camp to witness hangings.

Everybody felt bad about the prisoners, Grethe says, and the local people tried to do what they could to help:

Every day the Russian prisoners came from the camp, marching past my mother's house. The local people tried to help them. They left food in the roads and in the fields for them. When they discovered prisoners were stealing food from the animal barns they would put more meat and fish in it. My grandfather was almost caught because he left food out in the fields and a German guard saw it, but he knew a higher officer who said: 'Just leave it.'

I don't think they [the older generation] wanted to talk about it because of the things they saw – the prisoners in the snow without enough clothes, the horrible things that happened to them. I think they just wanted to forget about it.

Grethe and I explore the vast and once-fearsome coastal fortification still dominating this headland, even despite being rent asunder at the end of the war by a British demolition team. The top of the hill is littered with concrete gun emplacements and bunkers, some shattered by considerable explosions, others intact, camouflaged even better against detection by the growth of moss and grass around their remains.

'The headquarters was the big one behind there,' says Grethe as we pick through the ruins:

They could see any boats coming in. They could see everything from here. It was an important lookout point.

It's so horrible and it's so beautiful: these ugly things and the beautiful mountains. As an artist I see what time has done with it. It's very interesting to do something a bit beautiful with this horrible history. How could this happen here, where the people just wanted to live in peace and do their fishing and farming and look at the Midnight Sun?

I take photographs as Grethe shows me the site. The power of the weapons of hate that were bolted into this hillside must have been phenomenal. The bunkers are made from steel-reinforced concrete varying from between 12cm to 1m thick. The tops of the bunkers hug the contours of the landscape well. In some places the walls leading to the living quarters are made from individual stones rather than concrete blocks, stacked one on top of the other and held together with a dark mortar, topped with grass, which gives it an almost prehistoric feel.

I think of the weak, emaciated Russian prisoners building this wall here, forced to live in such misery amongst such beauty. A rising, curving entrance to one of the gun installations has been assembled from local stone of all different shapes and sizes: it's quite a piece of craftsmanship.

Different coloured moss and lichen has grown on some of the stones. I can see how an artist might be attracted by some of the contrasts here, like the thick steel baseplate with five bolts sticking up where the guns would have been bolted down. The baseplate and bolts remain; the guns and their crews are long gone. This headland is like a ghost town silenced and abandoned, but nature has been unable to reclaim it entirely. Seventy years is not long enough to smooth out the harsh contours of a pit for a heavy-calibre cannon.

A crude, ugly concrete blockhouse still has the steel housings for an anti-aircraft gun. Grethe shows me where the minefields were and the gate to the prison camp, where on Sundays local people could buy carvings from the prisoners. Briefly we poke our heads into one of the bunkers where the gun crews would pass the time between shifts, expecting an invasion and bringing up ammunition that would never be used, for guns that would never be fired.

'People tell me German soldiers have been coming back here for many years,' Grethe says:

I think many were very fond of Norway and went fishing and hunting and became fascinated with this country. The German children and grandchildren are sorry for what their parents and grandparents did. My project has brought some of this into the open. It hurts us all but we must remember. My grandmother and grandfather had to be very strong to protect their home and their family, and not give up. It moves me very much.

We are strangers standing side by side staring out across a misty fjord, sharing thoughts so close to a person's heart. As we look at the mountains, the fjord and the sky Grethe tells stories of cruelty and brutality, of hurt, pain and anguish. In this area of remarkable natural beauty stories like this seem unimaginable:

My uncle told me about the time they had to go as refugees. The Germans told them to bring all their animals to Birtavarre [a town on the same fjord about 10km south] so they went there along the road. But he didn't want the Nazis to take his horse Guri, because he loved her so much. He said he would prefer to shoot Guri himself than let the Germans take her and maybe mistreat her. So he took a gun and walked with Guri to the field and shot her. Afterwards, some of the neighbours said they wished they'd done that to their animals too. My uncle was 70 when he told me this story and he was crying as he told me.

The Germans slaughtered the livestock and made the horses work for them. My grandfather also had a beautiful traditional boat and he didn't want the Germans to take that either, so he took the family to Birtavarre in it with everything they could carry, like the sewing machine, and then he took it out to sea and sank it with stones. After the war he went and got it back. We still have it in the barn.

The Germans set fire to Birtavarre and slaughtered all the animals. The fjord was red with their blood. Then the Germans put everyone on a boat from Birtavarre to Tromsø. They sailed past this spot on the boat, not far out on the fjord from where everyone used to live, and the teacher was singing a song called 'Oh I know a land far up north' ['Å eg veit meg eit land']. It's a song every person from the north knows, it's the national song of north Norway, written by Elias Blix [a hymnwriter and politician credited with translating the New Testament into Norwegian]. Everyone in the boat was singing it. The teacher was conducting. Everyone loves this song:

Oh, I know of a land far away to the north,
With a shimmering beach between mountains and fjords
Where my heart wants to stay, when I'm far, far away
Tied with the finest, finest bands.
Oh, I remember, I remember
I remember this land so well!
And I long to see this land so often, and it tugs at me gently when I am far away.
With awakening spring my longing turns strong
So that all I can do is cry
All I can do is cry

The emotion of the moment seems to be getting the better of Grethe. I can feel several lumps in my own throat, not least for Guri the horse. We both gaze at the spot in the fjord where such a dramatic and emotional moment happened. As we look, a shard of sunlight breaks through the clouds and lights up the waves exactly where we're looking. It's like a scene from a film: a boat carrying people forced to leave their village – their world – having shot their much-loved animals themselves to spare them cruelty and mistreatment, their homes burned or destroyed, possessions buried, having walked to Birtavarre where the fjord is running red with the blood of butchered animals. As they sail past the homes they had to leave, the teacher bursts into a song of their much-loved homeland they are now leaving and they all start singing too. It's impossibly heart-rending and powerful against the backdrop of this grey, misty fjord with its single ray of sunlight.

Grethe stares out across the fjord with a faraway look in her eyes and says: 'My mother says to me: "When I die, play this song at my funeral."'

Grethe takes me to meet a friend of the family in the next village who is willing to share his stories. Roald Berg went to school with two of Grethe's aunties and was just 10 when the Germans marched into Djupvik. Now in his 80s, Roald has a little difficulty moving around, but he's a big man and would clearly have been a considerable physical presence in his younger days. We share coffee and cakes as Grethe translates his stories.

'The Germans came on 29 August 1940. My youngest brother was born that night,' he says:

> In one night my whole world was turned upside down. From being a quiet place to having hundreds of soldiers here, with cars, tanks – we'd never seen things like that. It was like a fairy tale for us young boys. We soon learned to say 'Heil Hitler' because the soldiers gave us sweets.

But the reality of the occupation soon sank in. Life under the Nazis became harsh and brutal, Roald remembers:

> You couldn't say a word. You had to keep your mouth shut – not a word about Hitler. We saw so much evil. Many of us saw the Russian prisoners being shot. We were so used to seeing the prisoners getting beaten. After a while it didn't affect us.
>
> One Russian prisoner was sick and wanted to go in to see the doctor. The guard on the door told him not to but the prisoner ignored him and pushed past, so the guard shot him. There and then. Many of us saw that.
>
> One guard wanted to shoot me because I gave bread to a Russian prisoner. The guard asked me: 'Where did you get that bread?' I said: 'I stole it from home.'

That wasn't true: my mother had given it to me. But if I'd have said that, she might have got into trouble.

He stood there pointing a rifle in my chest, but I didn't think he would shoot a 12-year-old boy. But afterwards I thought: 'If I had run, what then?' Perhaps I wouldn't be sitting here. They would have shot me.

The German deserters were treated the worst of all. We saw Himmler's SS watching these people. They were like devils, the worst. The Germans had strict discipline and were very tough on their own troops. They would never have conquered so much of Europe if they didn't have such tough discipline.

We pass round more coffee and cakes and switch to talking about the evacuation. Roald's family was evacuated first to Tromsø and then to Lofoten: thirty-two people in a fishing boat 15m long. Among the occupants were his extended family and the people who owned the boat, as well as other people from Djupvik. When they got to Tromsø the battleship *Tirpitz* was capsized in the fjord and rescue operations to free the sailors were still underway. They left for Lofoten and spent the next six months there, returning when peace came.

Many of the younger generation round here escaped into the mountains and made their way to Sweden, Roald says. 'The Germans didn't catch many of them. Have you heard of Jan Baalsrud?'

I nod. I've heard about him a few times since I've been in this part of Norway. Baalsrud was a Resistance hero here, one of many legendary wartime Norwegians – and for good reason. Betrayed by a shopkeeper they thought was their contact, Baalsrud and his Resistance team were ambushed on a mission to destroy an aircraft control tower at Bardufoss airbase south of Tromsø in 1943. Baalsrud was wounded but escaped into snow-covered mountains where, despite frostbite and snowblindness, he hid for two months helped by local sympathisers. Fearing gangrene was setting into his toes he hacked nine of them off with his penknife. Having saved his own life, Sami guides took him across the border to the safety of Sweden. After seven months in hospital he trained Resistance recruits in Scotland, then, having learnt to walk again, returned to active service. He lived in Tenerife after the war but returned to Norway to die, aged 71, asking to be buried among the people who had helped him.[2]

Roald's most vivid and shocking memories are reserved for the scenes he and his family sailed away from: the burning and destruction of the place they called home. Roald delivers these stories in bursts, pausing for Grethe to translate:

The German withdrawal went past here on Road Number 50 in a stream of horses and donkeys, trucks, Germans and equipment. For the snow and winter the Russian prisoners built a tunnel 70km from here high up in the mountains – 1,100m up – a snow tunnel to keep the road open. They had huge snowploughs to clear the snow away.

The people in the south know very little about what happened to us but they are beginning to understand that this was madness. The world thinks it was Germans that did this but they were Austrians. The soldiers were veterans of the Murmansk Front, fighting the Russians and evacuating from Kirkenes.

There was burning either side of the valley. Olderdalen and other places at the bottom of the fjord were in flames. They cut the heads off living sheep and hung them in the trees. The cows were howling because they hadn't been milked. The soldiers from the Murmansk Front were not human. They had seen so many bad things they didn't have any feelings left.

I often think about my parents and the other parents who had to get their families through the war. It was hard – it was tough – and they didn't talk about it. It was a common experience: they didn't have to talk about it.

Our parents didn't want any memories of the Germans and if they could have buried these bunkers [on the hill we visited] at the bottom of the sea they would have done. Even now, like my parents, I don't want to talk about it much. We'll never know what they took with them to their graves. They came back to nothing, but that didn't matter. We were free.

The mood has darkened. Roald stares out of the window towards the fjord, a distant look in his eye. I sense he has travelled back to a time of turmoil and it might be time for us to finish. I ask him for his memories of the end of the war and Roald becomes animated again:

> There was an explosion of joy when the war was over. You never forget some-thing like that when you experience it. Our house was filthy. The soldiers had put hay on the floor to sleep and the next soldiers had put more hay on top and so on. We started to clear the hay out when we came back and there was a dead dog in the hay.
>
> But when the war ended, how we danced. We danced and danced and danced. We played records all night and when the gramophone broke we span them with our finger. There was a man with a harmonica whose lips were so sore because he was playing all night. How we danced, and sang – because of what we had got back. Our freedom.[3]

The 83-year-old man finishes his story with a flourish, transported back seven decades to a night he will never forget, his eyes filled with a mixture of exhilara-tion and, at the same time, sadness. I put my microphone away, finish my coffee and start to pack my bags. Roald looks exhausted.

12

EVEN IN THE WILDERNESS, THERE WAS WAR

From Djupvik I drove forty minutes further up the fjord to the town of Storslett, one of the few towns in this area with a hotel. Roald had told me Storslett still had one of the two colossal German snowploughs from the war. Apparently the Germans asked for it back, but the Norwegians refused and it has been sitting outside the local council's offices ever since – part trophy, part-reminder. To my regret I didn't go there and check it out first.

Not wanting to be late for my next rendezvous I went straight to the Storslett Hotel, a large but basic hotel in the centre of town. Once checked in I made the mistake of peeling off my wet socks and sitting down to catch up on any emails. Before long it was 6 p.m.; not really enough time to go out before the arrival of Nord Troms History Society guide Pål Fredriksen, who had offered to take me out along sections of the Lyngen Line the following day. We had agreed to meet up at the hotel and discuss a plan in advance.

My room was the last one on the left down a long corridor and had the feel of a Soviet-era hotel. There were two single beds: narrow, basic, with spare blankets of almost military feel. The radiator was old-fashioned and, at this time in late August, cold. The bathroom had a shower, wc and washbasin – everything I needed – but nothing was flamboyant, just 'adequate'. I thought of Jan Baalsrud hacking off his toes with a penknife in a wooden hut high up in the sub-zero, snow-covered mountains. This was hardly slumming it. There was even Wifi.

An air-conditioned coach had pulled up an hour before in the large car park outside the hotel and offloaded – to my surprise – sixty elderly German tourists. Suddenly I was not alone anymore. Now small groups of them were strolling round the car park, some smoking. A dark-blue saloon car pulled up and a wiry looking man jumped out purposefully. That had to be Pål.

I walked down the corridor to meet him and we poured ourselves coffee from the flasks laid out for the German guests, then walked to a wooden verandah where Pål unfolded a large map of the region.

'This is Storslett here,' he said. 'These mountains here, to here' – he ran his finger along the contours of the hills to the south – 'this is the Lyngen Line. There are bunkers up here.' He pointed to an area I had studied many times on my map at home at the neck of a fjord:

> Tomorrow we go here: Skibotn. I will meet you at a petrol station outside Skibotn and we will drive to the start point from there. It's a two-hour climb, but there is a bunker at the top. It's not original, it's been reconstructed, but it's like it was. This is the Russian Road, built by the prisoners. Many of them died. They were treated very badly by the Germans.

That settled, we talked a little longer then replaced our coffee cups on the side dresser in the main hall. Then Pål said: 'Would you like to have a drive up the valley tonight? I can show you some places that are important in the history of Nordreisa county.'

Offers of local knowledge should never be refused and Pål was clearly a man of action, so we climbed into his car and he accelerated away, swinging onto a well-surfaced road splitting a wide valley between two mountain ranges. The rain earlier in the day had cleared and it was actually a lovely evening for a drive.

'The Germans camped here, here and here,' he said, waving his arm at clearings to our left; fields between forests of pine trees:

> There is nothing left of it now. Russian prisoners were kept here [he waved to the right], 100, 200. In Nordreisa there were about 1,000 German soldiers. They had German prisoners too – deserters and criminals. Political prisoners too – homosexuals.
>
> This road goes into the mountains, to the border with Finland. But the road stops and then you can only walk. The Germans were terrified of the Russians coming this way after them, so they put guns here, here, here.

He gestured towards woods of pine trees on one side and small farms on the other, pausing only to change gear as we hammered through the countryside.

'This road, the 865, was the one they expected the Russians to come down so they had guns aimed at it all the way along,' Pål added. 'And on the right, in the mountains, is the Lyngen Line.'

The mountains to my right are 1,000m high and very steep. It would be quite a job to climb them, let alone fight your way up against well dug-in and heavily armed defenders. It was easier to climb the mountains from behind, where there are paths up, Pål said.

'All these trees are from the period after the war,' he said, pointing to the vast green forests lining the road:

> The Germans needed a lot of material to build the barracks and warehouses and all the things they needed. They also built a tunnel along the road, at Kvannes, a snow tunnel. They took the wood for that from here. They cut all these trees down to make the tunnel, but they set fire to it when they withdrew in 1944. They didn't want the Red Army to use it.

A silence fell over us as the scale of the German work sank in. We are doing 110km/h along a smooth road through a valley lined with pine trees, occasionally slowing to cross the river on narrow concrete bridges. The vast mountains flashing past my window are formidable: steep, solid and rocky with a belt of dark-green pine trees separating them from the valley. Higher up are sheer cliffs trimmed with sparse scrub vegetation. Little whiffs of mist are starting to linger as the light fades:

> Young people in the war would walk up the mountain, turn south-east, cross the river at the border between Finland and Sweden and then they were safe. Norway established an army or a police unit in Sweden of 15,000 soldiers who were sent back to Norway when the war was ending to take control of the Finnmark region.
>
> I think Road 865 was made in the 1930s and when the Germans came they improved it a lot. In 1944 they were scared the Russians would come down the valley so they had military positions facing in all directions. They cut everything down and destroyed it all. Houses, power lines, everything. Some of these houses were 200 years old. Before people were forced to leave they tried to hide their belongings in the forest but the Germans searched for everything, then burned it or smashed it.

We have left the smooth road for a bumpy gravel track, but Pål has continued driving at the same speed. Finally he stops the car in a clearing in the forest where a dozen wooden fishing cabins are arranged into groups. A short distance away a small fleet of long, Viking-style salmon-fishing canoes have been pulled up onto the shore.

'Here we are,' said Pål, scanning the treeline:

From here there are no roads. This is all national park now. Up in the moun-
tains – that's where Norway meets Sweden and Finland. You can walk 116km to
Kautokeino, which is Sami country. Here it's all forests and lakes and mountains.
And even here the Germans were scared of the Russians coming.[1]

At 9 p.m. on a late summer's evening the light is starting to fade. The trees and
mountains are merging, one dark shape bumping into another. The air in this
remote forest at the far end of this road – Saraelv – is clear and fresh. It's so beautiful, so natural. The silence is overwhelming. It must have been tough to go from
this natural beauty to the butchery, horror and privation of the LitsaFront.

We head back to Storslett at the same breakneck speed Pål seems to drive
everywhere at. He talks with passion of the simple pleasures to be had here:
weekends camping in the wooden cabins that line the riverbank, catching salmon
from traditional narrow canoes, picking berries, enjoying the outdoors. It seems
a world away from the misery inflicted on this region seventy years ago – trucks
full of soldiers carrying machine guns on a one-way rendezvous with death; prisoners of war beaten and bedraggled, breathing their last, unable to satisfy guards
with the power of life or death over them; the camps, the guns, the orders, the
flames crackling, the people forced to leave their homes.

It all seems so out of place in this lovely peaceful valley where the air is clear,
new trees have replaced the felled forest and Nature has shaken those cruel times
from its mind.

As far as I can see, there are no memorials to what happened here in the war.
It's all carried in the heads of people like Pål; people who believe it's important to
remember that this did happen.

I'm tired when I get back to the hotel but I want to check something out
before I head to the Lyngen Line. Sitting at the desk in my room I look through
the Imperial War Museum's online collection for paintings by the British war
artist Stephen Bone. Bone was a landscape painter born in London who served
as a camouflage officer in 1939–43 and was then attached to the navy as an
official war artist: he painted scenes of the D-Day landings before being sent up
to Norway.

I've not had time to look at his paintings in detail until now, but I like them:
very natural sketches in chalk and ink of mountains, trees and fjords, with simple
scenes of human activity in the foreground. The chalk gives an air of natural calm
and coolness in which the landscape dominates. A series of watercolours empha-
sises the green of the countryside.

Bone was in this area just as the war ended and a dozen pictures deal with the
aftermath of what happened here. His eye for detail adds a powerful sub-text to
paintings that seem at first little more than impressionistic sketches. One picture shows the *Tirpitz*, keel up in the fjord at Tromsø. There are German camps

at Kvesmenes, alongside the Lyngen fjord. *A Farmhouse at Mandal, Lyngen Fjord, Burnt by the Germans* shows the ruins of a wooden cabin around a chimney and hearth which are still standing. In the foreground there are charred timbers, a partially burned desk and a family portrait lying in the grass.

Cable Railway Built by the Germans in Kitdal shows the ski-lift-style cable winch that helped the POWs move guns, timber and construction materials into the mountains to build the Lyngen Line bunkers at the top. The cable car runs along the Kitdalen to the back of the picture, with planking under the metal cable supports on the valley floor and German POWs standing near a small wooden hut. Then there's a painting which seems to show very little at all, but is entitled *Death Camp at Kitdal*. It shows a clearing in a wood with shelters dug out of the ground and covered with wooden supports and turf. Around these shelters are tree stumps, broken saplings, piles of rubbish and cloth. It's a sombre scene, but without any human presence at all.

One of the watercolours is of the Russian cemetery at Kvesmenes. It shows a memorial seat in the shape of a heart set into the boundary fence of a cemetery for Soviet prisoners who died in the camps. A red flag flies above the seat, which has red stars on its corners. Behind are the hills of the Lyngen Alps, which I was photographing earlier today. A second watercolour from Kvesmenes, entitled *Types of Plywood Hut*, is of a camp of curved plywood huts in a clearing edged with saplings. A Norwegian soldier is emerging from one of the huts, while a second soldier unpacks a backpack next to a pole hung with Norwegian and Soviet flags.

German Guns at Djupvik is a dramatic landscape of the Lyngen Alps, their jagged snowy slopes blue and grey and white in the background, with a powerful field artillery gun front and centre pointing out across the fjord, in a circular base so it can be pointed in any direction with ease. With a start of recognition I realise these are the positions Grethe and I walked through this afternoon, except this painting shows them as they would have been with the guns in place. To one side is the bunker for the crew to shelter in that we looked at less than ten hours ago.

But my favourite of this collection is of two soldiers standing in a Russian graveyard with the midnight sun high in the sky, yet long shadows stretch from the wooden crosses in the field. The twin, sharp peaks of the Otertind Mountain in the Signaldal are slightly off-centre in the background. It's almost an idyllic evening scene, except for the dozen crosses of dead men that stretch the width of the picture.

The paintings are understated, dignified and calm, finding beauty in the aftermath of the wretched events that Bone has catalogued. I'm surprised more British people don't know of Stephen Bone. His work is fantastic.

13

INTO THE VALLEY OF THE DAMNED: THE MALLNITZ DEATH CAMP

I woke up to rain and dark clouds. Slate-grey skies, grey fjord, dark-grey clouds with black hearts and a lingering wispy, white mist. The air was clear, fresh but wet. I thought I might beat the rush but at 6.30 a.m. the sixty-strong coach party of elderly German tourists were all having breakfast too, so I gathered scrambled egg, toast, yoghourt, fruit and coffee where I could and made an early exit. I backed out of the car park and headed onto the E6 for a two-hour drive south.

In the grey morning rain this road did not look like one of Norway's premier tourist routes. In summer tens of thousands of people drive along here hoping to see the Northern Lights, that mysterious magical dance of light, colour and movement in the sky – but there was little to interest a tourist just now.

Ahead was a left turn for Birtavarre, that settlement now synonymous in my mind with blood, Nazi savagery and Norwegian despair. As I drive by I imagine the flames and smoke rising from the wooden houses. I am crossing the river that was stained red with the blood of slaughtered animals; this is the pier where people gathered in small, shocked groups waiting for a boat out of here. All for what? The people who lived here for generations were uprooted and forced into boats, cleared from the land they loved, their homes and fields transformed into a field of fire so a second set of invaders could be mown down more easily by the first. They became inadvertent and inconvenient trespassers into a military and geopolitical struggle not of their making which would, in some cases, shape their lives for the next six decades.

War, and then the Cold War, put an unremarkable river bend on the map – but those maps would remain secret for many years. The bloody turmoil of the scorched-earth clearance would be promptly forgotten as fresh defenders rushed to aim a new generation of rifles at the same enemy.

I turn off the E6 a little further south and head for the offices of Storfjord Council in a small hamlet called Hatteng, alongside a petrol station, grocery store and tourist trail office. The office is a modern, two-storey block with a large stuffed polar bear in reception. I take the lift to the second floor for my meeting with Storfjord's mayor, Sigmund Steinnes. He is a man in his early 50s who looks determined and energetic. He welcomes me with a handshake and coffee and we sit down and start talking.

Within its boundaries Storfjord had twenty German prison camps during the war, housing around 5,000 prisoners. Of these about 800 died, 150 of them in the last six weeks of the war.[1]

Russian, Yugoslav and Polish prisoners were used as forced labour on Nazi construction projects, but only the Soviets worked on the building of the Lyngen Line fortifications high in the mountains that we can see from the office window. These camps were at the extreme end on the scale of brutality. This was not forced labour with proper rations, clothing, shelter and medical attention. This was slave labour, with prisoners being worked to collapse, and even death, fed little or nothing in freezing conditions and treated worse than dogs. When they were of no further use they were shot. Conditions were unspeakable.[2]

The Lyngen Line consisted of 550 defensive bunkers built across a narrow stretch of land at the very north of Norway. It traced a line from the Alpine mountains surrounding the Lyngenfjord across the valley at Skibotn and up into the mountains on the other side which led to the Swedish and Finnish borders.

To build these bunkers the Germans brought in 7,000 to 8,000 prisoners of war. Work camps were set up hurriedly in the area surrounding the Lyngenfjord from the autumn of 1944, most of them run by the Nazi military specialist construction company, Organisation Todt.[3]

Much of the research into what happened to the prisoners in this area has been done by Michael Stokke, who runs the POW history section of the Narvik Centre, and by the Falstad Centre, another POW remembrance project.

By far the biggest camp in the Lyngen Line region was at Skibotn, with 1,385 prisoners. Alongside the fjord Kvesmenes had 890 prisoners in four camps and the Kitdalen valley had 515, split across two camps: Mallnitz and Kitzbuehel. Nearby Signaldalen had 728 prisoners and there were 465 in camps on the Falsnes mountain.[4]

The prisoners were split between Organisation Todt and army construction battalions across the region, coastal artillery units in Djupvik, Rottenvik and Lyngseidet, the field hospital in Overgard and technical and supply battalions responsible for keeping the Wehrmacht fed, housed and fighting.[5]

Many of these prisoners died during the winter of 1944 working on the construction of the Lyngen Line. The work was physically demanding, the weather was harsh, they were not fed enough, were poorly housed and clothed, and the pressure and cruelty from the guards was unrelenting.

Colonel Edgar Johnson was one of the senior Allied staff officers taking control of Norway immediately after the German capitulation, and oversaw the release and eventual repatriation of the Soviet prisoners:

By December [1944] the Germans had retreated to the Lyngenfjord and here in the winter a defensive system – the Lyngen Line – was built from the Finnish frontier to the fjord. Some eight thousand Russian prisoners were set to work building an aerial tramway to lift cement, lumber, steel, guns and supplies to the crest of a high plateau where other prisoners were used to build elaborate defensive works. Until April of 1945 the work went on, with prisoners toiling as virtual slaves until they were 'unable to lift a log or swing a pick'. Those incapable of further work were shot and hence the upper work compounds became, in effect, extermination centres.[6]

Prisoners too sick or too weak to continue were shot and dumped in makeshift mass graves where they had been working. As the war drew to a close, things got even worse. Those too sick to leave the work camps were moved to Mallnitz in the Kitdalen where they were fed virtually nothing and left to die. Amid the beatings, brutality and sudden ending of life with a German bullet, some even resorted to cannibalism.

Kitdalen, this valley of death, is about 7km from Mayor Steinnes' office. The Mallnitz camp was named after the town in Austria where many of the soldiers came from. There were others, all named after Austrian towns and villages in the Tyrol – Wörgl, Gastein, Spittal, Kufstein, Windeck – but none were like Mallnitz. Mayor Steinnes is determined that this particularly brutal and sickening chapter of Norway's history should be preserved. The story doesn't make for easy reading.

The Mallnitz camp had been established in November or December 1944 as a labour camp for the construction of Lyngen Line bunkers. Until April 1945 it was used to house 160 'Vlassov' Russians, followers of the Red Army General Andrei Vlassov, who turned against Stalin when he was captured by the Germans and established the Russian Liberation Army to fight for a non-communist Russia.[7]

After April 1945 it became in effect a death camp. Of the 272 prisoners from the camp working on the Lyngen Line construction, only 67 emerged alive.[8] Following an outbreak of typhus in February 1945, which was finally brought under control in April, the Germans separated the prisoners into two groups: those who could work and were worth feeding, and those who were too weak or too ill and not expected to survive. The German commandants fed those who could work and halved the rations of the sick. These unlucky souls were dumped at Mallnitz to die, and die they did, in many ways: from sickness, overwork, exhaustion and malnutrition. Some were beaten to death and some were shot.

It was a journey into hell. Russian prisoners who survived long enough at the end of the war to be winched aboard the *Stella Polaris*, once used as a German troopship but converted into an emergency hospital ship anchored a few kilometres away from the camp at Kvesmenes near Skibotn, told Allied investigators about one mass grave they said had more than 100 bodies in it.[9]

The Allies set up a commission in May 1945 to gather evidence. Led by an English officer, Captain McGill, it also included an American captain, a Russian, the county doctor, the police chief and the local prosecutor. In addition there were interpreters, photographers and specialist pathologists.

Captain McGill's investigation now lies in a brown folder in the British archives at Kew, London. The original typed statements from German officers and Russian prisoners describing the macabre horrors of Mallnitz are with it, amended in some places in pencil.

The prisoners lived in makeshift cabins with walls a metre high made of earth and turf. The roof consisted of branches from birch trees that were no protection against rain. Dozens of prisoners were forced into four of six cabins in the camp, each measuring approximately 30m². Beds were netting or wire mesh strung between birch tree trunks. One witness said that sixty-eight men had slept in one hut on the night of 29 April 1945. When he left the camp on 11 May – less than a fortnight later – only ten had survived.[10]

Rations were pitifully poor for men engaged in hard labour in challenging physical conditions. Breakfast was hot water, sometimes tea. Lunch consisted of 800g or 900g of soup, made from 2kg of dried peas and bad flour stirred into 150 litres of water. An evening meal was 100g of bread, 800g of canned meat or 500g of margarine shared between four or five men.[11]

The prisoners were sent into the hills in working parties to cut wood to be used in road construction. The camp was under the control of the 6th Mountain Army, with Battalion 55 replaced as guards from March 1945 by Battalion 428, who ran it until 1 May, when they were replaced by Organisation Todt Battalion 204. It's during the period of control by Battalion 428 that Mallnitz became a death camp and the worst incidents occurred.[12]

War crime investigators visited Mallnitz on 2 June with several German officers present, among them Colonel Remold, who had taken over as divisional commander of 6th Mountain Army from 28 April. Medical Colonel Lauer and Medical Lieutenant Colonel Brunner, who had overseen Mallnitz from their HQ at Kvesmenes, went too. The inspection found 143 bodies in not one but four mass graves. Of the dead men, sixty-two had died violently: fifty-four of them had been shot. The other eighty-one had died non-violently, mostly through starvation.

The mass graves had originally been excavated by explosive charges being detonated and the rubble dug out. The dead were stacked on top of each other in the graves in rows. Unburied bodies lay in heaps nearby.

Grave number 1 was 100m from the camp and split into two: there were eight bodies in one small section and ninety-six in another, covered by large boulders, loose turf and earth. Grave 2 lay 500m up the hillside and contained twelve bodies. Grave 3 was 400m up the hillside with two bodies buried there. Grave 4, containing twenty-five bodies, was found 550m in the same direction. Attempts had been made to burn the bodies in this grave.[13]

The corpses were taken to Kvesmenes for examination and autopsies. Inquests showed the scale of the barbarism meted out to the wretched human beings: 'Causes of death listed as extreme emaciation, multiple fractures, bullet wounds, internal haemmorrhaging due to clubbing, scurvy, pneumonia, starvation, frostbite and gangrene. There was even evidence of cannibalism …'[14] One case of cannibalism involved a prisoner shot by guards in April 1945. The force of the shot split his skull and spilled his brain onto the ground. The inmate who buried him removed it, fried it and ate it. He survived the death camp.[15]

Another incident occurred just days before the war ended, in early May 1945, with the death of a Russian medical orderly. When another prisoner was seen cutting a piece from his thigh the German guards ordered all the prisoners back into their huts where they discovered human flesh in the eating bowls of three prisoners. These three prisoners were marched outside and executed.[16]

The 4th Company of the 428 Battalion commanded by Captain Max Kluge and Oberfeldwebel Kurt Teubel was in charge of Mallnitz from 6 March until 3 May, when responsibility for the camp was handed over to the 204 Battalion. On seeing conditions at Mallnitz, the CO of 204 initially refused to take responsibility for the camp. It was closed on 11 May.

War-crimes investigator Captain McGill carried out interviews with thirty of the surviving Russian POWs. The following precis offers a glimpse of the starvation, degradation and sickening brutality overseen by the Nazi guards:[17]

Witness 9: Iwan Kratschewski was among the first prisoners at Mallnitz, part of a group of 120 who arrived on 6 March. He'd been in Norway since 10 December 1944 but had been a prisoner of the 4th company for much longer. He gave war crimes investigators a picture of what life had been like in the camp.

Captain Kluge was the camp commandant. Oberfeldwebel Teubel was a member of the Nazi party, and head of the Russian POW section. Feldwebel (later Oberfeldwebel) Butzki, nicknamed 'The Pope', was the leader of some of the working parties up in the mountains. Feldwebel Backenstos was a work leader responsible for removing snow and getting wood out of the mountains. His nickname was 'Krivonogi', meaning 'ape' or 'monkey'. Kurz was another work leader. Staffgefreiter Schmidt was a guard commander and a POW foreman. Unterofficer Staib had the nickname 'Sacrementi'. Oberfeld Pfarrow had the nickname 'Rat Hyena.' Kratchewski saw Kurz give the order to shoot a POW who couldn't lift a bundle of wood. The POW – Alexij Pochvalon – was shot in the head at close range. One guard named 'Sok-Sok', who he believes to be Unterofficer Mabitz, commanded a group of ten POWs who dug grave number 1. He gave the order to shoot the prisoner Iwan Tabunstshak, who was shot in the head and whose brain was eaten by another prisoner.

Kratchewski said that until 17 April the camp had not been too bad. He'd been given injections in the arm of clear liquid and in the chest of white liquid, like milk. Other men given injections had been dead by the following morning. Unterofficer Kubiska who 'had not been too bad' said the big grave was for all of them. He was witness to the cannibalism when prisoners cut flesh from the leg of one dead man. Traces were found in the mess tins of three men. They were shot on the spot. He and five other POWs buried them in grave number 1. One of the dead men was Stephen Dyrkatsch. Teubel and Backenstos led the search for the men who ate the flesh.

Witness 22: Victor Murashenko arrived in April 1945 with fifty other men. His duties were around the kitchen. He was interviewed with two other POWs as together they remembered the Germans. Captain Kluge was nicknamed 'Kasol'. He stared fiercely at the men and wore an Iron Cross. Teubel was commandant of the Russian part of the camp and was nicknamed 'Bobik'. They had all seen him kill Russians. Steib they called 'Sacrementa'. They knew Backenstos too, the one who looked like a monkey. He was a feldwebel. They had heard that he'd killed several times but had never seen him do it. When the investigator mentioned an Unterofficer 'Alfred' Gebauer they said his nickname was 'Damotschka' because of his feminine looks. They claimed he used an eyebrow pencil. He issued tools, picks, shovels and axes, and beat the men when they didn't stand up straight. The cook was Mikolajczyk (Nikolaitschik) and was nicknamed 'Koch' ('Cook'); he beat the men when they stood in line for food. 'Sok-Sok' they knew was a work leader with five groups of ten men under him. They suspected he was a killer but had never seen him do it. They thought his name was Serisch or Berasch.

Witness 14: Iwan Korolew, b. 1911. Went to Mallnitz 6 March 1945 with 130 other POWs. Most of the POWs in better condition were sent away to other camps. This POW ate the leather shoes of dead prisoners, once on 28 April and again on 3 May. He also said he ate human flesh, part of a leg and fish bones taken from garbage cans. Mentioned most of guards above, but also one nicknamed 'Molotschik' or 'good fellow' because he would pat prisoners on the back then strike them. Korolew said, 'He was always mean to the POWs and beat them on many occasions.' One Gefreiter was nicknamed 'Boxer'. There was one called 'Subnoiwatsch' ('the Dentist') because he would hit everyone in the mouth. There was a Gefreiter nicknamed 'Memstskaja Oftscharka'

('Dachshund') because he beat the prisoners then yelled very loudly at them. Another German was called 'Prokuror' because of the vicious stares he would give the prisoners, trying to scare them.

Witness 7: Sergei Kusmin. Was captured 23 July 1941, moved to Norway in autumn 1944. Arrived 17 April 1945 sick and hungry but worked to avoid being killed. Prisoners who didn't or couldn't work were killed. He talked of food: no breakfast, dried pea soup at 12 noon, one loaf of bread between 15 men, 8g of margarine or jam for each man at 9pm. He shared a barracks with thirteen men sleeping in two tiers with a stove inside. He had plenty of blankets because so many had died leaving them behind. He saw Sok-Sok killing a prisoner with a pistol. Another one was killed with a rifle by a cross-eyed soldier with a red moustache.

Witness 5: Iwan Ducpanin: arrived at Mallnitz on 25 April 1945 with fifty others. Stated that he heard Kluge give orders to Kurz to shoot POWs who couldn't work. He reported that a POW who was the camp tailor was too sick to work: Kluge responded with the statement: 'Kaput – schiessen'. The prisoner was then shot.

Witness 6: Michael Seredenko: arrived 21 April 1945. Sixty-eight men slept in his barracks on beds made from wire netting stretched between poles. There were no mattresses. He was given warm water for breakfast alongside the usual rations: watery soup, small pieces of bread with meat or jam. He said guard Sok-Sok shot two POWs too sick to work on the mountain on the orders of Captain Kluge.

At the end of the thirty witness statements, the pathologist's report sums up the final moments of some of these unfortunate men.

Grave number 1: 104 bodies were found, 96 in one site and 8 in a smaller section. Of them 79 died non-violently, from exanthematic fever [typhus], pneumonia or TB; 17 died violently, including 13 who were shot – 11 by one bullet, usually to the neck, temple or chest. One man, who was found to have human flesh in his stomach, had his cap pulled down over his eyes, suggesting he had been executed. And 4 men were beaten to death, probably with the butt of a rifle.

Of the 8 men in the second part of grave 1, only one had died non-violently, of starvation and 6 others were killed by shooting, 3 with one shot, and 3 with two or more shots. The seventh death was due to blunt violence against the cranium.

Grave 2: 12 bodies, all presenting signs of starvation. Only one died non-violently, the other 11 had been shot, mostly at close range in the head, neck or chest. In one case the bullet passed through the man's hand before hitting him in the head, suggesting he was trying to protect himself when he was shot. In the 3 other cases one was bayoneted, another was hit with a powerful blow and then choked, while the third was strangled.

Grave 3: Only 2 dead. One was shot twice, once through the chest, the second time through the neck, as in a coup de grace. He had his cap reversed and pulled down over his eyes. The pathologist writes: 'The situation indicated even more pointedly at an execution than the corresponding case in grave one.' The second man had been shot even though he was even more starved than the first man, and was probably killed with a shot from a rifle. He was partly in the grave.

Grave 4: 25 dead, apparently pressed together and entangled in the grave, suggesting they were all thrown in at the same time. They were doused in petrol and set alight. All were shot, at close range, mostly in the neck. The injuries to some indicate they were probably trying to escape. Some had straps or pieces of wire around the neck suggesting they had been dragged to the grave. The pathologist suggests that perhaps these men were all killed at the same time.[18]

British war crimes investigators issued a list of German soldiers, officers, NCOs and ordinary ranks accused of murder in connection with these crimes. Kluge, Teubel, Berisch, Kurtz, Nikolaitschik, Alfred, Steib and Backenstosz are on the list.[19]

There was little respite for those prisoners who survived Mallnitz. Sickness and malnutrition were so advanced that even when liberated the prisoners were so ill they died. Of 550 sick prisoners sent to the German field hospital at Overgard at the war's end, 97 died. Another 200 ex-prisoners from the Storfjord region also died in other German field hospitals while waiting for proper medical help to arrive.[20]

Prisoners at Mallnitz were also given injections – sometimes one, sometimes a series – by German medical staff wearing armbands with red crosses on them, sometimes of a dark-brown liquid, sometimes white, sometimes clear. Prisoners reported feeling unwell afterwards: in a significant number of cases, they died. In one period, 1–5 May 1945, twenty prisoners were given injections: eighteen were dead by the next morning. It's not clear what they were given or why. In the Porsangerfjord region, Roger Albrigtsen has examined the captivity cards of prisoners at Billefjord and found 'poisoning' given as a cause of death in an unusually high number of cases, including several deaths on the same day.

Michael Stokke of the Narvik Centre believes the injections at Mallnitz were of camphor oil, which was widely used as a medicine until the 1950s, but which were administered by inexperienced medical assistants unaware that large doses of camphor oil led to poisoning and death.[21] He believes the poisoning at Billefjord is due to prisoners drinking methanol, and discounts the possibility that the injections were part of Nazi medical experiments on prisoners similar to those being carried out at concentration camps elsewhere in Europe around this time.[22]

In his office just a short distance from this valley of death, Mayor Steinnes reflects on this dark history, of which he is a guardian. The true picture of what

happened here has only emerged recently, he says. After the war people wanted
to forget the horror and get on with their lives. The Cold War made Russia the
enemy and the valleys around Skibotn once again became the front line. This
time NATO soldiers rather than Germans were staring down the barrels of the
guns facing towards the Russian border, often in the same positions as their Nazi
predecessors.

'I stopped the Norwegian Defence Ministry clearing everything from here
[when the Cold War ended],' he says:

> We're going to look at every site and camp in the area and we will decide what
> to do with it. We must preserve the camps and some of the bunkers the Russian
> prisoners built in the mountains.
>
> It was terrible for the prisoners here in Storfjord, especially at the death
> camp. They were sent there to die. There was no food for them, nearly nothing
> to eat. But cannibalism? I cannot accept it, but I can understand it. I have asked
> the Norwegian War Department not to destroy anything more here. We cannot
> allow everything to be cleared.

He jabs at the map with the end of his pen:

> It was the Austrians from the *Gebirgsjäger* who did this, the ones with the
> edelweiss [the mountain flower insignia] on their uniforms. They don't have
> empathy for their fellow humans. I don't understand how they could do this.
> What happened here in Storfjord is nearly the same as in Auschwitz.

I suggest that it takes some courage to compare what happened in your own
town to Auschwitz.

> It was a death camp. It wasn't as big, but it's the same history. I've been looking
> at this since I became mayor two years ago. We must consider what we want to
> preserve and the rest can go, but we must do it now, because nature is taking it
> back and then it will be gone for good.
>
> The Mallnitz death camp is a big part of our history. You have Mallnitz camp
> here, Kitsbühel here. They all had the name of German cities. [These areas of the
> Austrian Tyrol were part of Germany following the 1938 annexation by Hitler.]

'Do you ever get letters from Germans or Austrians, getting in touch to say
they're sorry?' I ask.

'No,' he replies. 'No, no, no.' He looks at me, almost shrugging his shoulders in
resignation. 'Nowadays we have good relations with Germany, no problem with
that, but the history is not good. We must not forget it.'

I wonder if the rapid switch of allegiances in the immediate post-war period caused the obscenities against humanity committed in the Skibotn valley to be forgotten. Worse, the people against whom these crimes were committed were Russian, and in the Cold War they were the new enemy. Even more perversely, the people who committed these crimes became Norway's new partners, so even more reason for letting this whole chapter slip from memory because everyone was too busy getting ready for the next war.

Two years after Norway joined NATO all the Soviet dead were exhumed and moved to one grave on a remote island, thus removing them from everyday memory; (see Operation Asphalt in Chapter 19.)

Mayor Steinnes laughs and sips his coffee:

This valley was a secret area in the Cold War. The Norwegian government built many installations here and everything was restricted. You couldn't just come in here. There were defences here – it was a secret military area. Until one or two years ago everything around here was top secret. Nobody knew what was in the mountains. Perhaps that's the reason the war history hasn't been remembered. In Skibotn valley in the 1990s you couldn't take a photo because of military restrictions – but now I have the map so there's no problem now.

He laughs again at what fate has dropped into his lap:

I'm glad that time is over but we must tell the next generation what we are sitting on. The history books don't have much about what happened in the north of Norway. There's plenty about Oslo and Bergen but nearly nothing from the north. We have a big history here but it's not in the Norwegian history books.

He pulls a file of papers from his briefcase. 'Here I have a map of the region. It was top secret two years ago but now I have it.' He spreads it out on the table. 'Here are Norwegian military installations from the Cold War. Listening positions, guns – all around, throughout the mountains. Everywhere. This was the front line of the Cold War. Here we stopped the Russians. That was the plan.'

It's amazing. These are military maps, stamped 'Top Secret'. No wonder I've not seen an accurate marking of the German Lyngen Line yet.

He laughs again. Clearly becoming mayor has been something of a journey of enlightenment for him. 'That bunker here and that bunker there, we are taking care of. It's our heritage – now it's protected.' He walks over to a map on the wall:

From here, to the fjord through the mountains to here in the Norddalen are the German Lyngen Line bunkers. Around Halordalvartnet and Skankemyra the bunkers are nearly intact. In the mountains here we have many German bunkers. After the war the Norwegian government built bunkers in the same places, round by the lakes: Govdajavri, Siktagura, Laukajavri.

'So the German defences against the Russians from the Second War were replaced by Norwegian defences against the Russians in the Cold War?' I ask. He chuckles:

> Yes, they were nearly the same. They say that after the war there was a German engineer helping the Norwegians build the defences against the Russians. They expected the Russians to come here and here, and this was our line to stop them, the same as Germans built. That's why you never saw a map of the Lyngen Line. Because it was secret.

We walk back to the table and sit down again. Death camps, top-secret military areas – how could all this be brushed under the carpet?

'I'm not an expert on history but this is our history,' says Mayor Steinnes:

> Yes, it's a dark history, but we must take care of it. We can use it in schools, we can use it in tourism but we must take care of it. We already have a big cycle race here round the valley and into the mountains. Maybe we will make a cycle route [around the bunkers in the mountains] with information boards along the way and a mobile app. telling of the history.
>
> After the war people wanted everything to go away but it gets more important every year that we do something about preserving this. We must have a museum here and rebuild the installations so people can visit, from France and England maybe, and you can tour the valley and perhaps stay in a cabin.
>
> Now we'll have everything out in the open and we'll work with our history. We'll gather the stories from the people who live round here and we'll tell the history from the Second World War. And we hope the Norwegian government will give us some money so we can use it in the project.

'Do people support you?' I ask.

> Yes, I feel that the people in Storfjord want to protect this history, I don't get any negative signals at all. Both young and old want it. The older people remember the war and they say: 'We must not forget.' But we must do it now before it's gone for good.

I read him the rations the prisoners at Kitdalen had. I still can't really believe it. 'Breakfast: hot water. Lunch: soup, which was flour stirred into water. Evening meal: 100g of bread, 800g of canned meat or 500g of margarine – shared between four or five men?'

Mayor Steinnes sighs and shakes his head:

You can't live on that. There's no chance to live on that. So it was a death camp.
Maybe you can work a little before you die.

    I don't understand it. It's not possible, but it was possible. They had a leader
– many leaders – so the German soldiers are following orders. But that's not an
excuse. You cannot do that to people.

He is genuine about his desire to preserve this unpleasant episode of man's capa-
bility to mistreat his fellow human beings. What happened in Storfjord is not on
the same scale as the industrialised murder camps of Belsen and Auschwitz, and
these were not camps for the extermination of Jews. But this is still a place of
unspeakable inhumanity. Mayor Steinnes believes Storfjord must face up to the
unpleasant facts about what happened here so others can learn:

    I feel it very deeply and I hope Storfjord means we can understand better how
    people could do this. Perhaps history will make us better people. It's a lesson to
    other people. This is real history – it's not plastic. And I think the tourists of the
    future want real history. We have to learn from this, and the world needs to learn
    from this. What happened in Yugoslavia in the 1990s – it's nearly the same. Do
    we ever learn? I hope we can. It's a hell of a job but it's an important job. We
    shall see if I can do it.[23]

With that we walk outside to take a picture of Mayor Steinnes against the mountains whose dark secrets he will try and expose. We shake hands and I climb into
my hire car again, turning right and taking the road for Kitdalen.

    The Mallnitz death camp was at the extreme end of the Nazi policy of using
prisoners, criminals and political opponents as forced labour. Since the occupation
of Norway in 1940, prisoners had been used to carry out building programmes
on a colossal scale, including a series of fortifications stretching along the west
coast called 'The Atlantic Wall'.

    A total of 100,000 Soviet prisoners were sent to Norway, of whom about
13,700 died, many in shameful conditions. More Soviet prisoners died than all
Norwegian war casualties put together.

    The Russian POWs were among the hundreds of thousands captured during
the German invasion of the Soviet Union in 1941. Ironically, the prisoners sent to
Norway were the lucky ones: often prisoners on both sides were executed on the
battlefield as the Eastern Front became a war of annihilation.

    The Germans had a network of 500 POW camps across Norway. In northern
Norway alone there were vast prison camps near Alta, Narvik and Kirkenes,

each holding 5,000 prisoners. North of Narvik and Bodø there were 23 camps housing between 500 and 5,000 prisoners. Narvik Centre figures estimate 110 camps in Finnmark, 75 camps in Troms and 120 camps in neighbouring Nordland county.[24]

Soviet prisoners were organised in work battalions from where they were used as slave labour for the air force, navy or the construction firm Organisation Todt.[25] They were housed in barracks which offered little protection from wind, rain and the winter's freezing temperatures. These conditions made it virtually impossible to rest and recover from a long day's strenuous labour. The constant humidity in the buildings created the ideal conditions for illnesses such as tuberculosis and pneumonia, which at the time were two of the most common causes of death.[26]

The only road through the north – Main Road 50 – was prone to winter closures because of drift snow, so a wooden snow tunnel was built to keep it open all year round. Main Road 50 was improved and completed all the way to Kirkenes. Railways, submarine bases and thousands of garrison blocks were built. Narvik harbour, through which vital iron ore from Sweden was shipped to arms firms back in the Reich, was deepened and improved. Airfields were constructed, as were enormously powerful coastal batteries capable of firing shells at enemy ships from 30km away. Some of these batteries remain.

Batterie Dietl was built on the extreme north-western tip of Norway on an island called Engeloya. Its guns – three so-called 'Adolf Cannons' named after Hitler – could fire a 40.6cm calibre shell all the way across the Vestfjord to the Lofoten Islands. This battery was capable of handling any naval approach or attack on Narvik but there was a terrible human cost in its construction. The manual labour was done by 2,000 Russian prisoners of war, of whom more than 500 died in the quarry hacking out the stone to build the battery fortifications and the quarters for the 5,000 to 7,000 German troops stationed in this remote place. Camp discipline at Engeloya was very strict, with even minor infringements of the rules punished with ten, twenty-five or even fifty lashes of the whip. Attempts to escape carried an automatic 50 lashes and worse. Camp survivor Viktor Petrasjevskyj said of it: 'Death ruled everywhere.' The irony is that the guns of Batterie Dietl were never actually fired in anger.[27]

Among Hitler's dream projects for Norway was a four-lane autobahn running from Berlin via Oslo to Trondheim with a new mega-city for 250,000 Germans and a major naval base at the Norwegian end of it. The Führer promised that he would 'never again leave Norway'.[28] Another was a railway running the length of northern Norway, an immense 1,200km project known as the 'Polarbanen' connecting Mosjøen to Mo i Rana and Fauske, then leading on to Bardufoss, Kvesmenes, Kautokeino, Karasjok and finally Kirkenes.[29]

The Trondheim super-city and autobahn never got off the ground, but the Wehrmacht adopted existing Norwegian plans for expanding the railway.

Work began north of Mo i Rana in 1943 involving 30,000 mostly Soviet and Yugoslav prisoners to incorporate an old mine railway into the line over the mountain at Saltfjellet, but progress was slow and the work was poor quality.

At one point the commander-in-chief of the German occupation forces in Norway, General Falkenhorst, demanded 145,000 POWs to get the job done. The line didn't get further than Dunderland by the war's end and didn't reach Fauske until 1958 and Bodø in 1962.[30]

To reduce German reliance on ferries and allow year-round movement of troops and supplies the roads were improved on the western coast of Norway, again with significant loss of lives among the prisoners. The construction of Highway 50 north (now the E6) over Korgfjellet at Helgeland was built by Serbian, Bosnian and Croat prisoners of war, of whom 618 died working on this stretch alone. The prisoners were kept in conditions of absolute misery, worked without pity and subjected to terrible ill treatment. The 'Blood Road' between Rognan and Langset to the south of Fauske is said to have got its name from one prisoner's chilling tribute to a lost friend – a cross daubed on the side of the mountain in his blood. The cross is now regularly repainted as a reminder of what happened here and there is a stone memorial cross to the Yugoslav prisoners who died close to a bridge over the Saltdal river.[31] Also 5km east of Rognan, in Botn war cemetery, 1,657 of the 2,368 Yugoslav prisoners who died in Norway are buried.[32] A Nuremberg war crimes trial in 1946 heard evidence from the Soviet Union's deputy chief prosecutor Colonel Yuri Pokrovsky about conditions inside the Yugoslav POW camp at Botn, which was established in 1942:

> Nearly 1,000 Yugoslav prisoners of war were brought into this camp; and in the course of a few months all of them, to the last man, died of illness, hunger, physical torture, or execution by shooting. They were forced every day to do the very hardest work on a road and some dams. Their working hours lasted from dawn until 1800 hours, under the worst possible climatic conditions in this far northern part of Norway. During their work the prisoners were beaten incessantly and in the camp itself were exposed to terrible ill-treatment.
>
> In August 1942 the prisoners were ordered by the German staff of the camp to have all their hair removed from their armpits and around their genitals, as otherwise they would be shot. Not one prisoner received a razor from the Germans, though the Germans knew well that they had none. The prisoners spent the whole of the night plucking out their hair with their hands and assisting one another. However, in the morning the guards killed four prisoners and wounded three by rifle fire.
>
> On 26 November 1942 German soldiers, in the middle of the night, broke into the hospital and dragged out into the courtyard 80 sick prisoners; after they had been forced to strip in the bitter cold, they were all shot.

On 26 January 1943, 50 more prisoners died in torment from the beatings received. Throughout the winter many prisoners were killed in the following manner: They would be buried up to their waist in the snow, and water poured over them, so that they formed statues of ice. It was established that 374 Yugoslav prisoners of war were killed in the above-mentioned camp in various ways.

On 22 June 1942 a transport containing 900 Yugoslav prisoners arrived in Norway. Most of them were intellectuals, workers and peasants, and prisoners from the ranks of the former Yugoslav army or else captured partisans or men seized as so-called 'politically suspicious elements'. Some of them – about 400 – were placed in the still unfinished camp at Korgen, while the other group of about 400 was sent 10 to 20 kilometres further on to Osen. The commandant of both camps, from June 1942 until the end of March 1943, was the SS Sturmbannfuehrer Dolps ...

Men were constantly dying of hunger. Forty-five were placed in a hut which normally accommodated six men only ... There was no medicine ... They worked under most difficult conditions on road building, in the bitter cold, without clothing and caps, in the wind and rain, 12 hours a day.

The prisoners in the camp at Osen used to sleep in their shirts without any underpants, without any cover whatsoever, on the bare boards. Dolps personally visited the huts and carried out inspections. The prisoners who were caught sleeping in their underpants were killed on the spot by Dolps with his sub-machine gun. In the same manner he killed all those who appeared on parade, which he reviewed personally, in soiled underwear ...[33]

Of the 400 Yugoslav prisoners held at Korgen, 205 died. Nine months after 500 prisoners were taken to another camp at Osen at the end of June 1942, only 30 were left alive.[34] Some 60 per cent of the 4,268 Yugoslav prisoners shipped to Norway as forced labourers for Organisation Todt's *Einsatzgruppe Wiking* in a ten-month period between June 1942 and April 1943 died. Most were Serbian, some as young as 13 or 14. Forced to work on construction projects without machinery, they had to do everything by hand, sometimes in temperatures down to -20°C or -30°C.

One 19-year-old prisoner recalled conditions in the camps:

We were only served enough food so that we would remember where we came from ... It was ordered that we, from morning to our bed time in the evening had to be half naked ... We woke up at five in the morning, and were not allowed to go back to our rooms before eight o'clock in the evening. This torture grew more dangerous for each day. Even when the sun did shine, it did not warm our bodies up.[35]

At the war's end there were 84,000 Soviet POWs and forced labourers (called *Ostarbeiter*, or Eastern workers) in Norway. There were 75,000 in 400 work camps on Norway's west coast alone. Most were soldiers from the Red Army, while around 7,500 were civilians, including around 1,400 women and 400 children.[36]

At the liberation many of the prisoners were extremely sick and in need of urgent medical attention. Relief organisers called in the Norwegian-American USAF air transport chief Bernt Balchen, whose team of pilots had been ferrying emergency food, medical and humanitarian supplies into Finnmark since November 1944. Seven planes were loaded with food, medicine and components for prefabricated houses made of wood. Outbreaks of sickness such as dysentery broke out and a humanitarian disaster seemed close.

The Germans were ordered to feed the prisoners from their own rations but things did not improve immediately. In one camp of 2,000 prisoners, 6 died during the night from overeating, unused to being fed properly.

Balchen sent a report about this to Allied control. With 80,000 Russian prisoners needing to be kept alive and eventually sent home, a meeting was sought with the commander of the Soviet Arctic army, Colonel General Shcherbakov. His reply seemed to sum up the Soviet attitude to its manpower:

> We have a policy that all Russian voluntary and deported workers on a prisoner of war status are not wanted back in Russia before we have considered this more completely. Furthermore the prisoner of war policy is this: a Russian soldier is not allowed to be taken prisoner, therefore he will only face court martial and a long prison term when he is returned to his homeland. I am not interested in them. They have served their purpose as far as I am concerned. You can do anything you want with them: we are not interested in them at all.

When Balchen questioned this, Shcherbakov spoke in German to reiterate his meaning: 'Sie sind verbraucht!' (They are used up, expended.')[37]

The Swedish Red Cross took over a German field hospital at Klungset, close to Fauske on the 'Blood Road', and within days 400 Soviet patients were being treated for severe tuberculosis and hunger oedema. The Swedish Red Cross also distributed food to prisoner camps.

Balchen gave a vivid description of one of the prisoner labour camps he visited, which is almost a perfect description of Stephen Bone's painting *Death Camp at Kitdal*:

> The men had been dumped there sometime in the spring of 1944 and told to make themselves homes. The only possible way they could get shelter was to dig into a clay bank with their hands. The front of the bank was pockmarked with holes from where the men had clawed their way into the clay to find some

shelter from the rain and sleet and wind of the Arctic. They had a few bits of wood to shore up the sides and roof, and where they needed protection they covered the entrances or roofs with turf. They had no heat, no way of cooking except with empty tin cans, and no sanitation facilities.

It must have been horrible in the summer, for anybody who has been in the north knows how punishing the mosquitos and flies can be. But in the fall, when it rained and sleeted, it must have been even worse. In a space ten by fifteen feet, at least twenty men would cram themselves, hoping to keep from freezing to death by mere physical contact. They were sick, suffering from scurvy and all sorts of filthy disease. At least 50 per cent of them died. We found their bodies, and even their skeletons, for if their own people did not bury them, the Germans let them lie where they fell. Helping to drive out the Germans who destroyed that area was worth all the dangerous flying we did.[38]

It's estimated that 2,000 prisoners escaped to Sweden, though escapees would have been seriously hampered by malnourishment, poor clothing and lack of shoes. It's likely that many would either have been caught, or died in the attempt. Norwegian newspapers carried warnings of the strict punishments for civilians helping POWs escape or for providing them with food on their march between camp and worksite. The Germans also paid well for information about escaped prisoners.[39]

The majority of the 83,000 Soviet survivors were sent home from May 1945 via Swedish ports on the Baltic, while those in the north travelled via Tromsø to Murmansk from June onwards, among them Ukranians, Georgians, Tatars, Byelorussians and other Soviet citizens. Some, however, evaded the repatriation process and stayed in Norway.

Other nationalities in the prison camps included: 10,000 Polish civilian forced labourers and 1,600 POWs; 5,000 to 6,000 Norwegian political prisoners; 3,800 Danish civilian volunteer workers; 1,400 French and 50 British POWs; 35 Dutch sailors; and 1,000 French, Dutch and Belgian civilians.[40]

Discovering what happened to the German and Austrian soldiers arrested in connection with war crimes in the Mallnitz camp is not easy, as many of the records are in Moscow. It's not certain that Sok-Sok, the Dentist, Rat Hyena, Boxer, Damotschka or the Dachsund ever faced justice.

The Narvik Centre says 264 Germans and Austrian soldiers were sent to the Soviet Union in January 1946 in connection with war crimes in Norway as a whole, both north and south; 36 for their activities in the Storfjord area. All were sent to gulags, and some returned in 1955.[41]

More than one Norwegian joked in conversation while I was gathering interviews for this book that they wished the war had gone on longer, as then they would have been able to get the train all the way to Kirkenes. But of course it was no laughing matter for the thousands who starved and died on those construction projects in the snow. Two prisoner memorial projects are working to ensure their suffering is not forgotten.

The Narvik Centre has grown from commemorating the Yugoslav POWs in 1949 with a small plaque to becoming a multimedia resource documenting this dark chapter of Norway's history. It's aim is to educate future generations and for scholars, human rights advocates and descendants of former POWs or their jailers to study the Second World War and 'make peace with the past'.

Michael Stokke, who runs the POW history section, will concentrate for the immediate future on the story of the Yugoslav prisoners but welcomes research help:

> Uncovering the true story of the POWs in northern Norway is an ongoing process and new information comes to light all the time. German prisoners for example were treated much worse than the Soviet prisoners. Death rates for the Yugoslav prisoners were as high as 60 per cent, while for the Soviets it was 13–14 per cent.
>
> At the Narvik Centre we are happy to share our information with anyone who wants to do research into the prison camp conditions. There is still much to do.[42]

The Falstad Centre, a memorial and human rights centre based in a notorious SS camp near Trondheim, is still seeking information on prisoners of war in Norway and, in a project named 'Painful Heritage', is aiming to give names to many of the 13,700 who died. Less than 3,000 have ever been identified.

Marianne Neerland Soleim has researched the story of the Soviet POWs extensively for the Falstad Centre and says the contribution their labour made to the modernisation of Norway should be recognised:

> The long rows of starving and emaciated POWs, staggering off to hard manual labour, were an appalling sight. The prisoners were regarded as work animals who could only expect fair and humane treatment if they followed German orders. The need for Soviet labour in Norway was closely connected to the German view that Norway was of strategic importance in the war. The efforts of the POWs contributed greatly to the development of the Norwegian infrastructure and thus in the long term helped to modernise Norway.[43]

With this catalogue of misery in mind I took the road for Kitdalen. As I drove slowly down the valley I imagined the columns of haggard, emaciated prisoners tottering along this same road seventy years ago. They would be great-grandparents now, had they lived.

The road curved to the right and then left between two mountains whose blunt peaks rose dramatically from the valley floor. There were trees growing in the valley but they looked like they had grown back, rather than being ancient and untouched. The fields alongside the road were clearly used for farming and livestock. I could see beyond one farm a track leading up into a neighbouring valley pass, but there was no road for a car. Further progress would have to be on foot, and today was not the day.

The drizzle turned to rain as I turned round in the driveway of one farm. A large white refuse van pulled up outside a farmhouse a little further along the road and a workman jumped out and fastened a wheelie bin to the back of it. A black and white dog began to bark at the both of us.

Although everything appeared to be a picture of normality, the truth was that this road had been a road to hell. When Mayor Steinnes had pointed out the death camps on the map to me, he had said, 'They are still there, but nature is taking them over'. I wondered if he had felt the weight of history when the secret plans of the Lyngen Line fell into his hands. Before that, only the farmers and the generals knew where these camps were.

Mayor Steinnes is right. The world should know about these despicable episodes.

14

WALKING IN THE FOOTSTEPS OF THE DOOMED: THE LYNGEN LINE

At just after 1.30pm Pål Fredriksen's battered blue car turned into the Statoil petrol station in Skibotn. In convoy we drove a short distance further south and pulled in at a parking place on the left. I had stopped here to eat a sandwich on the way up to Djupvik the day before. This was the 'Russian Road' – so called after the Soviet prisoners who died building a transport road up the mountain for materials to build the Lyngen Line bunkers. The road also goes by the name of 'Bollmannsveien' after the engineer in charge, Bollmann.

The rain clouds had cleared and it was a sunny day with blue skies now. Even so I pulled on a fleece and waterproof jacket. Pål had warned me that the mountains made the weather very changeable. He pointed to a path up a slope by the side of the road, overgrown on both sides by trees and bushes.

'That's the Russian Road,' he said. 'It takes about two hours to get to the top, then there's a bunker like the ones in the war. If you like we can try and reach it.'

'Sure,' I said. 'Let's give it a try.'

In walking trousers and army boots with a forage cap, all-weather fleece, waterproof jacket and handy-looking rucksack, Pål looked ready for anything. We began walking up the slope, Pål picking berries from the bushes as we skipped through puddles and teetered along planks laid across flooded paths beside waterfalls cascading down the mountainside.

The path rose at an angle of about 30 degrees from the road and was wide enough to fit a van or truck along. Along the way information boards related the wartime history here and marked significant places on the route to the top.

There was plenty of history to tell. The Germans occupied Storfjord from the 1940 invasion but only really began construction in this region in 1943–44, setting up camps in Skibotn, the nearest big town; in Kitdalen and Signaldalen, which later became the death camps; on Brennfjell overlooking this valley; and also high on the Fals mountain, which Pål and I were now climbing. The valleys were heavily guarded by troops and the road through the Skibotn valley across the border to Kilpisarvi was improved to get supplies to German forces in Finland.

Huge barracks were built close to one another on farmland with stables made from brushwood and temporary camps alongside. A water tower was built to supply the camps but was sabotaged during construction: nothing ever came out of it. Skibotn Kommune (the local council) has kept the tower as a war memorial.

Here at the Bollmannsveien the information boards relate stories of prisoners being worked until they were too weak to work anymore, then being shot where they fell and dumped in mass graves. These graves were said to be by the side of the road and sometimes actually in the road as it was being constructed. At each new section I wonder if I am walking on the bones of unfortunate men who never made it back down the mountain.

We have been climbing steadily for some time before the road switches back on itself. At the bend is what looks like a destroyed gun position, made of dark-grey slate tiles stacked like sandbags. After another switchback, the road flattens out into a plateau. There are more concentrations of slate tiles here, arranged in piles which could have been bunkers but which have been clearly been shattered and then collapsed. There is a rusty old metal wheelbarrow with a hole in it next to an information board. This flat area looks like a work camp or staging post up or down the mountain for prisoners, mules and horses carrying timber, construction materials, guns and ammunition: perhaps higher up the mountain things would have to be hauled by hand. We pause to look down the steep incline we have climbed which, stripped of vegetation and saplings, would give clear sight of any soldiers trying to attack.

To this point the gun positions have been at each switchback, but at this plateau there were bunkers every few metres. With large numbers of troops on hand the defensive fire from here would have been highly concentrated. We press on to the edge of the mountain where we get an unobstructed view across the fjord. The weather is changing rapidly and, even though it's cloudy and misty now, the views are remarkable. From here I can see everything moving on the road on the other side of the fjord. At night a light could be spotted a long way away. From over there to the left Jan Baalsrud made his way across the fjord and through the valley below us, up the side and across the border to Sweden. He couldn't have crossed the fjord during the day – everyone for several kilometres around would have seen the boat. From this gun position he could have had shells raining down on him in minutes.

There was a significant Resistance presence in Skibotn, despite the area being a military base and bustling with construction activity. Agents heading for Sweden needed guides to keep them out of the way of the Germans, and local Resistance sympathisers would oblige, sometimes bringing back post from Norwegians exiled in Sweden. A lengthy spell in jail or perhaps worse awaited those who were caught engaging in illegal activities. Many people were tipped off about impending arrests so they could escape. When an intelligence base on the Swedish side of the border called Sepals 1 began operating in 1944, it was mostly men from the valleys around Storfjord guiding the missions. Sabotage operations were run from here which sometimes included blasting important installations involved in the building of the Lyngen Line. All the operations were carried out at night, in bad weather or during snowstorms, and none of the saboteurs were caught.[1]

We stop at more information boards showing the spread of the 550 bunkers of the Lyngen Line, dotted across this mountain and the surrounding hills and into the valley between the Lyngenfjord and the border with Sweden.

The scale of the project is incredible. These mountains reach 1,200m and are capped with snow at their peaks, with relatively steep gradients down to rocky, lake-filled plateaus at about 1,000m. There are steep drops to the valley floor. The bunkers were made from laminated girders covered with planks and half-split logs covered with stones, like a form of camouflaged, reinforced living space high up the hill. Wooden bridges crossed inaccessible areas between observation positions, bunkers and guns.

The Lyngen Line was manned by 14,500 Austrian mountain troops of the 6 Gebirgsdivision, split into two regiments, the 141st and 143rd, with artillery regiments and air defence batteries, anti-tank cannons and regular support troops such as engineers and communication and transport specialists.

Observation posts were set up throughout the mountains from 500m above sea level to 1,200m, giving mostly unobstructed views of the main roads leading to and through the valleys and along the fjords. Artillery spotters would have had an easy job.

Each regiment was split into four battalions deployed in a variety of mountainous or valley positions. The second battalion of the 143rd manned the front across the border at Kilpisjarvi in Finland. The first battalion defended the valley behind them leading west to Skibotn. The third battalion blocked the main road south along the fjord by the Fals mountain, the road Pål and I travelled down from Storslett to get here.

The third battalion of the 141st Regiment was deployed along the Kitdalen, Midterdalen and Norddalen valleys, in effect the valleys we were looking at now from our vantage point. The second battalion was in the adjacent Signaldalen. More third battalion troops were in the bunkers along the top of the Fals mountain by Gavdajarvi ahead of us, with the 118th Artilleriregiment Battalion along the west side of Storfjord.[2]

Prisoners were held in camps on the mountain to supply ammunition to the guns, with large amounts of blocking materials like barbed wire ready to break out in an emergency, but minefields were not sown in the bunker regions in the mountains.[3]

The chief of Gebirgsdivision 6 was the vastly experienced Major General Max Pemsel, best known for his role opposing the Normandy landings in June 1944 which features in the film *The Longest Day*. He was sacked and posted back to the Arctic for failing to repel the Allied landings and stopping the American breakout later that month.[4]

Born in Bavaria, Pemsel served in the First World War at the Somme and across the Western Front. A career officer, he fought in Poland, France, Greece and at the Litsa Front in the Arctic North. He was a fearless commander mentioned in despatches in November 1944 for his fierce rearguard action against the Soviets during the Petsamo–Kirkenes offensive, single-handedly preventing his men being encircled and wiped out during the retreat.[5] In December 1944 he was awarded the Knight's Cross of the Iron Cross, among Nazi Germany's highest military honours, for defending against Russian attacks during the retreat from Finland.[6]

In April 1945 he was due to be posted back to take command of Berlin in the Reich's last days, but luckily for him his plane was delayed by bad weather and he was posted to Italy instead, where he surrendered to the Americans.[7]

Pemsel was one of the few senior Nazi commanders who later served in the peacetime West German army.

So these Germans – Austrians actually – knew what they were doing. They were vastly experienced mountain troops hardened in combat who had escaped capture or death on the Arctic Front, and who were now digging in for what they thought might be a final battle against their Red Army foes. Years of front-line conditions and combat stress would surely make a man aggressive, unpredictable and ruthless. Life would be cheap: the stories of Sok-Sok and the Dentist at Mallnitz were still fresh in my mind. Shooting Soviet prisoners would probably hardly register. They were, after all, the enemy.

We had been climbing again for some time and by now the going was getting tough for me. The views though were breathtaking. We paused at a rocky lip over the mountain's edge from where we could see right down almost to the fjord's entrance near Djupvik 30km down the coast as the crow flies; in 1944 we would certainly have been able to see the smoke and the boats full of evacuees coming from Birtavarre and Olderdalen, half that distance away.

Despite the low cloud ceiling, it was still possible to pick out individual houses way down the valley in Skibotn and along the main road to and from Finland, the E8. We scrambled higher still – or rather, I scrambled, while Pål hopped and jumped over the small streams flowing down from the summit.

We came to a flat area at the top of the mountain overlooking the whole of the fjord. Levelled and offering a perfect shot at any oncoming traffic, it could only have been a gun platform hewn from the rock. Just a short scramble away was what I had toiled for two hours to reach – the reconstructed bunker at the top of the mountain where the troops would have weathered the snowstorms and slept.

The bunker itself was quite a feat of engineering, even though it looked like a capsized boat under a pile of rocks. Access was through a door on one side. The other side was butted up to a large rocky outcrop, no doubt offering protection against bombs or rocket fire from attacking aircraft. Two wooden shutters each half a metre wide opened out from a glazed window. The hut's wooden frame appeared to be weatherproofed with tarpaulin and then covered with flat, stone blocks, giving it the appearance of a low profile makeshift pyramid fitting snugly alongside the mountain.

Pål unfastened the catch on the wooden door and swung it open. 'Shall we have a look inside?' he said.

We stepped into the cabin. Long timbers formed a whale jaw-shaped frame on a wooden-planked floor set on joists with planking for the walls and roof. There was a table by the window and room to cook, perhaps for a heater too, and space for maybe three reasonably sized men to sleep side by side. It was basic, but it was pretty good accommodation for the top of a mountain – and certainly better than the shelter offered to the luckless prisoners further down below.

We signed our names in the guest book and took photographs of each other at the top of the mountain. Pål produced some sticky buns, two chocolate bars and a bottle of orange juice from his rucksack and placed them on the table.

'Well, we did it,' he said. 'We're now about 800m up in the mountains. That's taken us two hours. What do you think?'

'It's amazing,' I said. 'It's like a fortified mountain. The effort to build this must have been incredible. And to do it all by hand? I'm really glad we did this.'

Pål looked pleased. 'Yes, it's quite an achievement, but very tragic. Lots of Russians died doing this.'

We enjoyed a rest while chatting about the last time he made the trip to the summit several years before. He told me that as a younger man he'd been in the army – these were his old army boots he was skipping around the mountain in – and that he was actually 67. I thought he was in his 50s, but looking closer when he took off his cap to wipe his brow he did seem older. It was me who was in my 50s; Pål, seventeen years older, had just shown me what a lifetime in the mountains really meant.

No wonder prisoners died, I thought, though I wasn't sure yet how many had actually perished here. The information boards made it sound like a lot but didn't give any figures.

Just climbing the mountain had required reasonable effort for a well-fed man in good weather in summer. Lugging a box of ammunition up these tracks in sub-zero temperatures, having not been fed properly for several years, sleeping in conditions worse than a cowshed and without proper footwear or clothing, watched over by sadistic guards who considered you subhuman – well, I wouldn't put my chances of survival very high.

There was one final story from the mountain: mutiny by the 118th Artilleriregiment at the very moment the war ended. When Austria declared itself a republic free of Germany on 27 April 1945, the new President Karl Renner made a broadcast in which he urged Austrian soldiers of the German armed forces to lay down their weapons and not to fight any more. Most of the troops in the Lyngen Line and in northern Norway were Austrians.

The broadcast was heard by the men of the 4th Battery of the 118th Artillery Regiment whose commanding officer Oberst Josef Remold ordered, '6th Mountain Division: do not obey this order, and do not capitulate. It is strictly forbidden to listen to the radio. The German salute is to be used! Oberst Remold. Heil Hitler!'

When the war ended on 8 May the battery greeted the news with relief. But in the afternoon came a telephone order instructing the men to ignore the surrender and keep fighting, as the Bolsheviks planned to fight on. Worried that in those circumstances they would be considered irregulars, the battery garrison NCOs planned a mutiny followed by an escape to the safety of neutral Sweden 17km away. The officers were to be overpowered, bound and gagged, but, when the mutiny began, a rogue NCO shot and killed both officers instead.

The unit split into two groups – one of forty-eight men, the other of eleven – making for the border with Sweden. The group of eleven were intercepted by German troops. A small number of the forty-eight turned back; the rest made it.

The captured men were court-martialled and sentenced to death. They were shot on 10 May 1945, two days after the war ended. The commander-in-chief, General Ferdinand Jodl, telephoned personally from his headquarters in Narvik to demand that the death sentences were carried out. 'The death penalty must be immediately enforced by shooting,' he ordered, 'because I refuse a pardon.'

Five of the defendants were given prison sentences of between six and ten years, two were acquitted. Rudolf Zatsch, 30, Josef Wenzl, 29, Leopold Wickenhauser, 29, and Helmut O'Neill, 28, were tied to stakes, blindfolded and executed at 10.16am on 10 May in northern Norway.[8]

Some 800m up the Fals mountain, looking down on the Norwegian fields the Nazis had turned into centres of inhumanity, the wind was starting to buffet us in strong gusts. It was 4pm and time to go. We took one final photograph and started back down the trail. As we did it started to rain, but the clusters of stacked tiles at various points now seemed to make more sense.

'This is definitely a bunker,' said Pål, peering into the disjointed mound of rocks. 'See – that is the frame. And all these rocks? After the war, the British – poom!' He made a gesture indicating that the bunkers were blown up by British demolition squads at the war's end.

Finally we reached the lower slopes. I was mentally congratulating myself on not having slipped on any of the rocks or on the planks across the streams when suddenly I lost my footing and tumbled over, hitting the ground momentarily but then regaining my balance. We both laughed.

'City shoes,' I said, wiping mud off my trousers. 'I thought it was too good to be true.'

When we reached the parking area below we stripped off our walking gear and said our goodbyes. Pål was heading back north to Storslett, where tomorrow he would continue teaching children about Norway's political system and also chair a debate about the forthcoming election. I was heading south, back to Tromsø, where I would continue my scorched-earth journey across Norway in a town that wasn't burned to the ground.

As I prepared to get into my car, Pål walked over with some hardback books. 'These are for you,' he said:

They are history books. They tell you all about this area: Skibotn, Nordreisa, Storslett. The Sami people, the reindeer, the fishermen. And war – lots of war. In the First World War this area was important for getting guns to the front in Finland. In the second war the same – and the Lyngen Line, of course. Then in the Cold War this was the front line again.

I was touched by Pål's generosity. The night before he had driven me deep into the Reisadalen, then he gave up his afternoon to climb the Fals mountain and show me the Lyngen Line. Now he was giving me a present of these beautiful books. I had nothing really to offer him in return apart from my appreciation. 'Thank you Pål,' I said. 'This has been really fascinating. It's been a real highlight of my trip. I'm glad I did it – and you made it possible.'

It would have been unthinkable for a passing Englishman to climb this mountain without a guide. Ever since I first heard about the Lyngen Line I had wondered exactly what those defences were like. Now I knew – bunkers dotted across snowy Alpine plateaus; gun positions clinging to rocky crags. Flushing crack mountain troops out of these positions would have been a nightmare. And now, having walked in the footsteps of the doomed, I had a better understanding of the misery those unfortunate Soviet soldiers endured.

The warmth and comfort of my hotel in Tromsø was less than ninety minutes away by car, and the only mishap over the past two days had been a muddy patch on my knee. I had seen the Lyngen Line and also reached the top of the mountain, but my satisfaction was tempered by the thought of all the men who, unlike me, did not come back down.

Later, the subject of the number of prisoners who died on the Bollmannsveien came up in correspondence with Michael Stokke, an expert on POW history at the Narvik Centre whose advice I had sought on events at the Mallnitz death camp (see Chapter 13). He wrote:

> The information boards on the Bollmannsveien say that a lot of prisoners died building that road but we cannot find evidence to support this.
>
> We have evidence of a mass grave of 30 men in a burial site south of Skibotn, on the way to Bollmannveien, which MAY be dead from the work site. This grave is mentioned in a British forces' report in September 1945. There were 39 POW dead at a burial site referred to as 'southern Quay', but it's not certain these were from Bollmannsveien. No POW graves were found up on the plateau, so any who died or were killed were all brought down and not buried in mass graves there. The total POW dead for the Skibotn area was 73.

But later he emailed me again:

> These were the figures from autumn 1945. Then in 1951 when the Norwegian authorities moved the bodies to Tjøtta, they found 80 dead at Skibotn, seven more than in 1945. There were also an unknown number of graves at Bentsjord that were presumably from the mountain. These dead are most likely to have been moved to Hatteng, to the large burial site there. But now the War Cemetery Service states that there were only 36 from Skibotn! So this is confusing.[9]

Whatever the true figure of dead on the Bollmannsveien, the appalling treatment, overwork and malnourishment of the Soviet prisoners is indisputable. Perhaps we will never know the true story of exactly what happened there.

15

A GUIDED TOUR THROUGH TROMSØ'S WAR

I parked my rented car at the hire firm and walked across Tromsø in the rain back to the comfort of the Radisson Blu by the harbour. These comfortable hotels were a world away from the stone bunker I'd eaten Pål's sticky buns in just four hours earlier. Those Austrians at the top of the mountain would have been the lucky ones, I thought. I was finding it difficult to imagine the misery of the Russian POWs in their huts made of earth; wet and weak, underfed, brutalised. I was certain I would have been a casualty early on.

Everyone was talking about 'the Germans' but in reality they were Austrian mountain troops, *Gebirgsjäger*, who'd been in Norway from Narvik 1940 through to the invasion of Russia, the years of stalemate on the Litsa Front and the retreat from Kirkenes and Finland to the Lyngen Line. It was Austrians in Nazi uniforms who were responsible for all this.

I looked at a map of Austria to see if I could find Mallnitz. No, it was too small. There was Vienna, Salzburg and the Berchtesgarden, Hitler's Alpine retreat. I switched to a bigger map. Mallnitz, Mallnitz – there it was! Smack in the middle of the Tyrol, on the floor of a valley between two mountains. A small, picturesque village in the Alps. Where the air was clear and the milk was fresh and the grass was no doubt very green. But men from that village had come to a similar setting in Norway and caused untold misery, suffering and death. How had Austria ducked the responsibility for this?

I looked to the north of Mallnitz. Perhaps that road north was the key to this. Only a matter of a few dozen kilometres led to Berchtesgarden and the cult of Hitler. Perhaps the troops who wore the edelweiss were considered ultra-loyalist keepers of the Nazi flame, like some Praetorian Guard to the Absolute Leader?

Whatever the reasons, these Austrians had certainly done a job on Finnmark. I'm sure their Führer would have been proud of their inhumanity.

Before I left for Norway I had contacted the Tromsø history society to ask if I might have a look around the Defence Museum one evening when I got into town. The chairman emailed me and gave me the number for a man called Gunnar Jaklin, who, I was told, would 'sort everything out'. This genial Mr Jaklin certainly did. I didn't realise at this point that it was Mr Jaklin, a former military officer, newspaper editor and journalist, who set the museum up and wrote all the information panels on its boards in several languages – as well as having been a member of the Norwegian 'police' at the end of the war and so able to give me vivid eye witness accounts of his experiences.

I called Mr Jaklin and he kindly agreed to collect me from my hotel. He drove me out to the museum over the skeleton bridge and along the coast for a few kilometres to an area called Tromsdalen. He pulled up outside what looked like an old barracks and unlocked the door.

'This is the museum,' he said. 'Please come in.'

Inside was an Aladdin's cave of war memorabilia. There were weapons and kit of all descriptions: knives, bayonets, submachine guns, shells, bullets, pistols, field guns, uniforms, water bottles, webbing, flags, code books, matchbooks. Mr Jaklin snapped on more lights and began to talk, so I quickly switched my tape recorder on.

'The Defence Museum has been open for about fifteen years,' he said:

A lot of the exhibits have been collected in the Tromsø area: all of it is from the time, some of it is very sought after by collectors. It's dedicated to what happened here in Tromsø during the war.

There was an organisation already set up in Tromsø to handle an evacuation from the north in case of Russian attack so they used that to deal with the Nazi evacuation. A reception committee was organised for 10,000 refugees to be registered on arrival in Tromsø and be given food and care. The committee arranged for them to be transported further south. At the peak of the evacuation there were 500 people in Tromsø working for the refugees. The evacuation office had a large fleet at hand for the journey from the north to Tromsø: there were up to 17 local boats running scheduled services and 290 requisitioned fishing boats. Before long 7 Hurtigrute coastal steamers, 12 freight vessels and 4 cargo vessels were made available for the transport south.

In autumn 1944 alone 29,400 evacuees came through Tromsø, nearly all by boat. The largest arrival in one day was 2,891. The Germans organised some transport on cargo ships but most came by fishing boats or small motorboats, in journeys of perhaps one or two days. The weather was extremely good; the sea was flat for months. That's never happened before.

Churches, schools, community centres and 240 rented flats were used to accommodate all the extra people. Some got seasick, but most arrived in good condition, except for those on the German cargo ships [the *Carl Arp* and *Adolf Binder*].

We move on, until we reach a model of what appears to be a camp. I ask him to explain.

'This is the prison camp my father was held in by the Gestapo,' he says:

It was called Sydspissen. The Germans took 120 well-known people in Tromsø, Harstad and Narvik as hostages when they attacked Russia and put them in the prison camp. My father [who was the editor of the newspaper *Nordlys*, or *Northern Lights*] was one of them. Both the editors of the papers in town were imprisoned, actually. The remaining prisoners and civilian workers had to make a new camp. It was a much bigger capacity – 2,500 prisoners passed through this camp between 1943 and 1945. Some were in for three months, some for six months. If they were sentenced to longer they were sent to Grini [the concentration camp in Oslo]. My father was in there one and a half years. He got some work when he was released, but in September 1944 the Gestapo started to arrest the same people who had been in prison before, so we decided to escape.

A Home Front [Resistance] group arranged for a car to get us out of town and a guide to take us across the border. We were told the guide would meet us at a church in a small village inland. We stole a boat, crossed a big river and cut the boat loose so they wouldn't trace us. We climbed a hill and slept out in the open air that night. It was completely dark and there was a German camp nearby. Because I spoke a little German I asked at the camp if they knew of a church in the area. A young lieutenant said he'd been patrolling down the valley and knew exactly: it was about 3km in that direction. Then he wished me good luck!

But there was no guide to meet us at the church in Målselv, so we walked from there to Sweden by ourselves, via Maukdal and across two lakes to cross the border there. The Lapps [Sami] near the border had an agreement with the Norwegian Embassy in Stockholm to take care of refugees and put them on a train to Kiruna. So we turned up at the police station in Kiruna and asked them to arrest us – which they did. We were in jail for three days, but conditions were good and we ate well.

In that jail there were people from fourteen different nations who had been forced by the Germans to work, mostly on the roads and airfields in northern Norway. There were even two Russians who had escaped from Alta and walked for two months living just on berries and roots. They had one loaf of bread with them. They were rather thin, but they were alive.

As we look around Mr Jaklin tells me that once the family reached the safety of Sweden he joined the ranks of the Norwegian 'police' training up for service because at 18 he was old enough. When he first picked me up in the car I would have put him at about 70, but if he served in the war and was 18 in 1944 he is clearly much older than that. My rough maths suggests he might be 87. We have reached a case with a small pocket-sized radio inside and some yellowing paper with fading type on it. Mr Jaklin taps the glass. 'A lot of visitors ask about the underground in Tromsø,' he says:

It wasn't on a very big scale because it was so visible and the city was so small. A lot of Gestapo officers spoke fluent Norwegian, dressed like Norwegians and mingled with Norwegians, listening all the time. They paid people – Norwegian informers – with money, tobacco and spirits to keep their ears open and report to the Germans. There were quite a lot of them.

There was an underground newspaper printed from a back yard in the city. This was produced by a man called Magne Jonsson from autumn 1943 onwards. There was a little radio called a 'Sweetheart' radio – this set here – which was smuggled into Norway. He sat late into the night listening to the BBC in Norwegian, writing it down and then making a newsletter which was copied using these old copying machines, and then it was spread among people who were reliable. It contained news from Europe, how the war was really going, what to do after the war ended and so on.

Magne Jonsson was his real name but he operated under a false Norwegian name, as 'Martin Jensen', with a fake permit as a carpenter which allowed him to enter the closed border area. He probably printed 150 copies twice a week from 1943 to 1945. But the people who got this newsletter in their postbox were told: 'Read it, remember it and tell good friends. But burn it.' It was very risky to have illegal newspapers. The Germans had strict punishments for people caught with them. This [tapping the glass cabinet again] is probably the only copy left. It's historic.

The Sweetheart radio was developed by the British Special Operations Executive (SOE) in 1943, designed by Norwegian electronics engineer Willy Simonsen. He had escaped to England the year before and began developing the radio using his knowledge and experience with Norwegian Resistance work. For the design of the Sweetheart, known as the 31/1, he was not allowed to use military grade components so he built it from everyday domestic components, such as a pocket-sized receiver with low power consumption that could work off standard household batteries. The receiver could fit in a pocket, the battery could be detached and low power crystal headphones were carried in a tobacco tin. Using these headphones – which had to be flown in from America – the batteries could last for 150 to 200 hours.[1]

Resistance units in the mountains tuned in to BBC broadcasts twice daily for coded messages at the end which carried their instructions, so the Sweetheart radio provided a vital communications link between fighters in the field and SOE HQ in London.

'When the Germans occupied Norway they made everybody hand their radios in,' says Mr Jaklin:

> But they didn't think it through, because of course many people had radios in their boats, so they carried on listening until the batteries ran out. After that they had to smuggle more batteries into Norway from Sweden. That's what Magne Jonsson brought back with him from Sweden as well.

Mr Jaklin smiles an enigmatic smile, waves a cigarette at me and excuses himself.

As he walked away I studied the information board intently: the Nazi penalty for listening to the radio or reading an illegal newspaper was death. More than 3,000 Norwegians were arrested for illegally distributing or issuing illegal newspapers, and, of the 212 who lost their lives, 62 were executed.

I look around and take some photographs while Mr Jaklin is outside having a smoke. The amount of information in this museum is overwhelming. Some of it is fascinating and full of tragic things I hadn't known. The Swedish border had not been open to all nationalities: German deserters trying to make it to the safety of a neutral country were turned back or handed over to German patrols – to almost certain death.

Mr Jaklin is now back at my side and keen to share more of his stories:

> When the Germans lost the Battle of Leningrad, 200,000 soldiers had to walk back to Tromsø through Finland and Norway. It took half a year to get them back through Finland because the Finns changed sides and started attacking them. The last boat with these troops arrived in Germany just a week before the German capitulation. But it saved their lives. The Germans lost 4,500 soldiers during the retreat, while the Finns lost 774 killed and 264 missing.

We stepped over to a double wardrobe in one corner of the museum. Mr Jaklin swung the door open; a rifle was slotted into clips on the inside, with a thick sheepskin coat hanging from a coat hanger. A German steel helmet fitted neatly into one compartment above, with shaving materials, boot polish and brushes and various military knick-knacks in other spaces.

'It looks as good as new,' I said. 'Amazing.'

Mr Jaklin smiled. 'Those sheepskin jackets are worth a fortune now,' he said. 'They are very warm.'

We moved on to a display showing pictures of a variety of wartime seaplanes. The Dornier Do 18 long-range flying boat had been used as a pre-war mail plane but proved too slow for wartime operations and was mostly used for air-sea rescue. There was the three-engined reconnaissance sea plane that replaced it; the Blohm and Voss Bv 138, known officially as 'Sea Dragon' but unofficially as 'the flying clog' because of its side view; and the twin-engined Heinkel 115 – looking like a Heinkel 111 'Flying Pencil' bomber fitted with floats.

Another was a vast seaplane like a German version of the Short Sunderland: the six-engined Blohm und Voss Bv 222 Wiking, which was both the largest plane and the largest seaplane to fly during the war.[2]

'There was a seaplane base in Tromsø called Skattora,' said Mr Jaklin:

> The Germans took it over and made it much bigger. It became the central seaplane base in the north and the largest in Europe. They used it for torpedo bombers, patrol planes and transport and rescue planes, and a squadron of fast rescue boats was based there too.

When the invasion came, the twelve Norwegian planes based at Skattora – including some of the six Heinkel 115s bought the year before from Germany – were used against the Nazi invasion forces until the capitulation, when they fled to Scotland.[3] The Germans took over the base and extended it, basing maritime reconnaissance, transport and rescue operations here involving a fleet of tankers, crane ships and catapult ships and more than 1,500 personnel.[4]

'These enormous Blohm und Voss planes patrolled the area to spot the convoys taking supplies to Russia. They could fly to Greenland doing reconnaissance – they had a range of 6,000km,' Mr Jaklin said:

> This Blohm und Voss Wiking [Viking] would rotate the troops from Hamburg to Tromsø. After a while they had two weeks' leave in Hamburg. Many of the German garrisons on these islands got crazy in winter. It was dark, there were no women, they had nothing to do. They had to change whole units with men from France. They lasted three months and then they got problems, so they had to change them again. At least 100 soldiers at a time could fit in one of these transport Vikings.

To protect the seaplanes at Skattøra from air attacks, the Germans constructed two blast walls made of stones about 6m high and 70m long, with a depth of 30m. The planes were parked up against the walls where they would be protected from anything other than a direct hit. To build them the Germans used Eastern European prisoners of war, living in barracks at Skattøra housing more than 200 prisoners. Some of them, it is said, were killed and buried under the walls. There has been a campaign to preserve the blast walls as a memorial to the prisoners, at what is the only remaining seaplane station in northern Europe.[5]

Finally we stop at a model of a soldier dressed in white-snow camouflage with special boots and mitts and a semi-automatic rifle slung across its body. Mr Jaklin says proudly:

> That was me. When I was 18 I joined the Norwegian 'police' in Sweden. There were 14,000 Norwegian troops training there in secret for the end of the war. The Germans knew nothing about it. The troops were mostly hidden in the forests in the middle of Sweden, with at least sixteen camps training soldiers, officially as police forces. That was a cover name: we weren't policemen, we were infantry; trained in shooting, military techniques, hand-to-hand combat. Most of us were infantrymen, trained in battalions by commandos dropped by plane from Scotland.
>
> About 2,000 of us went to Finnmark to make a supply road 80km long through the tundra near Kautokeino to move 400 tonnes of provisions, tools and material for building barracks for civilians in the inner areas, far from any major towns. Mostly we used horses and reindeer transportation. That was in March to April 1945. Then we were in the tundra near Aidejavre guarding the main radio station for the Norwegian liberation forces but we also patrolled across to Alta to get information about the German withdrawal.
>
> I was in Narvik for the capitulation. The top Nazis, the German civilian administration and even German officers shot themselves, a few took poison. A lot of German and Norwegian Nazis were brought to court. Around twenty-four or twenty-five people were executed as traitors, mostly Norwegians in German service, in the German SS or very high in the Quisling civilian administration. They were shot by my colleagues in the police.
>
> We toured the camps trying to identify the Nazis from the troops waiting for repatriation. We learned how to spot the Nazis, and the Norwegians returning from the concentration camps in Germany helped us find them too.[6]

There was that smile again ...

16

SCORCHED EARTH STORIES AT FIRST HAND

The next afternoon I boarded bus number 24 from Tromsø harbour and asked the driver to drop me at 'Steirvegan'. He flicked through his list but couldn't find a stop called that. Mr Jaklin had said it was about five or ten minutes out of town, near the airport, and had told me to ask for that. 'Star Way,' he'd said. It sounded magical.

'Stay-er-vey-en' – I hadn't checked the map as I'd been running late. Mr Jaklin said he had had done 'a little research' that he wanted to share with me. As we'd been in the museum so late after my day climbing the Lyngen Line mountains, we'd agreed to meet the next day. As the driver waited I tried calling him to check the street name but he didn't answer. 'Oh well,' I thought. 'Here we go again.'

For the first five minutes the bus drove up a hill through a university area, then down into a housing estate. One stop looked like 'Styrveien'. Perhaps that was the Norwegian spelling: 'Stirr-vayen.'

I asked the driver.

'I don't think that's it. It might be,' he said. 'Who knows?'

I'd expected a bit more from a bus driver but I thanked him and stepped off. The road was 'Styrmansvegen'. I called Mr Jaklin, who this time picked up straight away. Was it the right road? No, it wasn't, he said. He lived on 'Stayer-vey-en'. So how could I get from where I was to where he was? Neither of us knew.

I looked around for landmarks. All I could see was the airport. Mr Jaklin had said he lived somewhere near there. Maybe I could walk it. I walked through the suburban housing estate and down a hill in a light drizzle and guessed at a left at the bottom, which led further down a slope to what looked like a supermarket on the corner. I spotted a sign. This road was called 'Winston Churchills veg'.

'Surely an Englishman can get directions on a road called Winston Churchill's Way,' I thought. A youth in his 20s was cycling up the hill towards me on a mountain bike. He had a ginger goatie beard like he played in an American hard rock band. These were promising signs.

'Excuse me mate,' I said, trying to sound friendly as I walked across the road and into his path. 'Do you know a road called 'Ste-yer-veien'? It's somewhere round here.'

The cyclist stopped, pulled his phone out of his jacket, switched his music off, then flipped open the front and jabbed the icon 'Maps'. Why hadn't I thought of that?

'Staere-vegen,' he muttered, tapping his phone. I looked on as the map dropped a pin the other side of the island.

'That can't be right,' I said. 'Star Way, it's called in English. Starveiein maybe?'

'Let's try it,' said the cyclist, using a different spelling. This time the pin dropped close to our current location. 'Hmm,' he said. 'Down there to the Monoprix supermarket. Turn right, then second left.'

I felt like punching the air. 'Thanks very much,' I said. 'Brilliant work.' Lucky for me that everyone in Norway speaks English.

By the time I reached Mr Jaklin's door it was raining quite hard. I rang the bell and waited for him to answer.

'You found it then!' he said. 'Come on in.'

We walked upstairs to Mr Jaklin's sitting room. He poured coffee while I set out the cakes I'd brought for us to munch while he told his stories. I settled my tape recorder on the table and switched it on as Mr Jaklin began to read from papers he had prepared:

> During two months of October and November 1944 these German fire patrols burned down more than 11,000 houses, 6,000 farms, 4,700 barns, 27 churches and 140 houses owned by religious organisations.
>
> Fifty-three hotels and inns, 420 shops, 21 hospitals and smaller medical institutions, 306 fish factories, 106 schools and 60 administration buildings like council houses or town halls.
>
> Two hundred and thirty buildings for craft and industry, 350 bridges, 350 motor boats and thousands of rowing boats, 180 lighthouses – and they also destroyed boats, telephone poles and harbours.

At this point he looked up at me and waved his sheaf of papers.

'These figures are mostly from *Norway at War: Liberation* (*Norge I Krig: Frigjoring*) but I have checked them against other figures.'

I laughed, appreciating that his newspaper journalist's instincts and his need to check facts hadn't abandoned him.

It was systematic destruction but they didn't have time to burn down the eastern part of Finnmark because of the Russians. These petrol squads were equipped for burning things down or blowing things up. Many of the soldiers who came from the Russian Front were sane but they were brutal and cruel. In a few cases in Eastern Finnmark they poured petrol onto the sheep, set fire to them and chased them up into the fields by night so you could see them like torches burning to death. In other cases they used submachine guns against cattle and sheep, not to kill them to eat them but just for fun.

In Kafjord, there was a very big pier or quay at a village called Birtavarre. They made a very big hole in that quay and gathered all the cattle in the fjord in that area, took them to the hole, killed them and dropped their guts in the sea. All the fjord turned red with blood. The crows found their bellies in the sea and sailed on them on the tide, in and out, for hours.

My jaw dropped. 'But I was in Birtavarre just a few days ago and heard that same story – about the fjord red with blood. How do you know that story about the crows?'

Mr Jaklin looked at me a little surprised:

I got it from a book. I read it in *They Burnt Our Homes* (*De brente vare hjem*).[1] It's mostly pictures but there are some stories too. From 1942 or '43 the German units had orders to collect iron for the war industry and they seized every stove they came across. If a house was left empty they'd take the stove. They had hundreds. I had an uncle who had a farm in Lyngen. He was a skipper on a fishing boat, and they had to let three Germans stay in their house – they just took it over. When he came back from a fishing trip he met these three pushing a wheelbarrow with his stove in it. He was a very big man and he shouted angrily at them, so the Germans took it back and even refitted it. But later the police came for him and he was put in the prison camp in Tromsø for three months.

Mr Jaklin looked up at me again:

This story about the reindeer – did you hear about that in Nord Troms? It's very famous. The Lapps [Sami] had tens of thousands of reindeer in the inner part of Finnmark, in the Karasjok and Kautokeino area. The Germans of course wanted these reindeer to feed their men on the way back from Finland. The Nazi authorities had a meeting with the senior people, mayors and others in Kautokeino to discuss where to drive the reindeer so they could get them – of course they didn't say too much about what they were going to do with them. They agreed that they should take their reindeer flocks to a place called Heligskogen – that means 'holy wood' – but there are two places with the same name. The Germans thought they meant 'Heligskogen, not far from Skibotn', but the Sami took them to the border area between Norway and Finland! Exactly the same name, but in completely the opposite direction. I think the Germans had paid quite a lot of money for the reindeer too, so they were double-crossed. I expect once the Germans had the reindeer they wouldn't have paid, but they would have had a lot of trouble because reindeer only understand the Sami language. They don't understand Norwegian, and certainly not German.

We paused for breath, then switched to another topic – the evacuation:

The evacuation chief in Tromsø was Ragnar A. Hansen, a hotel owner and manager. He did a very good job. He wasn't afraid of the Germans at all. Several times the Germans tried to seize all the ships and fishing boats that were earmarked for the evacuation. He went to the commander-in-chief and said it was impossible to give them any ships as the city was so crowded there was a great danger of an epidemic breaking out. The Germans accepted that and gave them back the ships they had seized. So they used the two big ships instead, the *Carl Arp* and the *Adolf Binder*.

There were too few nurses in Tromsø with that great number of evacuees, so Chief Hansen appealed to the Quisling authorities in Oslo to send more nurses. He asked for fifty nurses – they sent five.

'The evacuation chief – he was a hotel man, an organiser. Was he a Quisling man?' I asked.

'He was a good Norwegian,' Mr Jaklin answered solemnly. 'He was brought in because he was a good administrator, and he did a very good job.'

'Not an NS man then?' I said. NS is Nasjonal Samling, a Norwegian Nazi, fascist or Quisling.

'Oh no. Far from it.' Mr Jaklin chuckled, it seemed, at the thought:

I met him but I didn't know him. He knew a lot of people in Tromsø. There were up to 500 volunteers working on the evacuation at one point: that's an enormous number in such a small city. They found accommodation for families, treatment for sick people, transport to the south. Volunteers organised the evacuation, not the NS. If the NS had organised it, people wouldn't have gone.

The police organised registrations and found food for the evacuees. They had 270 houses at their disposal for the evacuees. One warm meal every day. It was amazing they could find food for the evacuees because the city was really empty. We lived more or less on fish and potatoes for the last two years of the war. The shops were empty and you couldn't get clothes at all. No shoes. Nothing left. Sometimes people were living on 800 calories a day. [This is less than people living in Kirkenes were getting, far to the north-east and not having the benefit of supplies from the south.] You didn't get fat. If you were going to make a sandwich you had to put cod liver on it instead of butter, and that doesn't taste good. If you had friends on farms you could perhaps get some cheese and milk.

'Was there much of a black market?' I asked:

Yes. It grew very much during the last part of the war. In 1940 the Germans proclaimed that they would take 50 per cent of every fish catch in Norway. They established an organisation for buying fish and they paid with money they stole from the Bank of Norway. In Tromsø we had a large number of fishing vessels and they were allowed to fish along the coast – albeit not very far away – but quite a lot of them had colleagues on the islands with their own boats who fished in the same area. So if the Tromsø fishermen were coming back with 20,000kg they'd call in at the island and unload 10,000kg. Then they'd sail back to Tromsø, declare their catch at 10,000kg and the Germans would take 5,000kg. These 10,000kg from the islands went onto the black market. I didn't know that till last year [2012] when I was told about it. That trick with the fish catch was done on a great scale. More coffee?

Mr Jaklin walked over to the kitchen to fill up our coffee cups. We chatted about power shortages in Tromsø due to attacks by the Home Front.
'What kind of things could you buy on the black market?' I asked.
'Meat, butter, milk, fish. And I think that's all.'
'No cigarettes? No nylons?

No. The Germans stopped all the imports into Norway when they occupied the country. Cigarettes were not produced in Norway. You could get them from Germans. If you knew a German he could bring you some cigarettes. You paid him in Norwegian kroner. The drinking: before the war a lot of people in the rural areas made their own liquor. The Americans call it moonshine. But you need sugar, and there was no sugar, so we didn't have that. Occasionally the state authorities would get some aquavit – very strong – but it tasted very bad. If you were lucky you could get a bottle now and then, but you had to queue up in the evening and stand there more or less all night. A lot of old women stayed all night to get a bottle. Not to drink it but to use it to get other things. You could get a quarter of a pig for a bottle of aquavit. That tells you something. You could get 40kg of pig meat for a bottle of aquavit. [He laughs.] And it was terrible stuff! I tried this aquavit after the war. It's one of the worst things I have ever tried drinking. You can't compare it with the aquavit we make today.

Kirkenes after the German withdrawal. The stone steps in the foreground are all that's left of a bakery: the brick chimneys survived too. Years of Soviet bombing and the especially heavy air raid of July 1944 started fires that left the town a virtual wasteland. Picture used with permission of the Grenselandmuseet (Border Museum), Kirkenes.

Kirkenes in October 1944. Only stone buildings survived the bombs and flames. Families made shelters in stone cellars, living under whatever cover they could find. Picture with permission of the Grenselandmuseet (Border Museum), Kirkenes.

A wartime scene at Kirkenes harbour, with supplies being unloaded as soldiers look on. Picture used with permission of the Grenselandmuseet (Border Museum), Kirkenes.

Children during the war: Knut Tharaldsen (right) watched the fighting at close quarters as the Red Army broke three years of deadlock at the Litsa Front and pushed the Germans back into Norway. Eva Larsen (left) witnessed the liberation of Kirkenes by the Red Army in October 1944. Picture: Vincent Hunt

One of the few pre-war buildings in Kirkenes that weren't destroyed in the bombing and burning of the town. There are no plaques to identify the buildings that are the town's link to the past, just local knowledge. Picture: Vincent Hunt

The concrete bunker this house stands on was part of the anti-aircraft gun defences around the harbour at Kirkenes, an important Nazi supply port for the troops at the Litsa Front. This building was a seaplane office for many years after the war: now it's someone's home. Picture: Vincent Hunt

Finnkonckeila, a remote fishing village near Gamvik built in a steep gorge and only reachable by the sea, was burned down by the Germans during the scorched earth campaign. This picture dates from 1935. The Norwegian government refused to allow the village to be rebuilt after the war because of the dangers of landslips. It's now a ghost town. By kind permission of the Gamvik Museum.

Torstein Johnsrud, curator of the museum in Gamvik, a small fishing village on the coast of northern Norway. Three times the 300 villagers managed to escape SS raiding parties which tried to force them to evacuate. Only 13 people were caught. Picture: Vincent Hunt

The memorial to six fishermen murdered by German commandos at Hopseidet two days before the war ended. The stone marks the spot where they were gunned down – the commandos were put ashore from a submarine which surfaced in the fjord. Picture: Vincent Hunt

Mette Mikalsen's father and brother were among the six men murdered at Hopseidet. Husband Øyvind was first on the scene. Both were interviewed by the author for this book at Skjanes, August 2013. Picture by Ãlf Helge Jensen of the Finnmarken newspaper.

Those who escaped the evacuation of Finnmark survived the winter in makeshift homes made out of destroyed boats, driftwood and rags, like this one, Oswald Johansen's hut at Tverrikvannet. The first night after the burnings 40 people sheltered in here in a space of 20 square metres. Used with permission of the Norwegian Defence Museum, Oslo.

Nazi officers inspect the planned location of a coastal fortress along the northern tip of Norway, possibly Porsangerfjord. Hitler ordered a series of colossal coastal fortifications to be built in northern Norway as part of the Atlantic Wall stretching to France. The date of the picture is unknown. Picture from a collection of photographs taken from captured German troops at www.krigsbilder.net, a gallery of more than 20,000 WWII images. Used by kind permission of Tore Greiner Eggan.

SS troops pose for a picture in Skoganvarre, a popular fishing area south of Lakselv, a Nazi garrison town. The strategically important Luftwaffe base at Banak lay nearby, from where air raids were launched on the Allied Arctic convoys to Murmansk. This picture was taken following the 1940 invasion and is from www.krigsbilder.net, a gallery of more than 20,000 WWII images. Used by kind permission of Tore Greiner Eggan.

German soldiers bury a comrade at a funeral in Lakselv, close to the airbase at Banak. Lakselv became the last resting place for several hundred German war dead. Date unknown. Picture from www.krigsbilder.net, used by kind permission of Tore Greiner Eggan.

The white wooden church in Honningsvåg was the only building to survive the scorched earth burning of the town. Today it's a symbol of the total destruction of northern Norway during the war. Picture used with permission of the Nordkappmuseet in Honningsvåg.

A German soldier took this photograph of the burning of Hammerfest. The building on fire is the Folketshus or People's House. Picture used with permission of the Museum of the Post-War Reconstruction for Finnmark and Northern Troms, Hammerfest.

The total destruction of Hammerfest. The town once stretched around the harbour but was systematically burned and blown up. The German general in charge of the operation insisted at his post-war trial his actions were justified – he was cleared of wanton destruction. Picture: The Museum of the Post-War Reconstruction for Finnmark and Northern Troms, Hammerfest.

Troops stationed in northern Norway often experienced what Norwegians called 'Arctic melancholy' because of the constant darkness, sub zero temperatures and difficulty of getting leave. The German term was 'mountain sickness' – bergkrank – and suicides increased from 1943. Taken in front of a Nazi swastika this picture shows a band from the garrison at Lakselv/Banak, with a guitarist, accordionist, fiddler and flautist. Picture from www.krigsbilder.net. Used by kind permission of Tore Greiner Eggan.

The remains of the bunkers for the enormous coastal guns at Djupvik, Lyngenfjord. The guns could fire shells at attackers 20 kms away. The crew sheltered in the bunker to the left of the gun position. Picture: Vincent Hunt

Artist Grethe Gunning from Djupvik with family friend Roald Berg, who was a child through the German occupation. Picture: Vincent Hunt

The Allies feared fanatical Nazis would attempt a 'glorious last stand' in the mountains around the Lyngenfjord. Hundreds of Soviet PoWs died building a defensive line here, but the last stand did not happen. Picture: Vincent Hunt

Pål Fredriksen of the Nord Troms History Group at the Lyngen Line positions on top of the Fals mountain near Skibotn, overlooking the Lyngenfjord. Picture: Vincent Hunt

A reconstructed German bunker at the Lyngen Line, on top of the Fals mountain 800 metres above Skibotn. Three soldiers could cook, sleep and shelter in relative comfort here, with the rocks on the roof helping protect against possible bombing raids by Allied aircraft. Picture: Vincent Hunt.

Gunnar Jaklin was a teenage volunteer in the Norwegian 'police' units formed in neighbouring Sweden. He served in Finnmark and later hunted Nazis post-liberation. This snow uniform is on display at the Tromsø Defence Museum. Picture: Vincent Hunt

The Valley of the Doomed: Russian prisoners of war were marched along this road every day to be used as slave labour in the construction of the Lyngen Line defences. This direction led to the death camp at Mallnitz in the Kitdalen valley near Skibotn. Picture: Vincent Hunt

Soviet PoWs at a barracks at Saltfjellet following the German capitulation in May 1945. Many prisoners were badly malnourished after years of cruelty, starvation rations and forced labour in extreme weather. Picture courtesy of Marianne Neerland Soleim at the Falstad Centre. Owner of photo: The National Archives, Oslo. More information at http://painfulheritage.no

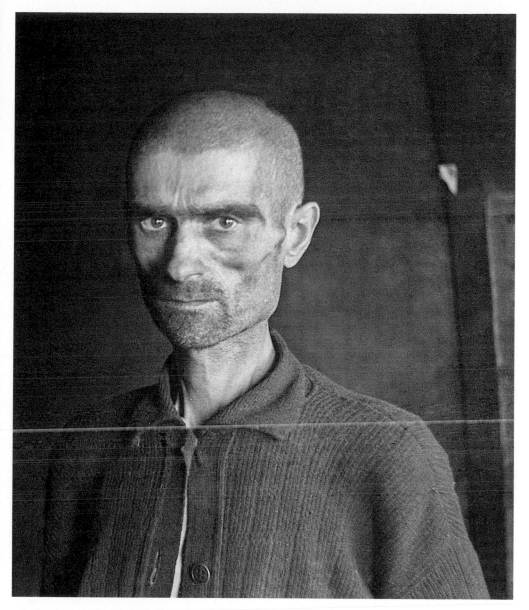

Soviet prisoner of war at Bjørnelva camp, 1945. There were 100,000 Soviet PoWs in Norway, of whom around 13,000 perished. The Falstad Centre and the Narvik Peace Centre are actively trying to document their stories. Photo: Leiv Kreyberg, (National Archives for Norway) courtesy of Marianne Neerland Soleim at the Falstad Centre.

Vidkun Quisling, the Norwegian Nazi collaborator who led the Nasjonal Samling party. Tried after the war for his crimes against Norway Quisling was executed in October 1945 by firing squad at Akershus Fortress in Oslo. His name has become a byword for collaborationist traitors.

Houses on fire during the scorched earth burning of Finnmark, 1944. Fire patrols soaked the wooden houses with petrol then set them alight. The location is unknown. Picture from www.krigsbilder. net, used with kind permission of Tore Greiner Eggan.

I'd brought with me a selection of cakes I bought in a shop by the bus stop in Tromsø – one chocolate, one macaroon and one fruit – so as we talked I cut them into sections and we munched on them. My jaw had dropped when the girl serving me asked for the equivalent of £15 for three pieces of home-made cake. Still, it was the only way I could think of to show Mr Jaklin how grateful I was for his amazing stories.

'I was a private at the end of the war, only 18,' he said, munching chocolate cake:

I ended up in Narvik as part of the police regiment based there so my job was paperwork and other things but whenever something was happening we were called out. We had to arrest some Russian prisoners who raided the bakeries and shops in Narvik. We arrested members of the Norwegian Nazi Party and put them in German barracks. We got them to clean our living quarters.

I think the Nazis were treated rather well but in a few cases some of the worst ones were put in coffins for a few hours. They were nailed up in coffins with the lid on, just to terrorise them, but of course you shouldn't do things like that. One sergeant who did that spent three months in prison afterwards. But mostly we didn't have trouble with the Germans at all. There were 16,000 of them in Narvik – a whole division – and we were a battalion, about 800 chaps.

There was one serious incident though. The Germans had a lot of alcohol. One night a Norwegian motorcycle despatch rider was riding through the streets when a door opened and a drunk German officer fired at him. He emptied the magazine of his pistol but didn't hit him. The Norwegian screeched to a halt, laid his motorcycle down, raised his submachine gun and fired a burst: brrrrrrrr!

He hit the German from his knees to his ears and left him very dead. The Germans didn't complain. They recognised that he was drunk and to blame. After that the British disarmed the Germans.

The chocolate cake seems to have triggered a passage of vivid memories for Mr Jaklin. I move the plate a little nearer to his right hand as he speaks:

Our most important job was to raid German camps and pick out Gestapo officers who had changed uniforms and were hiding among regular German troops. We had people who knew their faces. We started these raids at five o'clock in the morning. They had to line up in their underwear in all kinds of weather. Some of them had been guards in the concentration camps and there were always Norwegians who could pick them out. We had three or four of them with us. We arrested sixty-three Nazis in the southern part of Troms and took them back to the old concentration camp in Tromsø. Some were tried, some were sent back to Germany.

At the beginning of June 1945 German troops were being sent back to Germany and others were being separated for trial. There were some Gestapo officers on a boat between Narvik and Tromsø and we were guarding them, the whole platoon, with the Gestapo officers sitting on either side of a big room. One of our chaps went to take off his jacket but he caught the trigger of his submachine gun with his thumb and fired off about 20–25 bullets by mistake. The bullets missed the Gestapo officers but they became quite hysterical. They cried like children. They thought we were taking them to kill them and drop them in the sea. They were really scared and some of them cried tears – Gestapo officers!

'Are you proud to have served in the Norwegian police?' I asked.

'Yes, in a way,' he says. 'There were dozens of men from Tromsø in the Norwegian police. I'm probably the only one left alive, because I was so young at the time. Most were aged between 23 and 35 in 1944–45.'

He looks at me seriously:

I have told some people about the training we had and they've been quite shocked. We learned how to kill people with bayonets, from behind. Knee in the back, cut them here on the side of the neck and so on – [he demonstrates. I wince] – but mostly we trained with explosives. We trained with something I'd never seen before – an explosive fuse. So if you cut a tree you measured how thick it was – say 13cm – and you would have thirteen rings on the fuse and you ignited it and boom – the tree would come down and you could set a roadblock.

We were in Swedish Karesuando for winter training. There we stayed together with a Finnish battalion 10km from the German lines. We were the first Norwegian platoon that had been co-operating with the Finns. They were very young chaps, just 16 or 17, and they had enormous losses, especially among the officers because they always went first when attacking the Germans. Their tents were full of holes – hole and hole and hole – hundreds, because they had been in the line and the Germans had been using machine guns against them. They lay flat on the ground and the bullets went over them but the tents were full of holes. They had been fighting the Germans up the valley to Skibotn. The battalion commander was only 26. They had lost so many officers that even chaps in their 20s got high rank. There was no one else left.

I joined the Norwegian volunteers in the October 1944 and served fourteen months. I lost a year at school of course. At the end of my service they tried to get a few of us directly to officer training but I wanted to do my exams first, so I went back to Tromsø to go to school. I started in 1950 with two officer courses. Later I was picked out by the commander-in-chief in north Norway to go to the highest military college in Norway. I was a major at that time. I stayed in the army for seventeen years then worked on the newspaper my father edited, *Nordlys*. It's been an interesting combination, newspaper work and military activities.[2]

The light was beginning to fade and it was raining quite hard. The clock on the wall showed it was after 6.30pm. It was time for me to go. I had stumbled across an amazing treasure trove of stories from someone who had witnessed the scorched-earth aftermath at first hand and told a series of extraordinary stories for me. I wished Mr Jaklin all the best and walked to the bus stop to wait for a bus back into town.

17

SLAUGHTER AND SUPPLY FROM THE SKY

I leave my hotel early the following morning to beat the traffic into Tromsø Airport. This is Monday morning and I'm catching an early plane, so I don't want to be caught in traffic jams in those tunnels leading into the city. The hotel has called me a cab.

My trip to Norway is almost over and I'm flying down to Oslo to have a few days in the capital before my flight back to Manchester. A long, white Volvo estate with a taxi sign on the roof pulls up and I jump in. We speed through the tunnels towards the airport making polite conversation.

I tell the driver I've been hearing stories about the *Tirpitz* in Tromsø. He looks over at me: 'The *Tirpitz* was capsized there, in the bay,' he says, waving his arm to the right.

'I've had Germans in this cab looking at that spot in tears. They ask me to pull up so they can look out over the water, and then they say, "My grandfather died here." The old ones say, "This is where my father died."'

I had read about the efforts to rescue the men trapped in the hull of the *Tirpitz* after the pride of the German fleet, the most feared battleship of the war, was ripped apart by RAF 'blockbuster' bombs in November 1944. Only seventy-six men escaped through a hole cut into her hull; nearly 1,000 died. I imagined the sadness of those Germans making a difficult trip to see where their forefathers had died.

When my plane is south of Bodø I look down at the sea below with islands scattered in clumps and realise I'm flying over the area where one of the most horrific incidents of the scorched-earth period happened: the bombing by the Allies of the cargo steamer MS *Rigel* with the loss of 2,250 lives, mostly Russian prisoners. Even now the sinking of the *Rigel* is considered one of the worst maritime disasters on record.

The incident happened at a time of great drama in the shipping lanes off the western coast of Norway, just a fortnight after the *Tirpitz* was sunk. The MS *Rigel* was a cargo steamer built in 1924, requisitioned by the Germans after the fall of Narvik. The boat was used during the evacuation of Finnmark and was on its final journey south carrying prisoners when disaster struck.

With two German escort boats, the *Rigel* and fellow steamer MS *Korsnes* left Bodø on 26 November loaded with German soldiers and thousands of prisoners of war picked up at three different stops along the western coast of Norway. It's thought the convoy was heading for Trondheim, where the prisoners would be split up into camps.

The next day the convoy was passing between the tiny islands of Rosoya and Tjøtta near Sandnessjøen when it was attacked by Fairey Barracuda dive-bombers from the aircraft carrier HMS *Implacable*, part of a Royal Navy force laying mines and attacking shipping along the coast.[1]

Rigel was hit by torpedoes and five bombs falling directly into the hold. Belching smoke, the captain tried to beach the stricken vessel on the island of Rosoya. The loss of life was terrible: 2,248 prisoners – Soviet, Polish and Serbian – died in the attack. Soviet prisoners alone numbered 2,098. Norwegian writers say there were also 8 Norwegian prisoners, 95 Germans (mostly deserters from the Finnish front), 29 crew, 3 pilots and 455 soldiers on the *Rigel*, including two women: 1 pilot and 1 crew member.[2]

Beaching the *Rigel* on the shore at Rosoya probably saved the lives of the 267 survivors, one of whom was a Norwegian prisoner, who escaped with the help of locals on shore and managed to survive the war.[3] Six crew on board the MS *Korsnes* died in the attack[4] and the German escorts NT-04 and V-6308 were damaged beyond repair, as was the freighter *Spree*, which was at anchor.[5]

The British said they thought *Rigel* was carrying German troops. The wreck was visible for decades after the war off Rosoya until it was broken up; what's left on the seabed is still visited by divers. The graves of the 2,098 Soviet prisoners were salvaged in 1969 and transferred to the Soviet war cemetery at Tjøtta.[6]

It was beginning to rain outside so I turned to a leaflet I had been meaning to read for some time. It was about private support from American Norwegians during the occupation of their motherland and had been sent to me by Jeff Sauve, archivist of the Norwegian–American Historical Association in Minnesota, with whom I had exchanged emails before I left. I reckoned that now would be a good time to read it.

The article, written by Jeff and entitled 'A Helping Hand: The Efforts of American Relief for Norway', was about the economic mobilisation of the enormous number of Americans of Norwegian descent across the United States. Together with public backing from a number of high-profile Norwegians, between 1940 and 1947 the humanitarian organisation American Relief for

Norway Incorporated (ARNI) gathered an astonishing 750 tons of clothing: 1,925,000 separate garments with a value of $3.67 million.[7]

Many thousands of Scandinavians migrated to America in the mid-nineteenth century, and in places like Minneapolis and Idaho some settlements were overwhelmingly Norwegian. Activists like Trondheim-born Reidar Rye Haugan and wife Hermana were key figures behind the establishment of ARNI just ten days after the invasion of Norway. Haugan moved to New York in 1915 aged 21 and then got a job on the largest Norwegian-language newspaper in America, *Skandinaven*, based in Chicago. He became editor in 1939 and when Germany invaded he established a network of American-based Norwegians to start a relief organisation.

With its headquarters in Chicago but working through local and state committees, ARNI became a coast-to-coast operation, joining with Norwegian special interest groups at home and across the Allied nations to send food, medical supplies and clothing to the homeland.

Over the next seven years, ARNI raised cash contributions from the United States totalling $3,886,642, mostly gathered in small donations of 50 cents here or $1 there. The group acted as a focal point for the fundraising activities of Norwegians far and wide, such as seamen's churches and missions, the 'Little Norway' military camp in Canada where Norwegian pilots trained and organisations of Norwegian servicemen in Britain set up to tackle war-related problems.[8]

Expatriate Norwegians – or for that matter, sympathetic Americans – could contribute to the effort by making quilts or selling raffle tickets, ribbons, lapel button badges and letter seals. Lectures, concerts and fundraising parties were organised. One minor problem was that, after the attack on Pearl Harbour in December 1941, the State Department recommended that charitable contributions be reserved for the home front, not for foreign nations.

Early fundraising was spurred on by the callous statements of the Germans now in charge in Oslo, notably Reichskommisar Terboven, who said in autumn 1941:'It is a matter of indifference to Germany if some thousands or tens of thousands of Norwegian men, women and children starve to death during this war.'[9]

Food shortages and undernourishment in the Nazi and Quisling era were a serious problem. A report for the Norwegian Ministry of Foreign Affairs in 1995 noted:'Statistics bear witness to the scope of the food shortage. From 1942 Norwegians lived on an average of 1,500 calories a day, compared with 2,500 normally. In 1944 the average daily consumption of food sank to 1,315 calories and in the winter of 1945 the figure was 1,237.'[10] At the same time Germany was stripping assets and iron ore out of Norway at nearly 40 per cent of its GDP.[11]

Norwegians in America began a huge clothing-collection drive to offset shortages due to rationing. In occupied Norway clothes had to be repaired repeatedly and replacements were made of low-grade wool and cotton substitutes. Children sometimes didn't have enough clothes, or clothes in good-enough shape, to attend school. The Germans confiscated woollen blankets for their troops fighting in Russia.

The Norwegian government-in-exile offered to pay the cost of sending donated clothes, so ARNI appealed for 'bundles', hosting event parties to boost donations. The advertisement for one 'Bundles for Norway' party in San Francisco held on 21 January 1945, read: 'Bring a bundle of clean or new clothing and enjoy the afternoon. Entertainment and refreshments free. Admission by bundle.'[12]

Among the prominent backers of the ARNI relief effort was acclaimed Norwegian writer Sigrid Undset, who had been awarded the Nobel Prize for literature in 1928, and whose outspoken opposition to the Nazis since the 1930s caused her to flee to Sweden when the Germans invaded. Her son Anders Svarstad was a second lieutenant in the Norwegian army and was killed in action aged 27 in a clash with German troops in May 1940, not far from the family home near Lillehammer. She made her way to America through Siberia and then Japan; during the occupation Undset's home was used as quarters for Nazi officers.[13]

Undset spoke at a Norway Day ceremony in New York on 11 May 1945 just days after the German surrender:

> The Germans have tried to break our stubborn people ever since [1940] by torture, tyranny, by hunger and cold and systematic looting and ruin inflicted upon Norway. Norway is grateful to you for helping us get to our feet again after we have been under the German military boot for five years of hell.

The following day she was quoted in the *New York Times* report of the event as saying, 'the Norwegian lion was not destined to become a lapdog for a dictator'.

In an ARNI pamphlet she wrote:

> Help from our kinsfolk in America will come as a blessing and will be received with fervent gratitude. It means clothing for our people, who must strive and toil as never before; food for hungry bodies, who, returning to their demolished homes, must clear away the ruins and try to rebuild that which was torn down.[14]

Public support for ARNI came from other Norwegian notables in America, among them Chicago-born musician Storm Bull – whose grandfather had been a nephew of the composer Edvard Grieg and who was schooled by Béla Bartók.

Another more controversial supporter was possibly Norway's most famous international sportswoman ever. Ice skater Sonja Henie won ten world championships between 1927 and 1936, six European championships and three Olympic golds, met kings and presidents, and signed film contracts that made her, at one point, the highest paid actress in the world. Although the films had limited appeal, her hugely popular skating shows and range of branded merchandise gave her an income estimated at $2 million a year.[15]

Henie had been received with special rapture by the Nazis at the 1936 Winter Games at Garmisch-Partenkirken, where she had caused a stir by greeting the German Chancellor with a 'Heil Hitler' captured on film. She was a controversial figure to be backing the ARNI campaigns.

When Norway was occupied by the Nazis in 1940, Henie apparently sent orders home that a signed picture of Hitler that the dictator gave her on a visit to Berchtesgarden four years previously was to be left on show in her Oslo home: the house was left untouched. The following year – now an American citizen – Henie was asked to contribute money to buy equipment for the Norwegian flight training school in Canada but refused, saying that as an American she was 'neutral'. When America entered the war after Pearl Harbour she began to support fundraising efforts but never quite shook off the negative publicity from her previous standpoint.[16]

ARNI's relief efforts began with shipments to Norway via Sweden of ascorbic acid and prefabricated buildings when 15,000 homes were destroyed in the German invasion. Shocked Norwegian-Americans read how thousands of Norwegians sought shelter in boathouses, barns or shacks when they were made homeless by bombing, evictions or military action.[17]

When the Americans and British lifted a blockade on relief shipments later in the war ARNI spent $600,000 on powdered milk and other food for children, plus books and comfort articles for Norwegian prisoners, refugees in Sweden and medicines, medical supplies and hospital equipment. Shortages of leather meant pre-war shoes were priceless possessions; the only ones available during the occupation were a wooden clog-style shoe, held to the feet by straps through paper uppers.[18] Imagine the scenes when at Christmas 1944 more than 28,000 pairs of shoes were delivered across Norway courtesy of ARNI.[19]

By the end of 1944 ARNI was sending $37,000 a month to Sweden to buy food to be sent across the border in Norway, but only where it would not fall into the hands of the Nazis.[20] After the German surrender ARNI stepped up relief to Norway, sending thousands of tons of clothes. ARNI records break down what they sent:

For men
21,458 pairs of shoes; 14,469 pairs of rubber boots and overshoes; 138,168 pairs of socks; 8,543 undershirts and T-shirts; 2,700 sweaters and 2,500 raincoats.
For women
22,672 pairs of shoes; 1,634 pairs of rubber boots; 30,164 pairs of stockings and anklets; 27,682 undergarments and 4,174 skirts.

For children

32,752 pairs of shoes; 33,372 pairs of rubber boots and galoshes; 6,411 pairs of stockings; 1,803 undergarments; 52,859 sweaters; 18,799 coats; 3,590 skirts and 16,107 baby clothes.

Medical supplies included 15,000 vials of penicillin, x-ray units, operating tables, lights and accessories and anaesthesia equipment for six hospitals, together with microscopes, electrocardiographs, dental equipment and instrument washers as well as 100 beds, mattresses and pillows for the Red Cross Home for Backward Children.[21]

While in Kirkenes I asked teacher Eva Larsen if she remembered any of this American aid coming from Norway. She laughed and said:

I do. I remember those aid parcels coming to Finnmark. The local priest handed them out in the tunnel at Bjørnevatn where we were all living [in the iron ore mine]. I remember opening them and they smelled funny. I couldn't work out why, until someone told me that in America they had these funny flies that ate the clothes – moths – and they had treated the clothes with naphthalene, which had a strange smell.[22]

I land at Trondheim to switch planes for my final flight with Widerøe. This is going to an airport called Oslo Torp, an airport apparently two hours south of Oslo. When I booked the flight the airport was listed as Oslo but now I'm at the departure gate it seems to say something different – now it's Sandefjord. The modern map of Europe has been redrawn by low-cost airlines advertising flights to certain cities, then landing 100km away. I realise my final destination is one detail I have paid scant attention to, and now I might end up in the middle of nowhere.

The rain in the north is entering its third day as, for one last time, I climb aboard the green and white turboprop planes that have become so familiar. These planes have taken me to places so remote I wasn't sure what would be waiting for me. Hasvik, Honningsvåg and Mehamn were little more than a runway with airport buildings next to them, but the Widerøe service has been superb. I will miss not flying Widerøe – instead of turning up two hours before a flight and queueing, the twenty passengers turn up thirty minutes before the plane lands, and they all know each other. It's all very good-humoured and friendly on these multi-stop hops in challenging conditions to remote Arctic communities. I'm used to transatlantic flights full of grumpy, over-tired passengers wanting three square meals, wine, hot towels and headphones that work. On these planes you could almost tap the pilot on the shoulder and ask him where we are. And the passengers look grateful to reach their destination. I prefer Norway, thinking about it.

I have been using my time at the airports between flights to catch up on research. In the Arctic Circle the airports are full of wooden designer furniture and floor to ceiling glass so you can watch the comings and goings of small aircraft and budget-airline jets while eating generous breakfast packs of fruit, cheese and bread prepared by the hotel you stayed in last night. It's all very calm, civilised and friendly.

I've been reading more about the remarkable Norwegian–American pilot Bernt Balchen, who became one of the heroes of the Norwegian Resistance and a significant figure in the relief operations immediately after the liberation. He seemed destined for a life of adventure and narrow escapes from an early age.

Born in Tveit north of Kristiansand in 1899, he joined the French Foreign Legion during the First World War and was posted to Verdun but transferred back to Norway before seeing action. He then fought as a cavalryman in the Finnish Civil War and was left for dead when his horse was shot from under him and he was seriously injured. An expert marksman, notable boxer and accomplished skier he considered a career in athletics, but was selected as a pilot on a mission in 1925 to rescue the explorer Roald Amundsen, missing in the Svalbard archipelago near the North Pole. He spent the 1920s and 1930s flying airships and planes on expeditions over the North and South Poles, earning a reputation as a safe pair of hands in a tight situation.[23]

After America joined the war, and by then holding joint Norwegian–American nationality, Balchen ran search and rescue operations over Greenland for B-17s and other planes running into trouble over the ice. In 1943 he was made Chief of the Allied Transport Command for Norway, Sweden, Denmark, Finland and the USSR, with a secret base in Scotland. Itching to play a more positive role in the Norwegian Resistance, he jumped at the chance in early 1944 of rescuing 2,000 young Norwegian aircrew exiled in Sweden where they'd fled after the 1940 invasion.[24] Five B-24 bombers were painted dark green, stripped of weapons and fitted with radar and bench seats to take thirty-five passengers at a time. All military markings were removed. Flights into Stockholm across Norway were planned only in bad weather and at night to avoid German fighters. Resistance units in Norway relayed information about ground defences. Balchen said of the operation, codenamed 'Sonnie':

> We knew where every gun was on the Norwegian coast, where every German division was stationed, how many planes there were on every field and what type, when they usually landed and took off and what bombers or transports went through Bergen or Oslo or other important field.[25]

The story of Operation Sonnie reads like a thriller in itself. Thanks to Balchen's extraordinary organisational skills, hangar space was found at Stockholm's

Bromma airport, despite the German agents everywhere. Overnight bunks and rooms were found for pilots and crew. Their secret passengers were kept away from the airport until the last possible moment to avoid the suspicions of German agents in offices nearby.

Between March and December 1944 Balchen's crews flew out the 2,000 Norwegian aircrew and also 900 Americans and 150 other nationals, including important diplomats, who had been interned in Sweden, once even borrowing parts from a crashed B-24 held by the Germans to repair a blown cylinder head on one of the engines of his planes. Of course, Balchen replaced the spares the next day.[26]

The next operation – with the codename 'Ball' – would be an even more tense affair. The continual daylight of the midnight sun and the mountainous terrain had taken a heavy toll on RAF aircrews trying to keep a supply line going to the Norwegian Resistance during summer 1944.

Balchen offered to take over the job of dropping agents, ammunition and supplies to the Resistance fighters on the ground. Another fleet of ten B-24s was supplied to Balchen, painted black and stripped of unnecessary equipment, with guns only at the front and rear.

This time the mid-gunner's ball turret in the belly was stripped out to make a hole wide enough for agents wearing a parachute to slip through. These holes were known as 'Joe holes' – 'Joes' being the anonymous agents, of whom nothing was ever revealed. Female agents were known as 'Janes' or 'Josephines'.[27] Agents were often loaded at the end of the runway before take-off to keep contact with the crew to an absolute minimum. Flights through the fjords were at a height of 50ft, just above the treeline to avoid radar detection. Canisters of supplies were dropped at 100ft; agents slipped through their Joe hole at 500ft, but only after Balchen had made contact with the Resistance group on the ground.[28]

On his first drop Balchen slipped a personal note from King Haakon into the container, which was received with great warmth by the Resistance. Balchen's personal daring and his regular presence in Stockholm led to one occasion when he flew to Sweden and then slipped across a remote border area to be met by car and driven to Oslo for a meeting with Resistance leaders to clear up confusion over signals. In one mission following the Normandy invasion, Balchen's crews dropped copies of *Life* magazine with extensive photo coverage of the Allied landings, which soon found their way into the receptions of the best hotels in Oslo, to the fury of the Gestapo.[29]

As the Germans began their retreat to the Lyngen Line, the Allies stepped up operations in northern Norway. The Norwegian government-in-exile was especially keen to re-establish Norwegian control in 'liberated' areas to deter the Russians from annexing them.

Balchen was made commander of a unit headquartered in Stockholm with bases across Sweden and in Russian-liberated Kirkenes. These fliers became known as the 'Ve Do It' squadron, a nickname coined after his catchphrase 'Yes, ve do it' every time he was asked whether a seemingly impossible operation could be mounted.[30]

Two operations ran side by side: the Sepals project and Operation Where and When. The Sepals project was a sabotage operation involving British and American commandos working alongside Norwegian Resistance fighters; Operation Where and When was relief and supply missions. In total, 'Where and When' C47s airlifted 1,442 Norwegian 'police' to bases across the north through airfields at Bodø, Kautokeino and Karasjok, Banak and Skoganvarre, together with 1,100 tons of military and medical supplies.

Operations began on 29 December 1944 with an entire field hospital, twenty-five stoves, fourteen nurses, twenty-eight doctors and various medical specialists being flown to northern Sweden, then moved through the mountains into the Norwegian wasteland. The first flights into Norway came in January 1945, when Balchen flew 19 tons of equipment and thirty-seven men into Kirkenes.[31] They found the town utterly destroyed, with all but two buildings burned to the ground. The town's coal store had been set alight in November and was still burning. Balchen brought tents for the Norwegian mission troops; the Russian liberators lived in shelters in the snow.

Communications between Russians and Norwegians were often not good and the Russians objected to having the Norwegians in their area of control – even though it was their own country. More than once Balchen was called in to negotiate during periods of tension between the two supposed allies: the Norwegians apparently hated the Russians almost as much as the Nazis. The Russians stole watches and personal effects, despite the brutal consequences of being caught. Thieves were shot dead on the spot, and left lying where they fell.[32]

In her memoir of a wartime childhood in Kirkenes, *Terror in the Arctic*, Bjarnhild Tulloch relates one story which shows the Russian intolerance of petty theft among the ranks. One woman disturbed a Russian soldier as he stole her winter coat from a peg in her house. She gave chase but could not catch him. Fuming, she went to the camp commandant and reported the theft. He asked if she would recognise the thief and she said she would:

> The officer assembled his soldiers and asked her if she could identify the thief. Mrs Johnson confirmed that she could and pointed to the soldier. To her shock and utter disbelief, the officer pulled out his gun and shot the soldier dead in front of her and the other soldiers present.[33]

On one occasion Balchen watched some Russian soldiers clearing an airstrip with a bulldozer and warned the colonel in charge that the field had been mined by the Germans before they retreated. The colonel paid no attention and shortly afterwards the bulldozer hit a mine and exploded, killing the men. The colonel shrugged his shoulders and said: 'We have plenty of men, and we can always get more bulldozers from America.'[34]

Balchen dropped equipment for a network of radio communication stations across northern Norway, and everything from potatoes, bales of hay, cigarettes and even blueberry soup.[35] Although technically under the control of the American Legation in Stockholm, requests for help reached Balchen through informal channels. One Norwegian major, John Giaver – with whom he had designed a sledge tent for use in Antarctica in pre-war times – wrote to Balchen alerting him to areas needing humanitarian aid:

> I have lately been engaged in bringing in supplies to the population of west Finnmark from Sweden. During the first month we are planning to take in 90 tons over Karesuando by reindeer; for the following months we are planning about 70 tons per month. It would be so much easier and simpler to take these supplies in by plane and drop them at Kautokeino and Karasjok. I know that your help in this matter is very much needed ... and I am certain that you would more than gladly like to transport in food for around 4,000 people.
>
> There is also a group of about 200 people in the mountains inside Revsbotten in Kvalsund [near Hammerfest] who are starving. At Sørøya there are about 2,000 up in the mountains and a couple hundred at Kvaloy [in the Tromsø area]. I cannot reach these people alone on account of the Germans leaving troops on the coast and also operating patrols. Can something be done from the air? Planes equipped with skis can be landed on the rivers at Kautokeino or Karasjok. There is also a small flying field to the north of Kautokeino. I expect this field is mined.[36]

The official Swedish report into Balchen's Operation Where and When – the supply flights between Lulea in Sweden and Kirkenes – described some of the items flown north to help in the relief effort:

> They transported big iron stove-heated tents, which the Swedish Red Cross had received from the Finnish military authorities, and they also received prefabricated houses and furniture that could be transported in the airplanes. Groceries and clothes were requested by the often-homeless population, that during long periods of time had escaped to caves and holes in the earth. They flew everything, big things as well as small things. It could be everything from houses and tools, machines and spare parts to needles and fish hooks.[37]

One of the more notable operations by Balchen's squadron, now known as 'Carpetbaggers', was Operation Rype, of 24 March 1945. A sixteen-man team of agents led by Major William E. Colby, later head of the CIA, were dropped

on a frozen lake near Trondheim. Their target was a railway bridge to be used by
retreating German forces heading south to defend the Reich in its last weeks.[38]
Colby's men blew it successfully, leaving American military badges at the scene
to make it clear this was a military operation, so the Germans wouldn't shoot
civilians in reprisal. The ruthless Reichskommissar Terboven was so furious at the
sabotage he wanted 10,000 Norwegians shot as punishment.[39]

The subsequent suicide of Hitler and the German decision to seek surrender
rather than stage a last stand – a decision which sealed Terboven's fate and led to his
bizarre but successful suicide by explosive – meant this threat was not carried out.

Inside my plane, passengers are getting ready for landing. There are forests and fjords
below me and the landscape looks lush and green. I have time to finish the Balchen
stories before we reach whatever lies aheaad of me at Oslo Torpedo This though is
a tragedy involving the deaths of dozens of men involved in mine-clearance oper
ations in the war-scarred north.

Five days before the war ended, Norwegian troops were de-mining the road
between Finland and Skoganvarre at Karasjok, loading the supposedly safe mines
onto a truck. But one went off, triggering the detonation of another fifty mines
on board, resulting in a devastating explosion. Twenty-two men were killed out-
right and nine seriously injured and in need of urgent medical help. Emergency
teams called Balchen. He flew in a volunteer medical team of doctors and nurses
who made their first parachute jump into Karasjok. Once the injured men were
out of danger, Balchen flew back in a short take-off reconnaissance plane and
airlifted the wounded to hospital.[40]

Much later, in his memoirs, Balchen offered a glimpse into whether the
Russians really intended to extend their occupation of Norway as they pushed
back Hitler's troops. On 3 May 1945 Balchen was invited to a dinner at the
Russian headquarters in Kirkenes. His diary entry has the reminder: 'Drink cod
liver oil first' – a precaution to offset the effects of the copious amounts of vodka
that each guest would be plied with, partly as a tradition and partly as a way of
loosening tongues.

As the dinner progressed, an official from Moscow began to show the effects
of the vodka. He leaned over to Balchen and nudged him: '"We push to Narvik,
Zhukov to Denmark. Come together. You understand?" He joined his hands in a
gesture like pincers closing.'[41]

Balchen understood what the Russian meant only too well and the next day
made a phone call to Allied headquarters to tip them off about the conversation.
In the end General Montgomery reached Denmark first, not the Russians, and
by doing so perhaps saved Norway from joining the Baltic states in spending the
next half century behind the Iron Curtain.

Another remark from dinner that night stayed with Balchen until late in his
life. A senior Soviet officer, Colonel Grigge, leaned across the table and clinked

vodka glasses with him. 'Colonel American Balchen, we drink to you,' he said. 'But one day in the Arctic we will be fighting you.'[42]

I look up from my book to see the ground approaching rapidly. The plane's wheels touch down on the runway at Oslo Torp airport. Now I have to figure out how to get to Oslo city itself from wherever I am. Already the north of Norway seemed like an adventure in a different land.

18

QUESTIONS MOUNT ON THE STREETS OF THE CAPITAL

The doors of the coach opened with a snort of compressed air. 'Oslo bus station,' the driver called. 'Everyone for Oslo bus station.'

It had been three hours since I landed at Oslo Torp from Trondheim. I spent an hour of that sitting on a bench at the bus station reading, waiting for the driver to allow me on board. I was determined not to miss the bus. The two-hour ride north to the capital had been very pleasant in the late afternoon August sun and the country looked beautiful, but I had had enough of travelling for a while.

I braced myself for the shock of the bill at the other end – everything in Norway is twice the price of the UK – and got a cab to my hotel. The driver did a U-turn on the tramlines outside and I walked into the reception with a twinge of regret. This would be my last stop in Norway.

When I got into my room I filled a kettle and put it on to boil to make some lemon tea. I stuffed the used travel documents, receipts and plans in my hold bag. Anything I was working on I carried in my cabin bag. This included some documents I'd been looking at on the flight down. They were from an American military collection relating to the end of the war in Norway. I pulled off my boots, made some tea and started to look through them.

The first was a statement by the Norwegian government-in-exile, issued in London at the end of the week of the German surrender. The headline read: 'After Five Long Years the Norwegian People are once more Free':

By virtue of Germany's unconditional capitulation, the German forces in Norway have laid down their arms. The Norwegian Home Front and Forces of the Interior are now in charge in Oslo and all over Norway.

The transition has proceeded with remarkable smoothness and ease, thanks largely to the discipline shown by the Norwegian people and to the careful advance planning by the Home Front [Milorg Resistance] and the Norwegian Government. An Allied Military Commission arrived in Oslo on Tuesday [8 May] to arrange the formal signing of the surrender instrument. On Wednesday the Commission issued a communique announcing the withdrawal of all German troops from all the principal towns by midnight on Friday.

Obeying the Home Front order that they should maintain calm, dignity and discipline, the Norwegians abstained from provocative acts and refused to take the law into their own hands. The people marched in processions and sang their songs in an orderly fashion, and no clashes or bloodsheds were reported. Even some German soldiers were carried away by the general enthusiasm and were shouting 'Hurrah for Free Norway!'

On the afternoon of 8 May, as vast crowds continued to celebrate in Oslo, two flying boats, with Norwegian flags on their fuselages and manned by Norwegians, circled over the city and then landed at Fornebu [Oslo's main airport then, now closed]. The Allied military delegation had arrived. They proceeded immediately to Oslo and continued later to the German military headquarters at Lillehammer to settle the formalities of surrender. Later they returned to Oslo and established headquarters at Hotel Bristol, where the British flag now waves alongside the Norwegian.

The reception of the delegation in Oslo was overwhelming. Never has the Norwegian capital witnessed such scenes of rejoicing. The crowds surged around their cars, cheering and singing the British and Norwegian National Anthems as though for five years they had lived only for this moment.[1]

I had read about the scenes of rapture at the liberation. It sounded like a great relief after so many years of misery at the hands of the Germans. Other documents in the collection detailed the arrival of the civil affairs representatives who would run the newly liberated Norway, including Lieutenant Colonel E.A.J. Johnson, the chief of the Economics Branch of Allied Land Forces and Lieutenant Colonel E. Ross Jenney, who would oversee the inquests of the Soviet POWs at Mallnitz. The initial reports of the civilian administrators mentioned fuel shortages hampering the efficient running of the rail network, but also the civilised transition of power back from the Germans following the surrender. That was the moment the Norwegian 'police' trained in Sweden and Resistance groups had been waiting for. The purging of Quisling collaborators from positions of power had been peaceful, the report noted, and women collaborators had not suffered badly:

The usual incidents of cutting of hair of women who collaborated or consorted with the enemy have taken place but with no great disturbances and regarded as rather a minor form of punishment. Towards women who married Germans, or who consorted with Germans during the occupation, no specific policy has been evolved.[2]

The report was made by the chief of the legal branch of the Allied Land Forces, Lieutenant Colonel John Enrietto, who concluded that, 'It seems to be the Norwegian attitude that these women will be such social outcasts that they will find it necessary to go to Germany or to emigrate elsewhere'.[3]

Those final words would be a chilling premonition of the hatred and hostility the children born to women branded 'whores of Germans' would suffer for the next sixty-five years. The *Lebensborn* 'war children' endured appalling treatment in an episode of deep shame for the Norwegian people to this day.

Other situations that needed settling resolved themselves on 8 May 1945. The day of the capitulation was the end of the road for SS chief in Norway, Wilhelm Rediess, who shot himself on the day of Germany's surrender. That evening Terboven blew himself and Rediess's body to pieces by detonating 50kg of dynamite in a bunker at the Skaugam Palace.[4] Three of twenty-nine paintings looted from the National Gallery in Oslo by Reichskommissariat enforcers were found in his flat a week later.[5]

The Quisling police minister Jonas Lie, who had led the evacuation of Finnmark, Justice Minister Sverre Riisnaes and Police Chief Henrik Rogstad retreated to an NS farmhouse outside Oslo with ten bodyguards. There were few options for such a senior group of Quisling leaders. Surrounded by 200 Resistance fighters they attempted to negotiate their way out but ended up settling for a suicide pact. Rogstad shot himself, Lie missed but died anyway of natural causes, possibly stress, heart failure and alcohol misuse.[6] Riisnaes gave himself up, claiming to be mad. Despite enabling the Nazi persecution of Jews in Norway and the subsequent death of 736 Norwegian Jews in concentration camps, he was certified as insane and escaped trial – and the death penalty – on the grounds of his mental health.[7]

The traitor Minister-President and Norwegian Fascist leader Vidkun Quisling surrendered on 9 May and was tried for treason in August that year. He was executed by firing squad at Akershus Fortress in Oslo in October 1945.

Norway purged itself of Quislings and collaborators. Charges were filed against 90,000 people with 46,000 sentenced for treason. Of these, 18,000 were imprisoned and 28,000 were fined and deprived of their rights as citizens. Thirty Norwegian collaborators and fifteen Germans were sentenced to death and thirty-seven of the forty-five death sentences were carried out: twenty-five Norwegians and twelve Germans. The Nazi police chiefs in Oslo, Trondheim and Kristiansand and Quisling's Minister of the Interior Albert Hagelin were among those executed.[8]

Those sentenced to death had been guilty of acts of torture, killing prisoners or causing the death of their countrymen by acting as informers. The

largest group of death sentences were handed down to members of the notorious 'Rinnan Gang', a fifty-strong band of traitors in the Trondheim area
led by the Gestapo agent Henry Rinnan. This gang was responsible for the
deaths of at least 100 Resistance members; hundreds more were tortured after
Rinnan's members infiltrated their networks. Rinnan was shot after being
convicted of thirteen murders; nine of his gang were executed, eleven were
sentenced to hard labour for life and many others were given long prison
terms. Some 40 per cent of the death sentences for war crimes in Norway
were connected to the Rinnan Gang.[9]

Another sixty Germans were jailed, most of them members of the security
forces. Arguments still rage over whether sentencing was consistent or became
more lenient with the passage of time and whether some of the charges were
illegal in the first place.

At the end of the war Norway was a busted flush: an economic basket-case.
One of the documents in my file – drawn up by the Civil Affairs department of
the Allied Land Forces – painted a particularly vivid picture of what Norway was
like immediately post-liberation. I could imagine the writer shaking his head as
he typed:

Norway has been thoroughly stripped of commodities of all sorts. There is a real
shortage of food and of all other items of supply. It has never been a country
which produced sufficient items of food and clothing for its own requirements
within its boundaries …

Immediately on liberation, six Allied destroyers moved into various
Norwegian ports. Each of these vessels carried a 'token' shipment of C.A. supplies. The composition of each of these shipments was:

	Tons
Coffee	10.0
Vitaminised Choc	1.5
Soap	2.0
Canned Meat	5.0
Evaporated Milk	3.0
Medical Supplies	0.5
	22.0

Within 10 days from Liberation Day, 12 vessels had been loaded with C.A. supplies and were en route to Norway. These vessels carried more than 20,000 tons
of basic supplies. They are being distributed from Oslo all the way to Tromsø.
Roughly, the shipments were made up as follows:

	%
Food	83
POL	9
Shoes & Clothing	3
Soap	3
Medical supplies	2
	100

The shortage of fuel – both coal and POL [petrol, diesel oil] – is one of the biggest problems here. Again and again, this obstacle is encountered. There is no indigenous production. Every gasworks in the country is shut down, not because of destruction but because there is no coal.

The railroads are in reasonably fair shape, in so far as equipment and right of way are concerned. But the shortage of fuel has reduced operations to a bare minimum of the most important lines.

The economy of Norway depends on its tremendously complex water transport system. Here again, the boats are adequate, but the scarcity of petrol, diesel oil and coal endangers operation.

Norway's fishing industry is the big potential source of thousands of tons of surplus food for world supply. The vessels and the gear, though worn, are serviceable. POL and coal are necessary to insure this activity.[10]

The last document in the collection was a report about the triumphant return of King Haakon to Norway and the simultaneous ending of the military phase of the liberation. From this moment on, Norway was restored as a democracy with a monarch as head of state. The horrors of the war and the scorched-earth policy could be tackled in times of peace. The report read:

The King Returns and the Military Phase is Ended

On 7 June 1945, five years to the day after the pressure of German invasion forced King Haakon VII and his Government to leave Norway to continue the war against the aggressor from the British Isles – and one month after the reception of the first news of the surrender of the German armies to the Allies – His Majesty the King returned to his liberated people.

About one hour before King Haakon VII set foot on liberated Norwegian soil, Brigadier P. H. Hansen, VC, DSO, MC, Head of Civil Affairs Norway, rode from his office through the flag-decked streets of jubilant Oslo to the Royal Palace. He carried with him a letter from SHAEF [Supreme Headquarters Allied Expeditionary Force, in effect Allied forces in north-west Europe] terminating the Military Phase of the Norway operation.

This letter announced to the Norwegian Government that the complete responsibility for civil administration in Norway was restored to His Majesty the King and to the Norwegian Government, confirming that the military situation was such that in accordance with para. 2 of the Inter-Governmental Agreements of 16 May 1944 full and complete responsibility of civil administration in Norway be exercised by the Norwegian Government, subject to certain arrangements necessary to enable the British–U.S. forces to conduct the following operations:

(a) The disarmament and removal of German army, navy and air force personnel, together with German auxiliary organizations and civilian agencies and the disposal of enemy property.
(b) The repatriation of ex-prisoners of war and displaced persons.
(c) The orderly withdrawal of army, navy, and air forces from Norway.

Of the many Civil Affairs responsibilities in Norway, which are now beginning to assume full shape, the more important are the following: To assist the Royal Norwegian Government with:

(a) The provision of supplies for the civil population, including coal and POL.
(b) Disposal of refugees and displaced persons.
(c) The establishment of military courts for the trial of Germans.[11]

This seemed an appropriate moment to go and look round Oslo. My hotel was at the junction of tram tracks close to the Royal Palace so a short walk past the Cultural History Museum would take me to Oslo's main street, Karl Johan's Gate, and from there I could explore town. Facing me as I strolled up the street on a warm and sunny evening was the Norwegian Parliament, the Storting. Campaigning was underway for the 2013 elections and leaflets were thrust into my hands by energetic young people enthusiastically trying to engage passers-by in discussing their voting intentions.

One woman with a handful of red roses waved one at me and urged me to vote for the Labour Party. Behind her was a caravan pasted with posters for the Arbeiderpartiet, the political party that had been in charge at the end of the war and that so many in Finnmark had complained about. The communist persecution, the idealised living standards, the enforced conformity, the refusal to allow evacuees home – surely here was an opportunity for the party to explain why it did this?

I stopped to speak to the lady. 'Ah, you're the Arbeiderpartiet? What Norwegians would call the Social Democrats?'

'Yes, that's right,' the lady said.

'OK, good. I'd be very interested in talking to you,' I said:

I've just come from Finnmark. The people there have a number of things to say about the Social Democrats, particularly about not being allowed to return home after the war and all having to live in the same kind of houses – particularly in Kirkenes, where they say communists were persecuted and subjected to surveillance after the war.

The lady – stylishly dressed, in her mid 50s, with lipstick as red as the roses she was brandishing – looked at me in surprise. 'But they're all communists!' she said, unexpectedly.

'I can see you're busy with the election,' I said, now surprised myself at her reaction. 'But I'd really like to talk to you about this. Perhaps I could email you some questions and areas to talk about and we might go through this when you have a little more time?'

'Sure,' she said. 'I'm a member of the parliament so you can write to me there.' She wrote her email address down on an election leaflet and gave it to me.

'Marit ... Nybakk ...,' I read it back to her. 'Great. Where do you represent, by the way?'

Marit Nybakk had returned to waving roses at passers-by. 'Oslo,' she said. [12]

Even better, I thought. It would be interesting to see what Marit said. (See Appendix Three.)

I walked over to the Akershus Fortress to ask in the Defence Museum about a photograph I'd seen in Gamvik of the house of rags that forty people had sheltered in immediately after the Germans burned their homes. The attendants gave me the email address of the picture curator and I looked round their displays before moving on to the Resistance Museum. I'd been there and remembered the spot where the Resistance members had been shot. There it was: a small paved memorial area with a cross backing up to one of the walls of the fortress. These execution sites seem more forlorn and lonely the older I get. The thought of someone's life ending here, blindfolded and tied to a stake, seems incredibly sad.

My intention had been to look at how this national museum reflected the war, and whether there was a bias in favour of the 'the boys in the forest' in Oslo compared with what happened in the north. But the truth is that so much happened in Norway during the war it was hard for me to keep track. The museum did what I thought was a reasonably thorough job of telling the story of the war and the part played in it by Norwegians, both north and south, both against the Nazis and for them. Even seventy years later, new research brings to light aspects of the Second World War in Norway, some of it distinctly uncomfortable. [13]

I walk back to Karl Johans Gate and to the benches in front of the Parliament building. This is a nice area to rest and relax, perhaps have a drink outside the Hotel Bristol or get an ice cream and sit for a while.

My mind drifts back to my conversation in Honningsvåg with the film maker Knut Erik Jensen, a man who has done a great deal of research into the war years and has met many influential people with a bird's-eye view of history. He'd said:

The war in Norway was the fight against Bolshevism. I interviewed the king about this. He described the scorched-earth period as the worst catastrophe in Norwegian history since the Black Death. He said he went up to inspect the damage in that area. I asked him what made the greatest impression on him and he said: 'When we passed over Hammerfest there was nothing. There was snow on the ground so there was nothing casting shadows. It was as if nobody had ever lived there.'

While making his series he said he'd met Jørgen Juve, one of Norway's most famous footballers, who went to Finnmark as a journalist and photographer with the 2 Bergkompani, the soldiers trained in Scotland who went back as Colonel Dahl's military mission. Juve is Norway's all-time international top scorer and played in the quarter-finals of the 1936 Berlin Olympic football tournament when Norway defeated Germany 2–0 in front of Goebbels, Goering, Hess and Hitler. Watching his first football match, and with Germany having won 9–0 against Luxembourg in the first round, Hitler left early in a huff. Juve came home with a bronze medal.[14]

'I met Jørgen Juve when I was making the series about Finnmark,' Knut Erik said:

He gave me all the pictures he took at the time, including some of the girls having their hair cut off. He arrived three weeks after the liberation and he said: 'This is not Norway, this is a strange place.'

When I grew up there was nothing in the history books about this time and no one was invited into the schools to talk about it. There are still old people around who remember the way it was. It's not long ago. I reached the age of 40 without ever having seen Nazi newsreel of the occupation – and it was just lying in the archives. I found 35mm colour newsreels of the German troops coming from Finland into Kirkenes, playing with Sami children with music and propaganda and everything – you know [he impersonates a German announcer from the 1930s], 'German troops leaving Finland' – and they said no one had touched this until I opened the box in 1980.

It was the same in Moscow, in Austria. It has been there all this time and no one had seen it. I took the photographs in my book from the original negatives. It's the history of this area, the war history of this area, partly recorded through the lens of the occupiers and the liberators.

It's been thirty years since my series was shown on TV. The film is out of print and the book – *Til Befolkningen!* – is unobtainable. Why?[15]

The questions in my mind were mounting. They'd been mounting since I arrived, really. I was particularly puzzled about the persecution of the communist partisans in Kirkenes. It seemed fairly obvious that if the Soviet Union was only 7km away you might try and help undermine the German occupation force.

Now a celebrated international film-maker was complaining that he couldn't get his Oscar-winning films about the scorched-earth period shown on TV, nor get his book reprinted.

Then there was the inability to prosecute anyone for the murders at Hopseidet, when there were witnesses and defendants and one soldier even confessed to firing at least some of the shots – and the Arbeiderpartiet government not letting people go home after the war, making them live in government-approved houses.

The questions were turning into quite a list, and I was far from the end of it.

19

DARK CHAPTERS AND COLD WARS

That strange phenomenon – when roles are reversed and the prisoners become the guards, adopting the same behaviour as their hated captors – seems to have happened in immediate post-war Norway. In the prison camps, manned by Home Front Resistance fighters and the Norwegian 'police' volunteers trained in Sweden, the Germans and the NS collaborators got a taste of what it was like to be on the receiving end:

> The guards … were mostly quite young men with no training or experience in the treatment of prisoners. Some of them had personal experience as inmates of prison camps and had acquired from the Germans and the NS police their ideas of how to treat prisoners. There were cases in which the guards made use of irregular methods of punishment, such as strenuous drill and in some cases, blows and kicks, or amused themselves by frightening the prisoners by firing over their heads or in other ways.[1]

Writing about the liberation twenty years later, in *Norway and the Second World War* – which dates from 1966 but which is still on sale today – Andenaes, Riste and Skodvin argued that these episodes were magnified 'out of all proportions':

> It could hardly have been expected that a settlement of such proportions, carried out with the assistance of thousands of young and untrained people – many of them with their nerves on edge after several years of active opposition to the occupation authorities – should have been accomplished without irregularities of any kind.[2]

Those 'irregularities' that did happen were sporadic incidents blown out of proportion at the time, which soon stopped, they claimed. 'There was hardly any country where the liberation and the reaction against enemy collaborators took place in a calmer and more disciplined manner than in Norway.'[3]

However, the use of German prisoners to clear their own mines – in contravention of the Geneva Convention – is another questionable episode in a series of dark chapters for the Norwegian government after the war.

At the end of the war in May 1945 there were 98,000 mines left buried in Finnmark alone. Work started to clear them within fourteen days of the war's end. German prisoners were assigned to clear the mines, many with no protective clothing and only the most basic of mine-detecting equipment – generally long-handled sticks with metal needles on the end to find the mines. The death rate among these prisoners was appalling.

Professor Anders Christian Gokstad examined records of the Allied Command that were held in Oslo and found that demining operations up to 21 June 1945 were responsible for the deaths of 119 Germans and 163 wounded; 2 Norwegians and 4 Britons were also registered as wounded. A month later, in late July 1945, the figures had risen to 179 dead and 292 wounded. However, by the time of the last registration before operations were suspended, on 29 August 1945, that figure had risen dramatically to 275 Germans killed and 392 wounded: a weekly average over the twelve weeks of operations of 23 Germans dead and 32 wounded. That's 3 Germans killed and 4 wounded every day.

In a 2006 interview with the magazine VG, Gokstad discussed his findings, published in a book for the University of Bergen's Department of Social Medicine. 'The subject is limited, but it is a bit questionable how this matter was handled,' he said. 'It is not just the trappings of our history. We were quite vengeful at the time, and it is a dark chapter.'[4]

The German High Command thought so too, and protested – ironic, given their use of Soviet prisoners of war – citing Article 32 of the Geneva Convention, which forbade the use of prisoners of war for dangerous or harmful work. But the Norwegians claimed the Geneva Convention did not apply, as the war was over and the Germans were 'disarmed combatants' who had surrendered unconditionally.

In May 1946 de-mining operations restarted after both sides reached agreement. This time a Pioneer Company of 600 former German prisoners was formed to clear landmines and ammunition in large parts of northern Norway. The men were apparently paid well for their efforts until demining stopped in September 1946.[5]
As the interviews in this book can testify though, there was still plenty of live ammunition to be found.

On 19 February 1948 the Nuremberg war-crimes trial found General Lothar Rendulic guilty of three charges of war crimes relating to the murder of civilians, shooting of hostages, execution of partisans and destruction of villages and towns in Greece, Yugoslavia and Albania. He was found not guilty of the destruction of Norway. The court said of him:

> The defendant is charged with the wanton destruction of private and public property in the province of Finnmark during the retreat of the XXth Mountain Army commanded by him. The defendant contends that military necessity required that he do as he did in view of the military situation as it then appeared to him.
>
> Villages were destroyed. Isolated habitations met a similar fate. Bridges and highways were blasted. Communication lines were destroyed. Port installations were wrecked. A complete destruction of all housing, communication and transport facilities was had. This was not only true along the coast and highways, but in the interior sections as well. The destruction was as complete as an efficient army could do it.
>
> While the Russians did not follow up the retreat to the extent anticipated, there are physical evidences that they were expected to do so. Gun emplacements, foxholes and other defence installations are still perceptible in the territory ... mute evidences that an attack was anticipated.
>
> We are not called upon to determine whether urgent military necessity for the devastation and destruction in the province of Finnmark actually existed. We are concerned with the question whether the defendant at the time ... acted within the limits of honest judgment on the basis of the conditions prevailing at the time.
>
> The course of a military operation ... is loaded with uncertainties, such as the numerical strength of the enemy, the quality of his equipment, his fighting spirit, the efficiency and daring of his commanders and the uncertainty of his intentions. These things when considered with his own military situation provided the facts ... which furnished the basis for the defendant's decision to carry out the 'scorched-earth' policy in Finnmark as a precautionary measure against an attack by superior forces.
>
> It is our considered opinion that the conditions as they appeared to the defendant at the time were sufficient upon which he could honestly conclude that urgent military necessity warranted the decision made.
>
> This being true, the defendant may have erred in the exercise of his judgment but he was guilty of no criminal act. We find the defendant not guilty on this portion of the charge.[6]

Rendulic was sentenced to twenty years' imprisonment, later reduced to ten, and on 1 February 1951 he was released from jail. He died in 1971 aged 83.[7]

In what can only be described as one of the darkest of the dark chapters of post-war Norwegian history, it was decided that in 1951 all the graves of the Soviet prisoners of war spread across Norway should be collected and placed in one mass grave. This was carried out in an operation called Operation Asphalt. More Russians died in Norway between 1942 and 1945 than Norwegians did at home or abroad during the entire war.

The place that was selected for this mass grave was the island of Tjøtta, an extremely remote location on the western coast, well away from any of Norway's main cities. Getting to Tjøtta today requires a great deal of forethought: it's possible to drive there but only from a certain direction, otherwise ferry connections are needed. There is an air link but only to a small airstrip at Sandnessjøen and from there a further journey by road is necessary.

Up to 8,000 Soviet POWs who lost their lives in German captivity were found in more than 200 different places in the country, mostly in northern Norway. In a rapid and secret operation overseen by then-Defence Minister and former chief of the Resistance Jens Christian Hauge, their bodies were exhumed, transferred to lorries and boats and moved down to Tjøtta. The operation was so fast that, when the decision to move the bodies was made in summer 1951, their final resting place had not yet been decided. Operation Asphalt got under way in the autumn of that year but was dogged with controversy and was deeply unpopular.[8]

According to author Halvor Fjermeros, who wrote *With Corpses in the Cargo*, the remains of the bodies were loaded into flimsy paper sacks and the crew of one of two freighters charged with transporting this grim and grotesque cargo was close to mutiny because of the stench and the sickening conditions.[9] The freighters were apparently followed by a marine vessel with orders to fire warning shots if unrest occurred in ports along the way and secret service agents were on hand to observe and report any 'communist resistance' to the transportation of the bodies. In the town of Mo i Rana, one of the largest population centres on the way to Tjøtta, protests were so strong that the operation was called off personally by Hauge, and 700 to 800 people staged nightly demonstrations in the local graveyard. These protests – dubbed 'the graveyard war' – were not mentioned in the media at the time.[10]

Many of the monuments that had been in place at the original burial sites were blown up or broken. One construction worker who questioned why a memorial stone at Bjornelva was being blown up was apparently told, 'It is unpleasant for these tourists to see these Russian grave memorials standing around like this'.[11]

The Tjøtta Soviet War Cemetery was formally opened on 8 July 1953. The removal and relocation of the bodies caused the deepest diplomatic conflict between Norway and the Soviet Union, according to Fjermeros, who says the operation has been consistently misrepresented to the public by the War Graves Service.

The grave site has not been treated with respect and does not do a proper job of honouring the memory of those it seeks to, he believes, noting that, in 2002, the Service removed prisoner name plates, citing maintenance considerations. After vocal criticism from local enthusiasts and in the national media, the name plates were replaced in 2008.

Fjermeros accused the Norwegian government of missing the 60th anniversary of the opening of Tjøtta in 2013 as an opportunity to right the wrongs of history by improving information and signposting about the dead – as well as explaining how they ended up in such a remote spot. He wrote, 'In this way the Norwegian authorities continue a history of silence and sadness when it comes to honouring those who suffered most in our country during the German occupation. Understand that, if you can.'[12]

The operation is still vivid in the minds of those who saw it. Eva Larsen remembered seeing the lorries arriving in Kirkenes to take away the war dead from the town, both German and Soviet. The German cemetery in the town, based in the garrison district of Prestøia, was particularly large. 'I remember the big lorries came to collect all the bodies,' Eva said. 'I was at school, but we saw some bones sticking out of the truck. They took all the Germans and all the Russians too. There are no signs of it now.'[13]

Historian Kristian Husvik Skancke believes the post-war government ordered Operation Asphalt due to a combination of factors: Cold War paranoia about the intentions of Soviet visitors, post-war opposition to the honouring of German war dead and a desire to consign the war to history. 'Some people feared that the Soviets would use access to war graves as opportunities for espionage,' he said:

> Because of that they relocated the bodies to one location. That's Cold War politics. The German dead were relocated too. After the war no one wanted to be reminded of the Germans so they were moved to a few cemeteries, like at Narvik. People didn't want grave markers with swastikas on them, for example in Hammerfest, where there were lots of German dead in the cemetery. They were all moved out, probably to the big cemetery in Narvik. They didn't want the memories of the war, or German tourists coming to look in the graveyards after the war. Germans were seriously unpopular in the immediate post-war period.[14]

Work on salvaging the 2,456 dead from the sinking of the MS *Rigel* – 2,098 Soviet prisoners, the remainder Germans and Norwegians – started in spring 1969 and was consecrated on 6 September 1970. The bodies that were found were buried in a separate war grave beside the Soviet cemetery known as the Tjøtta International War Cemetery.

War historian and author Roger Albrigtsen from the group FKLF considers Operation Asphalt a kneejerk reaction to the new politics of the Cold War, which stands as a shameful episode. 'If the Cold War hadn't happened, the partisans in the north might have been heroes,' he said:

> We might not have had the prisoners of war who died in Lakselv dug up in 1951 in some kind of panic operation because we didn't want Soviet spies coming in to spy on us.
>
> The book *With Corpses in the Cargo* has opened up the stories of the people who dug up all those prisoners. I've done some work on 'Asphalt' and I spoke to a man who worked on this in Porsanger. I called him up and he said, 'I don't want to go into this, please. It was so terrible.' I could tell by his voice that he's been suffering trauma about what happened in 1951, and no one has been talking to the guys who dug up the corpses of the prisoners.
>
> Bodies were dug up and put into poor quality asphalt bags, sometimes paper bags. There's one story where they get to Tjøtta [where the mass grave is] and they're hoisting a load of partly decomposing bodies, and the rope just slipped off the bags and a guy underneath was just covered in, well, decomposing body parts.

'Do you think Norway's shown respect to those Soviet prisoners of war with that memorial at Tjøtta?' I asked Roger.

'No. It's tragic – a terrible story,' he said:

> It's a shame really. It was a panic act from the Cold War. In one sense you can understand it happening: 'We don't want these spies to come in.' People suddenly found that these prisoners had been removed from their minds, the collective recollection of the war. A lot of these stories just disappeared from these communities.
>
> There are no memorial places, there are no graves to visit. It's quite extraordinary really. How do you keep up the memories of the war if you have nothing to go and look at?[15]

20

THE WAR IS NOT OVER

In Oslo I receive an email from the man currently in charge of clearing war-time munitions in Finnmark, Lieutenant Commander Wiggo Korsvik of the Norwegian Explosive Clearance Commando. He's a munitions clearance diver and was in charge of ammunition clearance operations in Finnmark in 2010 and 2011. He has been kind enough to answer some of the questions I asked him relating to Second World War munitions remaining in the region.

'Yes, we do find and clear up many tons of all types of ordnance and ammunition in Finnmark still,' he wrote:

> There have been many others involved in the clearance of wartime munitions in Finnmark and I have only taken part in some of it.
>
> Clearance operations have been done from 1945 up to 1999, but we have very few statistics from that period. Reports have been written but they are not in the database. They are probably stored in some boxes deep in the State archive.
>
> We used to work two or three weeks in the spring or early summer to clear explosives in the eastern part of Finnmark County on behalf of the police. In Norway it is the police who are the 'owners' of explosives found outside military areas and they have to request support from the Armed Forces to deal with these munitions.
>
> Here are some examples of what we found and cleared during 10 days of clearance operations by the Explosive Clearance Commando in Finnmark in 2011 (600 explosive devices in total):

Various hand weapon ammunition	13,412
13 mm HE shells (HE = high explosive)	3
20 mm HE German FLAK shells (anti-aircraft)	41
25 mm AP French shells (armour piercing)	122
25 mm HE French shells	68
37 mm HE German PAK (anti-tank) shells	2
37 mm AP shells	11
37 mm SAP German shells (SAP = semi armour piercing)	1
47 mm German SAP shells	1
50 mm HE German PAK shells	20
50 mm SAP German shells	70
60 mm French HE Mortars	65
75 mm HE German shells	2
75 mm German Shape charge (highly concentrated steel or concrete-busting charges)	2
81 mm HE (Unknown nationality) mortars	3
88 mm German SAP shells	2
88 mm Rocket Propelled Grenades	1
105 mm German HE shells	56
105 mm German SAP shells	6
Detonators	67
Igniters for hand grenades	28
Landmine igniters	45
Various fuses	14
German bomb fuses	4
German egg hand grenade	1
Various explosive charges	9

In previous years we also have cleared many kinds of air-dropped bombs, sunken contact sea mines, depth charges, anti-tank landmines, all sort of projectiles ranging from 12.7mm up to 240mm, RPGs and hand grenades. There have also been empty container-bomb shells with live fuses, all sort of projectile fuses, bomb fuses, igniters, detonators and pure explosive charges. These are mostly of German origin but there are also French, British, Russian, Polish, Dutch and Italian munitions.

Lieutenantt Commander Korsvik has sent me details of where his team looked for munitions in 2011. Searches were concentrated in the areas around Hasvik near Sorøya, at Berlevåg near Neiden (where the final battle was), and around Kirkenes at Vadsø, Straumsfjellet, Kjelmøya and Storskog. There are pictures of rusty shells and bullets and also of fairly large detonations in fjords and off various coastlines. In one picture a diver in scuba gear is attaching what looks like a fishing net to a sea mine so it can be lifted from the seabed. A picture alongside shows a powerful eruption of water possibly 50m high from the fjord as the mine is safely detonated.

I wrote back to him and a conversation I hadn't expected began to develop. 'How dangerous is it for your teams to disarm or destroy these munitions?' I asked 'It's very dangerous,' he wrote:

Our motto is: Initial Success or Total Failure. The munition is often in a very good condition when we find it. Everyone who deals with EOD [Explosive Ordnance Disposal] knows that ordnance which isn't in its original packing must be treated as armed and dangerous – and deadly in the worst case, because it is exactly that!

Military-trained EOD operators have all the necessary education and training in how to deal with this problem and of course in the safest way possible. We sometimes have to destroy the ordnance in place, because it's not safe to move it. This is of course if the area can withstand a High Order detonation, otherwise we can do a 'Render Safe' procedure using Low Order techniques. But very often we consider the ordnance to be safe for transport and we move it to an approved demolition site or to a safer area nearby for disposal.

We clear minefields using a variety of methods – metal detectors, ground penetrating radars, sometimes mechanically or with explosives), but sometimes we are forced to it manually. We have to get down on our knees and use a prodding stick (a thin metal rod) and stick it gently into the ground with a 30-degree angle. It is a very slow and time consuming process and in order to clear just 1 square metre it's necessary to do 1,090 inserts.

I wonder if this ammunition must be quite unstable by now. I have heard stories from kids in the 1960s putting the shells and machine-gun belts on fires on the beach to blow them up, I tell him.

He wrote:

This is true, even though I can't confirm it. But every year we send out warnings about the danger of putting up bonfires on soft ground, due to the possible danger of explosives lying in the ground. There have been fatal accidents due to explosives found by civilians in Finnmark and other places in Norway too, due to the remnants of war.

I started my career in the Navy as a diver because this was my hobby. First I became a ships' diver, then a 'Hard Hat' diver (like the 'siebe Gorman' antique diving helmets) and finally a clearance diver. The interest for working with explosives has just gradually grown in me together with my training and education. It feels good when you are able to make life safer for others and it's very good when this takes effect both in a military as well as a civilian way.

Best regards
Wiggo Korsvik
Lieutenant Commander
SO EOD-IEDD, J3-5 Protection & Security
Norwegian Joint Headquarters[1]

I stood up and looked out of my window, watching students crossing the triangle of tram lines on Tullins Gate to meet friends in the café bar across from this Holberg hotel, passing a homeless guy sitting in a doorway. So the stories in the north were true. There was still tons of ammunition in the ground from the war.

High on the list of truly depressing episodes from Norway's war period – and the last in this collection of scorched-earth stories – is that of the '*Lebensborn*' war children, fathered by German soldiers with Norwegian mothers.

Their crime – to be, as was so delicately put, a 'Nazi bastard' – led to lifetimes of rejection, persecution and discrimination. A legal challenge to the European courts in 2007 claiming a breach of their human rights was rejected on the grounds that it happened too long ago, but these children – who call themselves 'the unwanted ones' – will never be able to outrun their history.

Official registers record 8,000 war children born during the occupation of Norway, a policy positively encouraged by the German authorities to generate more blond-haired, blue-eyed children to replace the 'Aryan blood' lost in the war. The real figure is probably 12,000; it may be more. Their stories – like so many of these Norwegian war stories – are tragically sad and full of cruelty, pain and brutality.

The SS organisation Lebensborn (meaning 'Well of Life') was the brainchild of Heinrich Himmler. It was established in Germany before the war as an instrument of Nazi racial policy for increasing the numbers of 'Aryan' children. Norwegians were ranked as 'racially desirable' among the populations of occupied countries alongside the Danish and Dutch; French-speaking Belgians and the French were less so.

Reichskommissar Terboven was an enthusiastic supporter from the earliest days of the occupation, seizing an opportunity to show how the Lebensborn programme should be organised outside Germany. By the end of 1941 there were about 730 '*Lebensborn*'; a year later 2,200. By May 1945 registered numbers had topped 8,000, with ten dedicated childrens' homes across Norway, spread around Oslo, Bergen, Kristiansund and Trondheim.[2]

But sleeping with the enemy did not go down well with the locals. 'Being pregnant and giving birth to a baby with a German soldier as the father created stigma: the women were condemned often by society as a whole and by their close family,' wrote archivist and author Kåre Olsen:

> German soldiers, members of an occupant force, were the enemy. Neither family nor friends would accept a girl with a German boyfriend. If the girl became pregnant, rejection by both family and friends might follow. The mother in many cases had nowhere to turn but to the German authorities.[3]

When mothers did ask for help, the Lebensborn organisation paid for clothes and prams and provided a place in a maternity home. Medical expenses were paid by Germany, which also covered the cost of bringing the baby up 'until the end of the war'. It was not clear what would happen after that, Olsen notes. Until then these children were to be regarded as 'German outposts in the Norwegian people'.

Around 100 children were given for adoption to Norwegian families and 200 were sent to Germany for adoption, with between 600 to 700 adoptions in preparation at the end of the war. Around 10 per cent of the 2,514 Norwegian women who had either had babies with or were pregnant by German soldiers at the end of 1942 went to live in Germany. However, at least 30 per cent of the babies were fathered by Germans who were already married. Some women did not want to marry or identify the fathers. The Wehrmacht did not allow soldiers to marry abroad until 1942 and after then only to 'racially valuable' women in Holland, Norway, Denmark and Sweden. After the bride's racial pedigree had been thoroughly examined – using photographs and racial certificates of the parents and grandparents – the German man had to guarantee that she could live with him in Germany. Hitler had the final say if all these conditions could be satisfied.[4]

With 350,000 Germans in Norway at the end of the war, some not leaving until 1947, Olsen puts the true figure of German-Norwegian children at 10,000 to 12,000. In a population of 3 million, he estimates that 1 in 10 Norwegian women between 15 and 30 – about 400,000 women – had a German boyfriend during the war. 'Such figures are important for understanding why the war children, their mothers and other women with German boyfriends became a central topic in heated public debate in Norway after the end of the war,' he wrote.[5]

Some mothers fled to Sweden with their children, only to be refused entry as Norwegian refugees because they had had relations with German soldiers. Their children were not accepted as refugees by the Norwegian authorities either. One case for rejection concluded with 'The child has a German father', thus contravening Norwegian law – legally, both mother and child were Norwegian citizens.

A famous *Lebensborn* case is that of Anni-Frid 'Frida' Lyngstad, one of the singers in the pop band Abba. She was a 'child of shame': her mother was Norwegian, her father was a Nazi officer. Her grandmother took her to Sweden to escape the abuse and mistreatment she experienced in her home village in northern Norway. Anni-Frid's mother died of kidney failure before her daughter was 2; three decades later she traced her father and was reunited with him.[6]

At the end of the war these 'whores of Germans' suffered public hostility in the street and in their neighbourhoods. Some were forcibly shaved and had their hair cut off publicly. This was despite the government and the Home Front forbidding vigilante settling of scores.[7]

'In order to avoid friction a large number of them were placed in protective detention, altogether over 1,000,' wrote Andenaes, Riste and Skodvin in 1966, 'but then many of these women were notorious prostitutes who were suspected of being carriers of venereal diseases. They were gradually released as the agitation subsided.'[8]

In August 1945 the government brought in a new law stripping Norwegian citizenship from women who married a German soldier and banishing them to Germany. Several thousand were sent packing. Some were imprisoned and many lost their jobs in state or municipal institutions. After the 1945 election, the government appointed a committee to discuss the war child problem, amid claims that they could become a 'fifth column' in Norwegian society. An editorial in the daily paper *Lofotposten* in May 1945 argued:

> All these German children are bound to grow up and develop into an extensive bastard minority in the Norwegian people. By their descent they are doomed in advance to take a combative stance. They have no nation, they have no father, they just have hate, and this is their only heritage. They are unable to become Norwegians. Their fathers were Germans, their mothers were Germans in thought and action. To allow them to stay in this country is tantamount to legalising the raising of a fifth column. They will forever constitute an element of irritation and unrest among the pure Norwegian population. Its is best, for Norway as well as for the children themselves, that they continue their lives under the heavens where they naturally belong.[9]

The committee decided Norway should take care of these 'innocent victims' – although its chairman suggested sending the 8,000 children en masse to Australia to help with its post-war labour shortage.

The twists and turns of the unfortunate *Lebensborn* children continued unresolved for the next fifty years. Some 'German brats' – as common parlance dubbed them – had swastikas daubed on their schoolbooks. One girl had a swastika carved into her forehead by a drunken fisherman with a nail.

Some children who went to Germany were brought back to Norway in a hamfisted virtual kidnapping; Norwegian mothers banished to the ruins of post-war Germany ended up living on food parcels sent from 'home'. There are shocking tales of sexual abuse and physical and mental cruelty towards these children, coupled with almost complete indifference from the Norwegian government until the turn of the twenty-first century, when a group of *Lebensborn* children filed a lawsuit in the European courts accusing the government of violating their human rights.

Randi Hagen Spydevold, an Oslo lawyer who represented 170 war children in the case, cited a speech broadcast on the BBC by the exiled government in London during the occupation, which warned Norwegian women they would be punished if they had relationships with German soldiers.

'Every society has its abusers,' Spydevold said in a newspaper article in 2001. 'But this was systematic and the government didn't do anything about it. It got legitimised because the government sent these messages to the man in the street.'[10]

Norway's parliament apologised to the war children in 2002 and awarded them compensation but the *Lebensborn* activists fought on, demanding proper recognition for the loss of their childhood and the disgusting episodes they have endured. The war children claim reached the European Court of Human Rights in 2007 but was turned down on the grounds that it was too long ago.

Finn Kristian Marthinsen, a member of the Justice Committee which recommended to parliament that the war children be compensated, said at the time:

> Norwegian society has to say that we are sorry. It was wrong because these children did nothing criminal. They have suffered because of their mother and father, and that is unfair. It is a black spot on the history of Norway.[11]

There are shocking stories of sexual and physical abuse meted out to the unfortunate ones growing up in childrens' homes. In one, children were force-fed until they vomited and were then made to eat their own vomit. In another, people came to the back door at night, paid staff half a ham and a bottle of alcohol and were let in to abuse the children. Other reports suggest the children were subjected to experiments with LSD in which at least five died.

One *Lebensborn* claimant, Paul Hansen, was categorised as 'mentally retarded' after a prominent 1940s psychologist argued that, as the mothers must have been retarded to go with Germans, the children must be retarded as well. He spent his early years growing up in a childrens' home where his fellow inmates relieved themselves in the room.

Another, Gerd Fleischer, registered as *Lebensborn* number 2620, realised at school that her classmates hated her. 'I was seven years old,' she said, 'and the first bad word I learned in Norwegian was "tyskerhore" [German whore]. I learned

very soon that there was something very wrong with me, basically wrong with
my blood. I was the child of the hated.'

Things got worse at home when her mother married a former member of the
Norwegian Resistance. 'My stepfather had good reasons to hate me, and he did.
He was violent to my mother and me,' she said.[12]

One war child who acted as a spokesman for the compensation claim group,
Bjorn Lengfelder, has resigned himself to getting on with this life. 'One myth
about the programme is that all *Lebensborn* homes were special brothels, where
German officers and soldiers could sleep with selected women of pure, Aryan
blood, so as to help build the aforesaid race,' he said:

> History has shown that this is not entirely correct but it is a fact that German
> servicemen were encouraged to sleep with as many suitable girls as possible. In
> Norway, as in other occupied countries, nature for the most part took its course;
> girl met boy, they fell in love – and there we were. Some 12,000 to 13,000 of us,
> all in all. Which makes us love children, and not the result of a systematic breed-
> ing system. Of course the result of most of these romances was exactly what
> Himmler wanted: pure, clean Aryan offspring to bring forward the thousand
> year Reich.
>
> At the end of the war there was one *Lebensborn* home in each country, except
> in Norway, where there were nine, with plans for another six. This large number
> stems from the fact that the Nazis considered the Norwegians to be direct
> descendants of the Vikings – obviously the 'original Aryans', in their view.

He too has sad tales to tell of brutality, sexual abuse and hatred being directed
towards children, particularly from those in positions of authority.

'In the Norwegian population, there was a hatred directed at us children,' he said:

> A brother and sister, 5 years old, were placed in a pigsty for two nights and two
> days. Then in the kitchen they were put in a tub and scrubbed down with acid
> till they had no skin left because 'we have to wash that Nazi smell off you'.
> Because he was a war child, the boy was harassed at school and in his close
> environment, without anybody trying to stop it. As a 9-year old he was, with his
> teacher's blessing, raped by some older boys at school.
>
> At one orphanage it was routine that members of a neighbouring Christian
> sect came to fetch children and bring them with them. Then they sexually
> abused them until they were unable to walk. On bringing them back, they were
> given 'fresh children' for the same purpose.
>
> Schoolteachers were also active with harassment and abuse. They would
> shout, 'You German offspring are too stupid to learn anything; go sit at the back
> of the room and shut up!' There are several examples that teachers and others,

who supposedly were to look after and care for the children, lined up the 'Nazi brats' – and urinated on them.

Even as late as the end of the twentieth century the hatred and hostility towards these children was still vicious, Mr Lengfelder says:

> For us the war is not entirely over. A few years ago a group of members of our union met at a café in Oslo, on their way to our annual meeting. A man at the next table heard what they were talking about and jumped up, furiously yelling, 'You Nazi bastards should get the hell out of here!' Then he tossed his hot coffee at them.
>
> We were children! We were placed in homes for the retarded and the mentally ill, got no proper schooling, were harassed, mistreated, sexually and physically abused. For one single reason: we had German fathers.
>
> Norway's treatment of us – the unwanted ones – is so bizarre and so far beyond civilised and decent behaviour, that in most ways it stands uniquely alone.[13]

I have been reading Knut Hamsen's strange novel *Hunger* while I've been in Norway and it's been at times a welcome relief from this seemingly unending stream of brutal treatment of fellow human beings. It's fairly safe to say that the story of Norway's war has not renewed my faith in human nature.

But Oslo is a beautiful city and I have a sunny afternoon ahead of me before my flight home tomorrow. The futuristic white Opera House is new to me, so I spend an hour walking over its roof and watching drama students perform theatrical moments for donations for charity, looking over the district of new high-rise office blocks that has been built for management consultancy firms along the downtown waterfront.

'Does the world need more management consultants?' I think to myself on the Opera House roof. 'And, if it does, why not put investment like this into somewhere that needs it, like Kirkenes?'

Oslo has changed enormously since I was last here in 2006, and I feel I have changed enormously too in the two weeks since I first touched down at the city's Gardemoen airport for my connecting flight to Kirkenes. Although the people I met in the north had harsh words for those running the country from Oslo, the capital is a pleasant place: relaxed, pretty and civilised. But physically and mentally there is a very wide gulf between the war in Oslo and the war in Finnmark.

I walk back into town from the Opera House, pausing to rest on a park bench looking back at the harbour. The words of Kirkenes businessman and film star Kåre Tanvik come back to me: '1944 is Year Zero here. Everything was burned. No memories, nothing. Everything was destroyed. We lost our identities in Finnmark – we don't have any history.'

I feel restless, so I get up and walk again. Down to Oslo's Old Town, up and down pavements, across tram lines, past the solid stone buildings of Christiania, historic banks and old doorways where *Hunger*, Norway's most famous novel, is set. I have that book in my pocket. Its Hitler-supporting author was tried as a Nazi sympathiser after the war, having backed the Nazi occupation. But being 85 he was fined rather than jailed. 'Terrible man, great writer,' I believe they say.[14]

Oslo has a sense of permanence. The old hotels, the restaurants, the main roads – everything has been here for 100 years, 150 years – looking just like this. Kongensgate, Kirkegate, Nedre Slottsgate, Radhusgata – these roads are the core of the city, its spine. The buildings are the product of human endeavour over time, built in different styles for different purposes. They have witnessed history. They are in old photographs and in records in the archives; in the stories that shopkeepers tell about their great-grandfather establishing the business and so on. There's a sense of history, of shared space, of significant events having played out here. In Finnmark most buildings don't date back earlier than 1956. The wind-swept, wave-battered wild north of Norway is a long way from the mild, pleasant, civilised capital with its lawned gardens, hanging baskets and pedestrian streets; its banks, restaurants and shops; its trams, trains and buses.

Imagine all this being shattered by shelling, dynamited, in flames, with smoke belching from the windows and slaughtered cattle bleeding into the tramlines. Imagine the horror that Finnmark has seen coming to these streets. Imagine 2,000 women, children and elderly of Oslo being packed onto a stinking freighter with only two toilets between them for three days.

By seeing what Oslo still has, I have a better understanding of what Finnmark has lost, and that is its sense of self. In Finnmark everything was swept away. Human history was erased and consumed by flames. Photographs of grandmothers and grandfathers were doused in petrol and devoured by the hungry fires. Personal possessions, letters, baptismal gowns, combs, family trunks were simply fuel to an unstoppable bonfire that bought fleeing Germans time to escape but wiped out three generations of toil and effort.

Everything in Finnmark has been replaced – everything. The originals are gone. No one has grandfather's books or great-grandmother's letters, because they all turned to ashes in the flames. Kåre Tanvik is right: in the bombs and burnings the people of Finnmark lost something they can never get back – their history, and their identity.

Hitler's scorched-earth order of 28 October 1944 didn't just systematically destroy almost every piece of human habitation in the north of Norway and set the region back half a century or more. It also wiped out the features of Finnmark's forefathers. The memories of the people who braved the stormy seas and weathered the snow and ice to build a proud, thriving community from iron ore and fish, whose possessions were kept in drawers and special boxes in wooden houses, were lost too.

But even then the damage wasn't done. The flames consumed the roots and origins of the people who came next. The children of the scorched-earth policy lost part of themselves: the proof of who they are, the essence of their identity - the pictures and personal things that explain who they are and the detail of where they come from. That is a lot to lose. They have lost their past.

And nothing can bring that back.

APPENDIX 1

THE COST OF THE SCORCHED EARTH POLICY

Evidence was submitted to the trial of the 20th Mountain Army commander General Lothar Rendulic at Nuremberg detailing the scale of the destruction of the scorched-earth policy and its impact on the population and geography. As an unemotional assessment of what the scorched-earth policy actually entailed, it shows just how comprehensive the destruction was.

It is a sobering document.

The estimated cost of the damage to Norway during the war of more than 3 billion Norwegian kroner (in 1940 prices) comes in the form of a letter from the statistical Office of Finnmark, addressed to the Supreme Court Attorney Ivar Follstad, Victoria Terrasse 7, in Oslo, dated 25 February 1947: 'War damages in Finnmark and North Troms.' It states:

> In connection with the claims of reparation by Norway on Germany the Town Council has collected information on the war damages. Those informations are, however, not complete concerning the distribution of the damages on the different districts, but, on the basis of the material produced, the Town Council has been able to put up the following survey on the damages especially as regard Finnmark and North-Troms. The informations are partly based on approximate calculations and do [not] pretend to be complete.
>
> Most of the damages are included in the war damage insurance for buildings and movables amounting to about 270 million Norway Kroner, for all the years of war. The Town Council has no special information about the part falling within the time of evacuation.
>
> *Roads and bridges*
> The road director has estimated the German destructions of roads and bridges in Finnmark during the evacuation in the autumn 1944 to approximately

altogether 24.7 million Norw. Kr. Of this about 11 million Norw. Kr. for roads and 13.7 million Norw. Kr. for bridges.

Telegraph and telephone

The telegraph director has estimated the damage on stations (inclusive radio stations) and on telegraph and telephone wires during the German evacuation of the Finnmark and North Troms in the Autumn 1944 to about 15.6 million Norw. Kr.

Harbours and harbour works

The port director has estimated the war damages on official bridges in the Finnmark and north Troms districts during the German evacuation in the autumn 1944 to approximately 2.2. million Norw. kr.

In addition to this there are considerable damages on private bridges and quays. The amounts for these damages are included in the figures mentioned below by the War Damage Insurance for buildings (risks on industry and civil risk).

Agriculture

The War Damage Insurance from buildings has estimated the war damages on houses and buildings in agriculture in the Finmark and north Troms districts to about 12 mill. kr.

The War Damage Insurance for movables has estimated the war damages on machines and farming outfits domestic animals, crops and furniture to about 6 mill. kr.

The damages to the forests of the Finnmark and the north Troms districts during the war, inclusive the devastation made by the Germans during the evacuation in the autumn 1944 and inclusive future losses due to exploitation of the forests, have been estimated by the Town Council to approximate 25 mill. kr.

Industry

The war damages on industrial buildings in the Finnmark and north Troms districts have been estimated by the War Damage Insurance to about 38 mill. kr.

The War damages on industrial movables in the Finnmark and north Troms districts have been estimated by the War Damage Insurance for movables to about 5 mill. kr

Houses and buildings, movables, civil risks

The War Damage Insurance for buildings has estimated the war damages on buildings in the Finnmark and north Troms (exclusive buildings has estimated the agriculture and industry and those belonging to the state) to about 114 mill. kr.

The War Damage Insurance for movables has estimated the war damages on general movables in the Finnmark and north Troms districts (farming and industrial movables excluded) to about 94 mill. kr.

Stocks

The War Damage Insurance for stocks estimated in September 1945 the evacuation damages in the Finnmark in the autumn 1944 to about 18.4 mill kr.

The actual amounts are now considered 2–3 million Norw. kr. too high, but if all war damages on stock in Finnmark for April 1940–May 1945 are taken into consideration, the amount can be accounted for. The war damages outside the evacuation damages only amounted to about 2–3 mill kr.

Goods on board ships

The State Goods War Insurance estimates the war damaged on goods onboard ships in Finnmark during the evacuation in the autumn 1944 to about 1.2 mill. kr.

Various war damages covered by private insurance companies are not to be obtained in detail on Finnmark. The amount of these damages is, however, not estimated to be very high, considering the total amount of damages claimed by all insurance companies together for reparation war damages to be about 16 million Norw. kr. for the whole of the country and for all the years of war.

Ships, freighters, larger and smaller fishing boats as well as all sorts of small vessels

All smaller vessels at a value under 250 kr. were included in the War Damage Insurance as movables and amounts for wreckages and war damages on such boats in the Finnmark are included in the amount of 94 million kr. under the item for movables above.

By the State War Damage Insurance the amount of 1.9 million Norw. kr. was mentioned as the sum that this institution has paid especially for war wrecked boats, but also for partial war damages during the war on boats having their basis in the Finnmark and North–Troms districts.

The reinsurance institute for the fishing fleet BERGEN states that the amount of reparation costs paid by it for totally war-wrecked fishing boats, etc. and for partial war damages on such boats having their basis in the Finnmark and north Troms districts for all the years of war amounted to a total of approximately 2 million Norw. Kr. Perhaps the reinsurance institution is now able to give more exact information and especially also for the damages during the evacuation.

In addition to the two amounts mentioned here of about 1.9 million Norw. kr. and about 2 million Norw. kr. are amounts paid by the private insurance companies for their insurance responsibility on war damages on fishing boats and other boats. As mentioned above no information has been obtained about this last amount.

When these above mentioned amounts are added, the lump sum is about 360 million Norw. kr. for the war damages mentioned under the individual items. It is to be mentioned that these damages cover direct war or direct destruction through war actions. Damages brought about in connection with requisitions of houses and grounds as well materials with special reference to the exceptional wear and tear following the German use for houses and buildings, roads and bridges etc. and material requisitioned is not included in this amount.

The amounts mentioned in most of the above are based on the information presented to the Town Council during the war and immediately after this and they are calculated according to the prices before 9 April 1940.

At present further additional amounts might have arisen by which the final figures would have been still higher.

As a comparison it can be mentioned, that the informations received by the Town, Council up till November 1945 represent the war damages for the whole country including the total losses of ships preliminarily calculated to more than 3 billion Norwegian kroner.

Rubber Stamp: OSLO TOWN COURT
Signature: A. Skien

Damage to medical institutions during the German withdrawal
This second report covers the destruction of the hospitals and medical institutions in Finnmark during the withdrawal: in effect, all of them. Only a small tuberculosis hospital in Nesseby and the hospital in Vadsø were spared:

Finnmark
The following institutions were razed to the ground:

Hospital at Kirkenes	23 beds
nursing home	4 beds
Vadsø	45 beds
another hospital at Vadsø	30 beds
Vadsø hospital	54 beds
another at Vardø	13 beds
Nursing home, Tana	22 beds
Gamvik Red Cross nursing home	7 beds
Mehamn nursing home	12 beds

Red Cross hospital, Kjøllefjord	8 beds
Red Cross hospital, Berlevåg	18 beds
Kjelvik Tuberculosis home, Honningsvåg	38 beds
Red Cross Hospital	18 beds
Hammerfest hospital, Hammerfest	94 beds
St Vincent Hospital, Hammerfest	20 beds
Hammerfest Mental Home	100 beds
Home, Alta	4 beds
Karasjok tuberculosis home	20 beds
another one	7 beds
Tuberculosis home with annex for children	83 beds

North Troms

Skjervøy nursing home, destroyed during the evacuation	12 beds
Målselv tuberculosis home. Used by the German Air Force and afterwards destroyed	14 beds
Lyngen tuberculosis home, badly damaged during the evacuation	18 beds

Source:

Reports submitted to the Nuremberg court in 1947: pp. 2749–59 in the Rendulic transcripts, at University of North Dakota online archive of Nuremberg trials, 1947: www.und.edu/instruct/calberts/Nuremberg/Rendulic.

APPENDIX 2

WORST CRASHES IN NORWEGIAN AVIATION HISTORY

The 1944 FW Condor crash at Lavangen remains the worst air crash on Norwegian soil in aviation history. Others include:

29 August 1996	Vnukovo Airlines Flight 2801 Tupolev 154 carrying 141 Ukranian miners to Barentsburg crashed into the Opera Mountain on approach to Svalbard Airport at Longyearbyen. All died.
6 May 1988	DHC-7 from Widerøe Airlines, 36 dead when LN-WFN crashed into Torghatten Mountain on approach to Bronnoysund Airport in northern Norway
23 December 1972	Fokker F-28 Fellowship from Braathens flying between Ålesund and Oslo crashed at Asker near Oslo. 40 dead – 5 survivors.
9 August 1961	The Holtaheia crash: Vickers Viking G-AHPM operated by Cunard Eagle Airways crashed near Stavanger killing 34 boys between 13 and 16 from Archbishop Lanfranc school in Croydon near London. The boys were returning from a school trip to Norway. Two of their masters and three crew died as well – 39 dead in total.
2 October 1948	Short Sandringham of DNL: the 'Bukken Bruse' tragedy at Trøndelag near Trondheim. 19 dead of 45 passengers, among the survivors the philosopher Bertrand Russell.
28 August 1947	Short Sandringham *Kvitbjorn* of DNL. Flying between Tromsø and Oslo, LN-IAV crashed in heavy fog into the Klubben mountain close to Lødingen, (North Nordland) leaving 28 passenger and 7 crew dead, a total of 35 dead.

APPENDIX 3

ARBEIDERPARTIET RESPONSE

I never did hear back from Marit Nybakk, despite repeated emails and phone calls after I returned to Britain. Several emails to the Arbeiderpartiet's (Labour Party) press manager explaining my interest in the party's post-war treatment of people from Finnmark – including not allowing people to return, restricting them to a shortlist of approved houses during the Reconstruction and the harassment of communists – went unanswered, until I rang her up. At this point she suggested my questions would be better addressed by Finnmark MPs than by Marit Nybakk, a parliamentary representative for Oslo. I would have liked to hear Marit's thoughts, to be honest.

Finnmark has two Arbeiderpartiet MPs: Kåre Simensen and Helga Pedersen. Helga Pedersen's political adviser told me she 'didn't have time' to answer my questions. I didn't hear back from Kåre Simensen. I will leave readers to draw their own conclusions.

Born in 1947, Marit Nybakk is a long-serving Arbeiderpartiet MP, the vice president of the Norwegian Parliament and a senior figure both in her party and the government. Her biography can be found here: www.stortinget.no/en/In-English/Members-of-the-Storting/Members1/N/Nybakk-Marit/

NOTES

1 'It was absolutely normal growing up playing with ammunition'

1. Bob Carruthers (ed.) (2012), *Hitler's Forgotten Armies: Combat in Norway and Finland*, Barnsley: Pen and Sword, chapter 10, p. 158. ISBN: 978-1-78159-143-7
2. Ibid., p. 163
3. Ibid., p. 177
4. Ibid., pp. 318, 328
5. Ibid., p. 331
6. Tiina Kinnunen and Ville Kivimäki (eds) (2010), *Finland in World War II: History, Memory, Interpretations*, Leiden: Koninklijke Brill, ISBN: 978-90-04-20894
7. Henrik O. Lunde (2011), *Finland's War of Choice: The Troubled German–Finnish Coalition in World War II*, Havertown, PA and Newbury: Casemate Publishers, p. 340. ISBN: 978-1-935149-48-4
8. Major James F. Gebhardt (1989), 'The Petsamo–Kirkenes Operations: Soviet Breakthrough and Pursuit in the Arctic, October 1944', a Leavenworth Paper written for the US Army Command and General Staff College, p. 25
9. Ibid., p. 74
10. Sør-Varanger Historielag (2001), *Sør-Varanger 1906–1939: Jernmalmen skaper et nytt samfunn* (in Norwegian), Sør-Varanger Historielag (Sør-Varanger Historical Society).
11. John Andenaes, Olav Riste and Megne Skodvin (1966), *Norway and the Second World War*, Oslo: Aschehoug. ISBN: 82-03-22163-7
12. Global Non Violent Action database: http://nvdatabase.swarthmore.edu/content/norwegian-teachers-resist-nazi-takeover-education-1942
13. Andenaes et al. (1966), pp. 92–4
14. Private history of Hurtigruten ships: www.hurtigruta.info/Velkommen_eng.html; Hurtigrute museum web pages: www.hurtigrutemuseet.no/en/node/25
15. Bjarnhild Tulloch (2011), *Terror in the Arctic: A True Story from Foreign Occupied Norway in World War II*, Kibworth Beauchamp: Matador, p. 112. ISBN: 978-1-84876-807-9
16. National Archives Tromsø 1941, quoted in Ingrid Immonen (2013), 'Nursing During World War II: Finnmark County, Northern Norway', *International Journal of Circumpolar Health*, 72: 20278. ISSN 2242-3982 (print volumes from 1972–2011): ISSN 1239-9736
17. Annual medical reports 1940, 1941, quoted in Immonen (2013)

18. Immonen (2013)
19. Tulloch (2011), p. 113
20. Ibid., p. 136
21. Kalle Wara (1994), *Kirkenes–Litsa: tur-retur,* Oslo: Falken Forlag. ISBN: 82-7009-280-0
22. Wartime German military map at Grenselandsmuseet, Kirkenes
23. Quotes from Hans Kristian Eriksen (n.d.), *The Second World War in the Borderlands,* Kirkenes: Grenselandsmuseet, used with permission
24. From web page of Lofoten War Museum: www.lofotenkrigmus.no/e_finnmark2.htm and www.visitnorway.com
25. Edvard Radzinsky (1996), *Stalin* London: Doubleday. ISBN13: 978-0-3854-7954-7
26. Gebhardt (1989), p. 76
27. Ibid., p. 142
28. Ibid., p. 123
29. Casualty figures taken from Gebhardt (1989), estimates and research, pp. 186, 168, averaging 16 per cent on each side
30. SHAEF military papers, Col Paul B. Boyd, Head 2/19 CA Unit on Temporary Duty North Russia and Norway, Rpt, 18 Dec 44, SHAEF files, G-5, 17.08, Hist Rpt, Norway, Jkt I
31. Interview with author, August 2013. NB: 'Destination Kirkenes' closed for business at the end of summer 2013
32. Varanger Museum (n.d.), 'Norwegian Partisans in Soviet service 1940–1944'; web page: www.varangermuseum.no
33. Ibid
34. Grenselandsmuseet exhibition, Kirkenes
35. Interview with author, August 2013
36. Yngve Gronvik private document written for this book, August 2013
37. Gebhardt (1989)

2 'Pity for the civilian population is out of place'

1. K.E. Eriksen and T. Halvorsen (1984), *Norge I Krig: Frigjoring,* Oslo: Aschehoug. ISBN-13: 978-8203111440
2. Nuremberg trial transcripts, 'The Hostage Case' – testimony of Ferdinand Jodl p. 2552: www.und.edu/instruct/calberts/Nuremberg/Jodl.html
3. Rendulic order exhibit NOKW 086 Nuremberg evidentiary documents, p. 2: www.und.edu/instruct/calberts/Nuremberg/NOKW_086.html
4. From University of North Dakota Nuremberg transcripts, the Hostage Case: www.und.nodak.edu/instruct/calberts/Nuremberg/NurembergMain.html#
5. Rendulic testimony at Nuremberg, p. 5352: www.und.edu/instruct/calberts/Nuremberg/Rendulic.html
6. Ibid., p. 5354
7. Testimony of Trygve Schance to Nuremberg war crimes trial 26 August 1947, p. 2693: www.und.edu/instruct/calberts/Nuremberg/Schance.html
8. Einar Richter Hansen (2003), *From War to Peace: The Second World War at Nordkapp,* Honningsvåg: Nordkapplitteratur, p. 5. ISBN: 82-7579-010-7
9. Ibid
10. Ibid, p 16
11. From declassified CIA file on Neumann (document 27612403) at Jewishvirtuallibrary. org online collection 'Nazi Perpetrators of the Holocaust': www.jewishvirtuallibrary. org/jsource/Holocaust/OSS/neumann071288.pdf

12. Anne Merete Knudsen (1995), *Refugees in their Own Country*, Alta: Alta Museum pamphlets, p. 8
13. Telegram contents submitted in evidence to the Nuremberg tribunal, Dahl section p. 2644: www.und.edu/instruct/calberts/Nuremberg/Dahl.html
14. Knudsen (1995), p. 10
15. Ibid. p. 11
16. Ibid.
17. Interviews with author, Kirkenes August 2013.
18. Knudsen (1995), p. 14
19. Hansen (2003), p.17
20. Knudsen (1995), p. 16
21. Ibid., p. 17
22. Ibid.
23. Ibid, p18
24. Ibid, p22
25. German Army report by Colonel Herrmann submitted as evidence to Nuremberg in Jodl section, p. 2561. www.und.nodak.edu/instruct/calberts/Nuremberg/Jodl.html
26. Ibid., Table of evacuees, enclosure to 25.
27. Knudsen (1995), p. 27
28. Report of police chief Vardø, evidence to Rendulic prosecution, Nuremberg hostage trial p. 2744: www.und.edu/instruct/calberts/Nuremberg/Rendulic.html
29. Knudsen (1995), p. 28
30. Ibid., p. 30, quoting Laila Thorsen (1981), *Finnmark is Burning: Recollections and Diary Entries from 1944–45*, Oslo: Tiden
31. Captured German Army documents submitted in evidence to Nuremberg trial, Dahl evidence p. 2642: www.und.edu/instruct/calberts/Nuremberg/Dahl.html

3 'The destruction was as complete as it could be'

1. Major General Arne Dahl, giving evidence to the Nuremberg war crimes hearings on conditions in the north of Norway at the end of the war. P.2655: www.und.edu/instruct/calberts/Nuremberg/Dahl.html
2. Patrick Salmon (ed.) (1995), *Britain and Norway in the Second World War*, London: HMSO Books, Chapter 15, p. 148. ISBN 011-701232-7
3. Ibid., p. 149
4. Norsk Biografisk Leksikon: nbl.snl.no/Arne_D_Dahl
5. Norwegian Government report on Alta Battalion, biography of Dahl: www.regjeringen. no: 2 Alta bataljons deltagelse i felttoget på Narvikfronten 1940
6. John F. O'Connell (2007), *The Effectiveness of Airpower in the 20th Century: Part Two (1939–1945)*, Lincoln, NE: iUniverse. ISBN 978-0-595-43082-6; and Earl Frederick Ziemke (1960), *The German Northern Theater of Operations, 1940–1945*, Washington: U.S. Government Printing Office, p. 103
7. Salmon (1995); H.P. Willmott (1995), *Operation Jupiter and Possible Landings in Norway*, London: HMSO. ISBN: 011 701232-7
8. Malcolm Mackintosh (1995), 'The Western Allies, the Soviet Union and Finnmark', in Salmon (1995), p. 229
9. Tonne Huitfeldt (1995), 'Between the Lines, North Norway 1944–5', in Salmon (1995), p. 233

10. Ibid., p. 234
11. Ibid., p. 234, quoted by Huitfeldt
12. Ibid., p. 234
13. Dahl testimony to Nuremberg, p. 2658, University of North Dakota archives: www.und.edu/instruct/calberts/Nuremberg/Dahl.html
14. Wartime Canadian forces newspaper in Europe, Belgian edition, reproduced at: news.google.com/newspapers?nid=1585&dat=19441120&id=B8Y6AAAAIBAJ&sjid=SyoMA AAAIBAJ&pg=1668,7436852
15. Figures quoted by Arnfinn Moland (1995),'Milorg and SOE', in Salmon (1995), p. 149
16. Samuel Mitcham (2001), *The German Defeat in the East*, Mechanicsburg, PA: Stackpole Publishing, p. 144. ISBN 0-81117-3371-8
17. 'The German Northern Theater of Operations 1940–1945' reproduced in Carruthers (2012), chapter 10, p. 216, and biography built from records of Böhme's service from Leksikon Der Wehrmacht website: www.lexikon-der-wehrmacht.de
18. Report of Böhme's death in *Sarasota Herald Tribune*, 29 May 1947
19. Telavåg: www.museumvest.no and Norsk biografisk leksikon;Terboven: http://nbl.snl.no/Josef_Terboven
20. Ole Magnus Rapp (2009),'Gransker nordmenns rolle i leirene', *Aftenposten* 17 September 2009 (translated) at www.aftenposten.no/nyheter/iriks/Gransker-nordmenns-rolle-i-leirene-5581010.html#.
21. Jens Christian Hauge (1970), *Frigjoringen*, Oslo: Glydendal quoted in Salmon (1995), p. 214.

4 The villagers that escaped and the town full of Nazis

1. Interview with author, August 2013
2. Ibid.
3. Nils Johan Ringdal (1995),'Karl Marthinsen' (in Norwegian), in Hans Fredrik Dahl, Guri Hjeltnes, Berit Nøkleby, Nils Johan Ringdal and Øystein Sørensen (eds), *Norsk krigsleksikon 1940–45*, Oslo: J.W. Cappelens Forlag
4. Cato Guhnfeldt (2005),'Skuddene som kostet 28 livet' (translated from Norwegian), *Aftenposten*, 2 August.
5. Ibid.
6. Lars-Erik Vaale (2006) 'Skjebnesvanger likvidasjon' (translated from Norwegian), *Dagbladet*, 2 November
7. Gjerdrum biography from 'Våre falne 1939–1945' (Our Fallen) webpage, at da2.uib.no p. 688
8. Biography of Haakon Saethre: Norsk biografisk leksikon nbl.snl.no/Haakon_Sæthre (translated)
9. Evidence in trial of Hans Latsa, Law Reports of Trials of War Criminals Vol. 14, Court of Appeal 3 December 1948, p. 8, www.worldcourts.com/ildc/eng/decisions/1948.12.03_Norway_v_Latza.pdf
10. Guhnfeldt (2005)
11. Vaale (2006)

5 Still mourning the men of Hopseidet

1. Finnmarken report of my visit 28 August 2013 at: www.finnmarken.no/nyheter/article6831235.ece

2. Lawrence Paterson (2009), *Black Flag: The Surrender Of Germany's U-Boat Forces*, Barnsley: Seaforth Publishing, pp. 100–3. ISBN: 978 1 84832 037-6
3. Brennpunkt (2005), 'Tragedien på Hopseidet' (Translated), Norwegian TV investigation: www.nrk.no/programmer/tv/brennpunkt/5167568.html
4. Paterson (2009), p. 95
5. Ibid., p. 100
6. Interview with author, August 2013
7. Ibid.
8. Paterson (2009), p. 101
9. Printed poster submitted in evidence to Nuremberg by Arne Dahl, p. 2677; University of North Dakota online archive: www.und.edu/instruct/calberts/Nuremberg/Dahl.html
10. Paterson (2009), p. 102
11. Brennpunkt (2005)

6 The white church of Honningsvåg

1. Tjøtta memorial and further details at www.powstories.no
2. Interview with author, August 2013

7 The destruction of Hammerfest

1. 'The Life and Times of Hubert Brooks', at www.hubertbrooks.com
2. 'Norwegian Home Fleet', at www.warsailors.com/homefleet/shipse.html
3. 'Feddersen and Nissen', at http://no.wikipedia.org/wiki/Feddersen_%26_Nissen
4. City engineer's report on the destruction of Hammerfest, 20 April 1945, submitted to the Nuremberg trial in Rendulic testimony, p. 2761. University of North Dakota online archive: www.und.edu/instruct/calberts/Nuremberg/Rendulic.html
5. Interview with author August 2013
6. Ibid.
7. Ibid.
8. Ibid.

8 Refugees, rescues and resistance

1. Biography of Johnson: Store Norsk Leksikon-snl.no/Gunnar_Johnson
2. Interview with author, August 2013
3. A definitive figure of merchant shipping losses varies: official Russian figures say 85 merchant ships and 16 Royal Navy warships (www.rusemb.org.uk/arcticalliedconvoys) while the War Sailors website lists losses by ship and includes Soviet losses: www.warsailors.com/convoys/arctic.html
4. Taken from introduction to exhibition at Royal Museums Greenwich: www.rmg.co.uk/whats-on/exhibitions/arctic-convoys/
5. Figures from Russian Embassy website: www.rusemb.org.uk/arcticalliedconvoys/
6. 'Arctic convoy vet gets medal', *Western Daily Mail*, 31 July 2013, p. 15
7. John Fearn interview with author, September 2013
8. Samuel Eliot Morison (2002 [1956]), *History of United States Naval Operations in World*

War II: The Atlantic Battle Won, Champaign, IL: University of Illinois Press
9. Nancy Eklund Later (ed.) (2007), *Breaking News: How the Associated Press Has Covered War, Peace, and Everything Else*, New York: Princeton Architectural Press. ISBN: 978-1-56898-0
10. From Uboat website: www.uboat.net/allies/merchants/ship.html?shipID=3356
11. Ibid., ID=3357

9 The death of Erika Schöne and other secret tragedies

1. Håvard Klevberg (1996), 'Luftmark i Flymark' (translated), *Forsvarsstudier* 4/1996. Norwegian Institute for Defence Studies. ISSN 0333-3981
2. Lunde (2011)
3. Ibid., p. 370
4. Ibid., p. 368
5. Details of flights from Albrigtsen, Second World War aviation crash website flyvrak: FW200 Salangen: ktsorens.tihlde.org and correspondence with Birger Larsen, curator of the Norwegian Aviation Museum in Bodø
6. Correspondence with Birger Larsen, curator of the Norwegian Aviation Museum in Bodø (see Appendix 2)
7. Roger Albrigtsen (2013), 'Story of Erika Schöne' in Albrigtsen, *Last Letter: Human Fates and German War Build-up Porsanger Area 1940–1945*, Narvik: Kristiansen Publishing
8. Interview with author, September 2013

10 'You must not think we destroyed wantonly or senselessly'

1. Alexander Mikaberidze (2013), *Atrocities, Massacres and War Crimes: An Encyclopaedia*, Santa Barbara, CA: ABC-CLIO. ISBN 978-1-59884-9267-4
2. Maj. John Rawcliffe and Cpt Jeannine Smith (eds) (2006), *Operational Law Handbook*, at http://www.fas.org/irp/doddir/army/law0806.pdf. ISBN: 978-1-42891-067-6
3. Jodl testimony to Nuremberg, p. 2578: University of North Dakota online archive: www.und.edu/instruct/calberts/Nuremberg/Jodl.html
4. Ibid., p. 2601
5. Ibid., p. 2607
6. Ibid., p. 2624
7. Abbreviated form of charges contained in UN War Crimes Commission (1949), *Law Reports of Trials of War Criminals*, Vol. 8, pp. 35–7
8. Istvan Deak (1990), *Beyond Nationalism: A Social and Political History of the Habsburg Officer Corps*, Oxford: Oxford University Press. ISBN 978-0-19992-328-1
9. Gordon Williamson (2012), *German Special Forces of World War II*, Oxford: Osprey Publishing, p. 40. ISBN: 978-1-78096-999-2
10. Bob Carruthers (2013), *The Wehrmacht Experience in Russia*, Henley-in-Arden: Coda Books. ISBN: 978-1-78158-115-5
11. Rendulic testimony to Nuremberg, p. 5341; University of North Dakota online archive: www.und.edu/instruct/calberts/Nuremberg/Rendulic
12. Ibid., p. 5345
13. Ibid., p. 5347

14. Ibid., p. 5348
15. Ibid., p. 5352
16. Submitted to Nuremberg trial as evidentiary document NOKW 086; www.und.edu/ instruct/calberts/Nuremberg/NOKW_086.html
17. Rendulic testimony to Nuremberg, pp. 5353–4
18. Ibid., p. 5359
19. Damage report of Oslo Town Council, see Appendix 1. A 1947 medical report submitted to the Nuremberg trials by Dr Karl Evang of the Norwegian Ministry of Social welfare, requested by Lt Colonel Ivar Follestad, Norwegian Attorney General's Office

11 'Oh, I know of a land far up north …'

1. Interview with author, August 2013
2. From information boards at Tromsø Defence Museum (written by Gunnar Jaklin)
3. Interview with author, August 2013

12 Even in the wilderness, there was war

1. Interview with author, August 2013

13 Into the valley of the damned: the Mallnitz death camp

1. Michael Stokke, Narvik Peace Centre, in questions; Asbjørn Jaklin (2012), 'Slik var dødsleiren i Norge' *Nordlys*, 22 April, reproduced at www.side3.no/ ipad/?articleId=3377272
2. Jaklin (2012)
3. Ibid., quoting Michael Stokke
4. Ibid.
5. Michael Stokke (2013), 'Breakdown of POWs per camp' lecture notes November, Narvik Centre, supplied to author during correspondence
6. E.A.J. Johnson (1971), *American Imperialism in the Image of Peer Gynt: Memoirs of a Professor–bureaucrat*, Minneapolis, MN: University of Minnesota Press, p. 114. ISBN: 0-8166-0-0608-0. (Johnson was Head of the Economics branch of Allied Land Forces Norway and deputy head Supply Branch.)
7. Vlassov: article Valeria Korchagina and Andrei Zolotov Jr. (2001), 'It's too early to forgive Vlassov', *St Petersburg Times*, 6 November, at www.sptimes.ru/index.php?action_id=2&story_id=5830; and Lt Gen. Władysław Anders and Antonio Muñoz (2002); 'Russian Volunteers in the German Wehrmacht in World War II', at http://www. mochola.org/russiaabroad/vlasan01.htm
8. Jaklin (2012)
9. Johnson (1971), Chapter 8
10. Jaklin (2012)
11. Ibid.
12. Report of Captain McGill, British military archive WO331/13, Public Records Office, Kew

13. Ibid.
14. Johnson (1971), Chapter 8, p. 113
15. Report of Captain McGill
16. Statement to British investigators by witness 12, Alexander Smirno, in British military archives, report of Captain McGill, Public Records office, London
17. All witness statements contained in report of British war crimes investigator Captain McGill, British military archives, London
18. Pathologist's report, Captain McGill investigation, as above
19. 'List of German officers and NCOs accused of murder by Russian ex war prisoners'. British military archive within Captain McGill's report, WO 331/13, PRO, Kew
20. From information boards at Bollmanveien memorial sites
21. Michael Stokke, in Jaklin (2012)
22. Michael Stokke, correspondence with author, November 2013
23. Interview with author, August 2013
24. Michael Stokke, correspondence with author, November 2013.
25. From Falstad Centre (u.d.) 'Soviet prisoners of war', exhibition brochure: ISBN: 978-82-92383-19-3, at painfulheritage.no/eng
26. Reinhard Otto (2011), 'Cemeteries of Soviet Prisoners of War in Norway', *Historisk Tidsskrift*, April, ISSN Online: 1504-2944; quoted in Isak Ladegaard (2012), 'Soviet prisoners of war in Second World War: nameless, until now', *Science Nordic*, 30 January
27. Ladegaard (2012), p. 7; Falstad Centre (u.d.)
28. Joachim C. Fest (2013), *Hitler*, Boston, MA: Houghton Mifflin Harcourt. ISBN: 978-0-54419-554-7
29. Alan S. Milward (1979), *War, Economy and Society*, Vol. 5 Oakland, CA: University of California Press. ISBN: 978-0-52003-942-1
30. From Jernbaneverket 50th anniversary web pages: www.jernbaneverket.no (www.jernbaneverket.no/no/startpage1/News/The-Nordland-Line--50-years/)
31. Cross location: www.saltdal.kommune.no
32. Ibid., Botn cemetery
33. Evidence to the Nuremberg trial Vol. 7 59th Day (14 February 1946), p. 433; Avalon project collection, Yale Law School: http://avalon.law.yale.edu/imt/02-14-46.asp: 'Colonel Pokrovsky's Presentation on Criminal Violations and customs of war in the treatment of prisoners.' Date ref amended in this text from original text: 'On 22 June 1943' to 1942 on advice of Michael Stokke
34. Revising down death toll at Korgen to 205 on figures provided by Michael Stokke, correspondence with author, November 2013
35. Rakel Kamsvåg (2012), 'Yugoslav Prisoners of War in Norway' essay for Belgrade International School at Norwegian government website for Serbia: www.norveska.org.rs
36. Falstad Centre (u.d.), p. 7, revising figure of 9,000 civilians on advice of Michael Stokke during correspondence with author
37. Shcherbakov, quoted in Carroll Glines (1999), *Bernt Balchen: Polar Aviator*, Washington, DC: Smithsonian Institute Press, p. 201
38. Glines (1999), p. 202
39. Falstad Centre (u.d.) p. 8
40. Johnson (1971), p. 23. NB: Figures revised on advice of Michael Stokke of Narvik Centre: 25,000 Polish POWs became 1,600 Polish POWs and 10,000 civilian forced labourers, and the Danes were not POWs but volunteer workers
41. Michael Stokke, correspondence with author, November 2013
42. Ibid.
43. Falstad Centre (u.d.), p. 8

14 Walking in the footsteps of the doomed: the Lyngen Line

1. Information boards, Russian Road, Fals mountain: August 2013
2. Ibid.
3. Ibid.
4. Samuel Mitcham (2009), *Defenders of Fortress Europe*, Dulles, VA: Potomac Books. ISBN: 978-1-59797-652-7
5. Pemsel biographical information from Leksikon der Wehrmacht: www.lexikon-der-wehrmacht.de
6. List of Knight's Cross recipients, at www.ritterkreuztraeger-1939-45.de/Infanterie/P/Pemsel-Max-Josef.htm
7. Samuel W. Mitcham, Jr (2006), *Retreat to the Reich*, Mechanicsburg, PA: Stackpole Books, p. 101. ISBN: 978-0-81173-384-7
8. *Der Spiegel*, 3 February 1972, at www.spiegel.de/spiegel/print/d-42853993.html
9. Correspondence with author, January 2014
10. Correspondence with author, January 2014

15 A guided tour through Tromsø's war

1. Sweetheart radio details at Cryptomuseum website: www.cryptomuseum.com/spy/sweetheart/
2. Seaplane details from Jean-Denis Lepage (2009), *Aircraft of the Luftwaffe, 1935–1945: An Illustrated Guide*, Jefferson, NC: McFarland. ISBN: 978-0-78645-280-4
3. Kjetil Korsnes (u.d.), 'Heinkel 115 in Norway' article for website 'Special Interest Group Luftwaffe', at www.luftwaffe.no/SIG/Artikler/115.html
4. LFT, the Society for Aeronautical History in Tromsø: www.skattora.com/tff-no3-splintmur/
5. Ibid.
6. Interview with author, August 2013

16 Scorched earth stories at first hand

1. Tore Hauge and Anders Ole Hauglid (1995) *De brente våre hjem*, Sorkjosen: Nord-Troms Museum. ISBN: 978-8-29914-541-1
2. Interview with author, August 2013

17 Slaughter and supply from the sky

1. From: Lt Cdr Geoffrey Mason (u.d.), 'Service Histories of Royal Navy warships in World War 2' at www.naval-history.net
2. From MS Rigel page at 'Norwegian Homefleet in WW2' online at: www.warsailors.com/homefleetsingles/rigel.html
3. Details of incident and naming of Norwegian survivor at Maritim magazine: http://maritimt.com/skipseksperten/skipene/rigel.html
4. The Korsnes casualties are named here: www.warsailors.com/homefleet/shipsk.html

They are named as: Stoker Alfred Mauris W. Andersen, Able Seaman Oddvar Martin Ellingsen, Steward Rasmus Græsdal, Mess Boy Martinius N. Haugland, Able Seaman Johan Edvard Karlsen, and Deck Boy Morten Reidolf Larsen. They are commemorated at this memorial for seamen in Stavern, Norway.

5.   Damage: Norwegian diving website dykkepedia.com/wiki/Rigel Spree www. naval-history.net/xGM-Chrono-04CV-Implacable.htm
6.   From MS Rigel page at 'Norwegian Homefleet in WW2' online at: www.warsailors. com/homefleetsingles/rigel.html
7.   Jeff Sauve (u.d.), 'A Helping Hand: The Efforts of American Relief for Norway' North American Historical Association pamphlet
8.   Ibid.
9.   Ibid., quoting NAHA pamphlet 'Look to Norway!'
10. Ibid., quoting report by Tor Dagre 'Norway and WWII'
11. Ibid.
12. Ibid.
13. Undset biography from Store Norsk Leksikon (sbl.no); Erika A. Kuhlman (2002), *A to Z of Women in World History*, New York: Infobase Publishing. ISBN: 978-0-81604-334-7; article by Gidske Anderson online at www.reisenett.no/norway/facts/culture_science/sigrid_undset
14. Sauve (u.d.)
15. Henie biography Norsk biografisk leksikon (translated) nbl.snl.no/Sonja_Henie/utdypning
16. Ibid.
17. 'Help Norway' pamphlet 1940, ARNI archives
18. Sauve (u.d.)
19. Dr A.N. Rygg (1947) *American Relief for Norway*, New York: Arnesen Press, p. 64
20. Sauve (u.d.), p. 38 quoting ARNI president John Asgaard letter
21. Sauve (u.d.), p. 39, quoting American Relief for Norway final report, by Andrew Wigland, NAHA archive.
22. Interview with author, August 2013
23. Glines (1999)
24. Ibid., p. 171
25. Ibid., p. 172
26. Ibid., p. 175
27. Ibid., p. 177
28. Operation Ball gunner A.L Sharps, quoted in Glines (1999), p. 181
29. Ibid., p. 181
30. Glines (1999), p. 176
31. Ibid., p. 192
32. Ibid., p. 193
33. Ibid., p. 196
34. Ibid., p. 195
35. Letter from John Giaver to Balchen, quoted in Carroll Glines (1999), *Bernt Balchen: Polar Aviator*, Washington, DC: Smithsonian Institute Press, p. 190
36. Glines (1999), p. 198, quoting 'Flygoperation Where and When', a translation of the official Swedish report
37. From Norwegian Operational Group online pages: www.ossog.org/norway/norso_01.html
38. Glines (1999), p. 196
39. Ibid., p. 195

40. Bernt Balchen (1958), *Come North with Me*, New York: EP Dutton, p. 291-292
41. Ibid., p. 296
42. Ibid, p297

18 Questions mount on the streets of the capital

1. From: US Army of Military History p. 843 online at www.history.army.mil/index.html. Ref: 'Statement From the Royal Norwegian Govt Info Office in London', 12 May 1945, as Quoted in HQ, Allied Land Forces Norway, CA, G-5 Div, Hist Rpt, 1–31 May 1945, SHAEF files, G-5, 17.08, Hist Rcds, Jkt 2
2. US Army of Military History p. 844, online at www.history.army.mil/index.html. Ref: 'Strict Legality Observed In Dealing With Quislings' issued by Lt Col John Enrietto, Chief of the Legal Branch, Allied Land Forces Norway, Rpt as Quoted in HQ, Allied Land Forces Norway, CA, G-5 Div, Hist Rpt, 1-31 May 45
3. Ibid.
4. Christian Goeschel (2009), *Suicide in Nazi Germany*, Oxford: Oxford University Press. ISBN: 978-0-19160-891-9
5. Looted paintings: From www.armyhistory.mil Chapter XXXVI: The Protection of Historical Monuments and Art Treasures: release entitled 'The Germans took even more art from Norway than was expected'. [CA, G-5 Div, Hist Rpt, Allied Land Forces in Norway, 1–31 May 1945]
6. From Norsk Biografisk Leksikon www.nbl.snl.no (translated)
7. Walter Laqueur and Judith Tydor Baumel (eds) (2001), *The Holocaust Encyclopedia*, New Haven, CT: Yale University Press, p. 450. ISBN: 978-0-30013-811-5
8. Andenaes et al. (1966)
9. Ibid., p. 148
10. US Army of Military History p. 845, online, from: 'The Supply Situation On Liberation' (HQ, Allied Land Forces Norway, CA, G-5, Hist Rpt, 1–31 May 1945) www.history.army.mil/index.html
11. US Army of Military History p. 846, online, from 'The King Returns And The Military Phase Is Ended' (HQ, Allied Land Forces Norway, CA, G-5 Div, Historical Rpt, 1-30 Jun 45, SHAEF files, G-5, 17.08, Hist files, Jkt 3,)
12. Conversation with author, Oslo, September 2013
13. 'Sadistic murder, torture, ill treatment and abuse of a sexual nature', *Nordlys*, 4 November 2013 (translated), in http://www.nordlys.no/nyheter/article6960785.ece
14. 'Hitler, huffs and Kanu's 'beautiful moment'', *The Observer*, Sunday 10 September 2000 at www.theguardian.com/sydney/story/0,,366607,00.html
15. Interview with author, Honningsvåg, August 2013

19 Dark chapters and Cold Wars

1. Andenaes et al. (1966), p. 125
2. Ibid., p. 126
3. Ibid.
4. Jonas Tjersland (2006), 'German soldiers used as deminers' by *VG magazine*, 8 April, at www.vg.no/nyheter/innenriks/artikkel.php?artid=166207. NB: The VG article also includes an astonishing video of the prisoners clearing minefields, some in their underpants.

5.   Ibid.
6.   Findings of the Hostages Trial: United Nations War Crimes Commission. Law Reports of Trials of War Criminals, pp. 69 and 70, Volume VIII, 1949. From University of the West of England archive www.ess.uwe.ac.uk/wcc/List4.htm#FINDINGS
7.   Howard D. Grier (2007), *Hitler, Dönitz and the Baltic Sea: The Third Reich's Last Hope, 1944–1945*, Annapolis, MD: Naval Institute Press. ISBN: 978-1-59114-345-1
8.   Halvor Fjermeros (2013), '60 years of silence and sadness', *Dagbladet*, 4 July 2013
9.   Ibid.
10. www.dagbladet.no/2013/07/04/kultur/meninger/hovedkronikk/kronikk/krigsfanger/28032175/)
11. Falstad Centre (u.d.)
12. Fjermeros (2013)
13. Interview with author, Kirkenes, August 2013
14. Interview with author, Bodø, August 2013
15. Interview with author, October 2013

20 The war is not over

1.   Correspondence with author, November 2013
2.   From 'Krigsbarnforbundet Lebensborn' website, the Union of Norwegian Lebensborn: www.lebensbornnorway.org
3.   Kåre Olsen (2005), 'Under the care of Lebensborn: Norwegian war children and their mothers', in Kjersti Ericsson and Eva Simonsen (eds), *Children of World War II: The Hidden Enemy Legacy*, Oxford: Berg. ISBN 13 978 1-84520-207-4
4.   Ibid., p. 23
5.   Ibid.
6.   'Abba girl's Nazi secret', *Daily Mail*, in http://www.dailymail.co.uk/tvshowbiz/article-126647/Abba-girls-Nazi-secret.html#ixzz2i1GCGriE
7.   http://www.dagbladet.no/nyheter/1998/10/18/135348.html
8.   Andenaes et al. (1966), p. 124
9.   *Lofotposten* article quoted in p. 94 Ericsson and Ellingsen (eds) (2005)
10. '"Master Race" children confront painful past', *Philadelphia Inquirer* online edition, 22 April 2001, at http://articles.philly.com/2001-04-22/news/25330617_1_german-soldiers-master-race-lebensborn-children
11. Gregory Crouch (2002), 'Norway tries to resolve a lasting Nazi legacy', *New York Times* online edition, 16 December 2002, at http://www.nytimes.com/2002/12/16/world/norway-tries-to-resolve-a-lasting-nazi-legacy.html
12. Ibid.
13. Bjorn Lengfelder, 'The Unwanted Ones', lecture notes supplied to author
14. Rob Woodward (2008), 'The Nazi novelist you should read', *Guardian* blog, 10 September, at www.theguardian.com/books/booksblog/2008/sep/10/knut.hamsun.nazi

INDEX